LITTLE-KNOWN
WARS
OF GREAT AND
LASTING IMPACT

LITTLE-KNOWN WARS

OF GREAT AND LASTING IMPACT

THE TURNING POINTS IN OUR HISTORY WE SHOULD KNOW MORE ABOUT

ALAN AXELROD

FAIR WINDS
PRESS
BEVERLY, MASSACHUSETTS

First published in the USA in 2009 by

Fair Winds Press, a member of

Quayside Publishing Group

100 Cummings Center

Suite 406-L

Beverly, MA 01915-6101

www.fairwindspress.com

13 12 11 10 09   1 2 3 4 5

ISBN-13: 978-1-59233-375-2

ISBN-10: 1-59233-375-3

Library of Congress Cataloging-in-Publication Data available

Axelrod, Alan, 1952-

  Little-known wars of great and lasting impact : the turning points in our history we should know more about /
Alan Axelrod.

    p. cm.

  Includes bibliographical references and index.

  ISBN-13: 978-1-59233-375-2

  ISBN-10: 1-59233-375-3

  1. Military history. 2. Low-intensity conflicts (Military science) I. Title.

  D25.5.A946 2009

  355.009—dc22

2009016107

Cover design by Peter Long

Book design by Sheila Hart Design, Inc.

Photo research by Anne Burns Images

Printed and bound in Singapore

DEDICATION

To Anita and to Ian

CONTENTS

INTRODUCTION

Although many think the deadliest American war was waged between the states in 1861–1865, it was actually fought between New Englanders and their Native American neighbors in 1675–1676.

The December 7, 1941, attack on Pearl Harbor, which brought the United States into World War II and doomed Japan to become the world's first victim of nuclear warfare, was firmly rooted in the Genpei War, fought on that nation's soil, not in the twentieth century but the twelfth.

In another early era, after Roman soldiers publicly whipped her and then raped her daughters in the year 60, the widow of a Celtic chieftain rose up as a warrior queen and led a bloody revolt that prompted the emperors to rewrite the rules of imperial conquest in ways that influenced empires for the next two thousand years.

And in a clash between Visigoth Christians and Umayyad Muslims on the bank of a Spanish river, modern Europe was born.

The Swiss historian Jean-Jacques Babel famously estimated that in the past 5,500 years—the period we call "recorded history"—the world has known a slim total of 292 years of peace—292 years in which the name of no armed conflict can be found. No two historians agree on a precise census of war, on just how many armed conflicts the human race has fought, but by conservative estimate, we can say that there have been some 2,000 wars sufficiently significant to have merited naming. Most of us can rattle off perhaps a half-dozen of them—and maybe a few more, if we think beyond those in which our home country was involved—but the rest that have been fought over the past five and a half millennia claim places in few minds. They are, for the most part, consigned to the vast category of "minor" conflicts, wars of relatively brief duration, producing relatively few casualties, and affecting the future minimally, if at all. And yet a handful in this category, though similarly little known, have had an impact on history that is astounding, profound, and life altering.

For example, asked for a quick list of U.S. wars, the typical American would mention the American Revolution, the U.S. Civil War, the Spanish-American War (possibly), the two world wars, the Korean War (maybe), Vietnam, and the ongoing wars in Iraq and Afghanistan. These represent about 1 percent of the wars in which Americans have fought from colonial times to the present, a total of 106 conflicts by my count.

Now some of these 106 wars, like most others fought elsewhere in the world over the past five and a half millennia, were "minor"—that is, of relatively brief duration, producing relatively few casualties, and affecting the future minimally, if at all. They are, therefore, deservedly obscure and of interest mainly to professional historians. But others, though similarly little known, have had a surprising, sometimes profound impact on the history that followed them.

We have alluded to some wars of this type in the opening paragraphs: America's King Philip's War of 1675–1676, Japan's Genpei War spanning 1180 to 1185, Boudicca's Revolt in the year 60, and the Muslim Conquest of Spain during 711–718. These, like the other dozen wars that are the subjects of this book, are well known only to the small society of historical specialists and but dimly familiar to the amateur history buff. Yet each made an impact on history and on ourselves, an impact out of all proportion to the limited knowledge we have of them. Call them "little known wars of great and lasting impact," as we do in the title of this book, or call them what they also are: the subterranean springs and hidden headwaters of the great river that is our history on this earth.

A WOMAN AGAINST ROME: BOUDICCA'S REVOLT

60

A fierce hinterland rebellion led by a warrior queen against the most powerful empire on Earth helped to reshape Roman imperialism, which provided a new model of enlightened conquest that would influence world history for some two millennia

Prasutagus, king of the Iceni people in East Anglia, Britain, and grudging vassal of the Roman Empire, died in the year 60. Within days of his passing, Catus Decianus, the chief Roman bureaucrat stationed in Britain, sent a detachment of heavily armed legionnaires to the door of his widow, Boudicca, the Iceni queen. They pillaged the royal residence, gathering up the few things Prasutagus had bequeathed to wife and daughters—the rest having become the property of Roman Emperor Nero the moment Prasutagus died.

When they had finished, the soldiers fanned out in platoons, running through the homes of Iceni nobles and stripping them of valuables as locusts strip a lush field to dry sticks and brittle straw. What they could not carry, they destroyed, and almost at random, it seemed, took captive family members to sell into Roman slavery.

Their work completed, the soldiers returned to Boudicca to demand of her the immediate repayment of loans the Roman treasury had made to her husband for the maintenance of the Iceni court. Boudicca replied that she could not pay—and how could she, because Nero had already seized everything of real value?—whereupon the legionnaires laid hands on her, took her prisoner, set her in the public stocks, and flogged her. In the meantime, her daughters were thrown to the soldiers for their pleasure.

Sometimes, rebellions are the bitter fruit of injustice meted out over many years. Sometimes, they result from the outrage of a matter of minutes. Boudicca's Revolt was the explosive product of both.

THE INVADERS

Rome's ambition was to rule the world, and in the first century, the world ended at the British Isles. The Roman legions took more than a few stabs at an invasion, beginning with Julius Caesar in 55 BCE, and getting serious in the reign of Claudius, one of whose generals, the future emperor Vespasian, marched his Second Augusta Legion in conquest of tribes as far as Exeter. Another Claudian army, the Ninth Legion, advanced north, eventually subduing the region around modern Lincoln. In 47, Ostorius Scapula, the freshly appointed governor of Britain, launched a campaign against the tribes of Wales, but was bogged down and held in check by Claudius, who did not consider subduing Wales worth the effort.

◄

This fanciful nineteenth-century engraving shows Boudicca rallying her warriors to resist the legions of Rome. No one really knows what the Iceni queen looked like, and because the Romans strove to obliterate all traces of her tribe, no one knows much about the Iceni, either.

Nero, who succeeded Claudius—assassinated by poisoning in 54—was determined to possess Wales and so resumed the invasion. It was, as Claudius had feared it would be, a long and bloody fight, and not until 60 was General Gaius Suetonius Paulinus in a position, his legions deployed, to commence the full occupation of Wales. He had just invaded Anglesey, an island off the northwest coast of Wales, and destroyed the Druid shrine and sacred groves there when news of Boudicca's revolt stopped him cold.

THE DEFIANT ICENI

Boudicca's people, the Iceni, lived in East Anglia, a broad peninsula that spread into the English Channel and included the modern counties of Norfolk and Suffolk, along with Cambridgeshire. Boudicca is the name by which the modern British know her. Suetonius Paulinus would have known her as Boadicea, and the Iceni themselves as Boudiga—at least, that is the name they had bestowed on her, borrowing it from the Druidical goddess of victory. Her name at birth, about the year 30, no one knows. She entered history only after she married Prasutagus, king of the Iceni, in 48 or 49.

Other than a sketchy history linked to the rebellion Boudicca led, the tribe bequeathed to posterity precious little evidence of its existence. Archaeologists have discovered torcs, which are thick, heavy, richly wrought rings of gold or silver meant to be worn around the neck and shoulders. By the first century, the torc was a warrior's

▲

Art historians believe the Roman emperor depicted in this painting by the early seventeenth-century Flemish master Pieter Fransz de Grebber is Nero, whose abuse of the Iceni and other indigenous peoples of the British isles was of a piece with his notoriously heartless and often sadistic approach to the governance of Rome itself.

accoutrement, so the survival of this ornament attests to the military orientation of the Iceni. To this may be added the coins the tribe began minting as early as 10 BCE. Some of these are inscribed ECENI, making them unique in the ancient world as the only money that bears a tribal name.

As a warrior tribe whose very coins proclaimed a kind of national pride or identity, the Iceni were not to be subdued easily. The Roman historian Tacitus wrote that the tribe was not among those conquered by Claudius in 43, but that King Prasutagus approached the Roman leaders that year, voluntarily and as an equal, to offer an alliance with the empire. The offer was accepted, and all apparently went well until 47, when the Roman governor Publius Ostorius Scapula, growing impatient with the presence of a stubbornly autonomous tribe within his province, made moves to disarm the Iceni. Prasutagus led his people in rebellion, but was defeated by Ostorius in a battle about which only two things are known. It was extraordinarily bloody for both sides, and it was fought at some fortified place, possibly Stonea Camp, a hill fort from Britain's Iron Age, located in the Cambridgeshire Fens and excavated by British Museum archaeologists as recently as 1980.

For some reason—perhaps in grudging admiration of the ferocity of their resistance—the Romans permitted the Iceni to remain at least nominally independent, even

The Divinity of the Druids

In the British Isles, most of the Celts—peoples who spoke the Celtic language—may be described as Druids. Although it is common to refer to the "Druid religion," the word "Druid" more properly refers to a priest, shaman, or priest-scholar who ministers to people practicing what can only be roughly described as Celtic polytheism—since no specific name for any of the early Celtic religions has come down to us. Very likely, the Celts themselves had no name for their beliefs, which were simply their perception of the world around them.

The religions the Druids served had two central features in common: a multiplicity of gods and an animistic world view, in which the gods or godhead (i.e., divinity) dwelled within the various manifestations of nature, such as the sea, the sky, land, the forest, lakes and rivers, and even specific landmarks, bodies of water, a particular hill, or an individual tree.

Fire had a special sacred significance because it was a natural manifestation that could also be created, controlled, and used by human beings. In this way, fire presented a communion with divinity, or godhead. Certain aspects of modern Christmas lore are survivals of Druid mythology. The Yule log and mistletoe both had animistic significance that has been carried over in the life-giving warmth of the blazing Christmas Yule log and the sexual power of mistletoe, under which it is not merely permissible, but obligatory, to kiss.

Julius Caesar's fascination with the Druids is recorded in his *Commentaries on the Gallic Wars (Commentarii de Bello Gallico)*, particularly the sacred and secular (governing) role of the Druid priests themselves and what he describes as the "principal point of their doctrine . . . that the soul does not die and that after death it passes from one body into another." Caesar made no note of a practice that shocked some other Romans—ritual human sacrifice.

This is a map of Britain under Roman rule, showing the principal Roman towns, including their Roman and modern names.

The unlabelled points are major Roman forts, but many towns served as fortresses as well.

in defeat. What this meant is that Prasutagus continued to rule, but his people became subjects of a client kingdom of the Roman Empire. The upside for the Iceni was this: they received protection against other tribes, improved education, greater employment, and the ability to draw on the imperial treasury for funds and loans. Most important, accepting client status was an alternative to conquest or even annihilation. Nevertheless, the bargain carried a heavy cost in the form of taxation and even some slavery—a certain segment of the Iceni population was liable to be sold to wealthy Romans. Despite this, Prasutagus and his queen, Boudicca, lived reasonably well as clients beholden to Rome, Boudicca bearing her husband two daughters, whose names are unknown to history.

THE ICENI BECAME A CLIENT KINGDOM OF THE ROMAN EMPIRE. THE UPSIDE WAS THAT THEY RECEIVED PROTECTION AGAINST OTHER TRIBES, IMPROVED EDUCATION, AND GREATER EMPLOYMENT... MOST IMPORTANT, CLIENT STATUS WAS AN ALTERNATIVE TO CONQUEST OR EVEN ANNIHILATION.

A WARRIOR RISING

With the death of Prasutagus, Nero received as a condition of the Iceni's client status all of the king's lands and real property, leaving Boudicca and her daughters a modest sum of money and various heirlooms. It was these few things that Nero's soldiers took—along with her daughters' honor.

However, if the abuse Boudicca had received at the hands of the Roman soldiers was intended to break her, it had the opposite result. She decided to rebel against Rome.

It is tempting to judge Boudicca's Revolt entirely as the impulsive act of a desperate woman, a queen who had suffered the cruelest of humiliations. While it is true that the outrages committed against her and her daughters galvanized Boudicca's resolve, the slender historical record leading up to the rebellion suggests that it was not driven solely by personal vengeance. The attack on Boudicca seems to have moved her to drink deep of Iceni warrior tradition and to transform herself into a warrior queen and a military leader.

She knew that a number of other tribes had risen in uncoordinated, scattered rebellion against Rome. She set about rallying to action the Iceni and also persuasively appealed to the chiefs of other discontented tribes. When she finally unleashed her rebellion, it was with a force of no fewer than 100,000. This was not a mob, but an army, and its assembly was not an act of desperation, but a thoughtfully organized revolution. As far as anyone can tell, it was the first instance of a genuine union among tribes for the purpose of driving the Romans out of Britain.

TOTAL WAR

Boudicca possessed an abundant willingness to wage what today would be called "total war," a war not just against the enemy army, but against the entire enemy population. She led an attack on Camulodunum Colonia, modern Colchester, at the time a colony populated by retired Roman legion officers and their families. Boudicca worked with spies inside the town, who gave her information that enabled her to plan the attack for maximum effect. Her army did not hit and run, but ravaged Colchester for several days.

A Roman runner managed to slip away and escape to Londinium (London), but he seems to have been incapable of conveying the horror of what was happening at Colchester. The procurator in London sent two centuries—200 legionnaires—who were simply consumed by an army that vastly outnumbered them.

The army Boudicca led—legend holds that she personally fought in battle, though Roman history does not record this—would have consisted of a relatively small contingent of charioteers driving two-wheeled *carpentom* chariots drawn by a team of two ponies. The tires of the carpentom were iron, and the chariot platform stood on a spring suspension—an innovation unique in the world at this time, which the Romans themselves later imitated. Two men, a driver and a warrior, manned the carpentom. The warrior was armed with at least four short spears (the *gaesum*), which he would launch on the fly. When he had exhausted this ammunition, he would dismount from the chariot and fight on foot with the longer *lancea*. The lancea could be thrown like a javelin, but, longer than the spear, it was also a formidable close-quarters thrusting weapon, its reach far greater than any sword.

Much larger was the Celtic army's infantry contingent, which fought with the lancea as well as the Celtic long sword. Most of these warriors were equipped with stout wooden shields sheathed in leather with an iron boss in the center. Officers wore bronze or iron helmets, and those of the wealthiest classes enjoyed the added protection of chain mail coats of armor.

The typical attack would begin with the deployment of slingers, who used large slingshots to shower stones upon the enemy as spearmen threw their long lancea. Boudicca's forces probably included archers as well. These initial attacks were made at a relatively long distance to weaken the enemy before the warriors surged in for close-quarters combat, which was accompanied by a cacophony of shield banging, shouting, screaming, horn blowing, and drum beating, all intended to strike terror in the heart of the already beleaguered foe.

ROMAN BRITAIN RAVAGED

Boudicca's forces destroyed Colchester and killed everyone in it. She then moved on, intending to advance against London, nearly 70 miles (113 km) away. En route, her advance guard sighted the 5,000 soldiers of Petilius Cerialis's IX Legion Hispana. Boudicca's troops were deployed in an ambush during which they killed in close-quarters combat all of the legion's infantry. Petilius, together with his cavalry, was able to retreat. Instead of giving chase, Boudicca continued toward London on the well-paved Roman road that was now wide open to her.

In the year 60, London was a market town that sprawled across 330 acres (1.3 km²)—a sizable city by Roman provincial standards. The news of Boudicca's slaughters preceded the arrival of her army, and the Roman garrison charged with London's defense deserted their posts, leaving the town entirely undefended. If Boudicca and her men were disap-

pointed at missing a battle, their actions did not betray it. She ordered London razed, and her troops were encouraged to kill every single Roman they encountered.

The fires of London must be accounted among the most devastating incendiary attacks recorded from the ancient world. They burned with a heat so intense that the city and its structures were not merely reduced but vitrified, as if in a giant kiln, creating a ten-inch (25.4 cm)-thick layer of hard red clay that, in places, still lies below the modern British capital.

THE NEWS OF BOUDICCA'S SLAUGHTERS PRECEDED THE ARRIVAL OF HER ARMY, AND THE ROMAN GARRISON CHARGED WITH LONDON'S DEFENSE DESERTED ITS POSTS, LEAVING THE TOWN ENTIRELY UNDEFENDED.

THE TIDE TURNS

From the ruins of London, Boudicca headed about twenty miles (32 km) northwest to strike Verulamium (St. Albans), a town populated by pro-Roman Britons. By the time she made her move against this town, Boudicca's army had doubled in size (according to contemporary reports), numbering perhaps 200,000. Against this vast force, Governor Suetonius Paulinus was able to muster just 10,000 legionnaires.

Boudicca was a determined and inspiring combat leader, but had she been a more competent strategist, she would have turned her attention to the Roman legion and attacked it. Almost certainly, she would have completely destroyed the force. Instead, however, she sacked St. Albans, which gave Suetonius time to deploy his soldiers atop a sloping hill located within what Tacitus called a "defile," which modern military writers interpret as a gorge. Suetonius was careful to position his legion with the troops' backs facing an impenetrable forest, so that any attacker would be compelled to approach straight on, uphill, and without the ability to simultaneously attack flanks or rear. It

◀

The fight between the Iceni and Rome was not the only clash between Druidic people and the forces of the empire. The so-called "Anglesy Massacre" in north Wales, in which Roman legionnaires under orders from Governor Suetonius Paulinus ravaged tribal locals, took place just before Boudicca unleashed her rebellion.

Icon of Misrule

With Caligula, Lucius Domitius Ahenobarbus—who ruled Rome as Nero Claudius Caesar Augustus Germanicus and so is known to posterity as Nero—figures in both lore and history as the epitome of depraved Roman tyranny.

Like so many other prominent Romans, he grew up amid familial chaos. Born in 37, he was banished by Caligula with his family in 39, and his father died a year later. Caligula seized the family's fortune, and Nero grew up in poverty, having for tutors a dancer and a barber. Claudius, who succeeded Caligula, restored the family to wealth and position, married Nero's mother, Agrippina, and adopted the boy, positioning him as heir to the throne. To accelerate her son's inheritance, Agrippina murdered Claudius in 54, and so Nero came to rule the empire.

Agrippina was the power behind the imperial throne until young Nero's advisers, Burrus and the philosopher Seneca (who had tutored the boy after Claudius restored the family), persuaded Nero to remove his mother from the palace. With the guidance of Seneca and Burrus, Nero ruled moderately and well—at first—but soon immersed himself in debauchery and extravagant luxury. When his mother returned to the palace to intervene in 59, Nero murdered her. Three years later, he may have poisoned Burrus as well. Without Burrus as an ally, and with Seneca's retirement, Nero was left in the hands of self-serving lackeys, who encouraged the emperor's excesses, which assumed megalomaniacal proportions. He immersed himself in the arts, in gladiatorial spectacles, in feasts, and in orgies, governing Rome—to the extent that he did govern it—through a class of secret informers, called the *delatores*, who created domestic terror by ratting out anyone who expressed the slightest dissent or dissatisfaction with Nero's rule.

When a catastrophic fire swept the city of Rome in 64, the people so despised Nero that they blamed him for the disaster, even though he had (according to Tacitus) financed relief for the homeless out of his personal funds. Tacitus relates that Nero sought to quell the rumors of his guilt by rounding up and inflicting "the most exquisite tortures on a class hated for their abominations, called Christians by the populace."

But it was the economic damage wrought by Nero's extravagant and financially ruinous rebuilding projects that turned the senators and other insiders against him. This, in turn, provoked Nero to order a string of revenge murders against those he perceived as conspiring against him—including his once-beloved tutor, the philosopher Seneca—but he did not in the least moderate his lifestyle, and soon the provinces were driven to revolt. As his empire crumbled about him, Nero, in despair, committed suicide on June 9, 68, with the parting words, "What an artist dies with me!". Ruinous civil war was his legacy to Rome.

is difficult to believe that Boudicca failed to recognize the poor ground left to her. That she decided to proceed with the attack, despite this obvious disadvantage, was almost certainly due to her faith that the overwhelming numbers she commanded would more than compensate for the adverse terrain.

Certainly, she was "up" for a fight. Roman historian Cassius Dio recorded that her appearance before and during the battle was "almost terrifying." Iceni warriors painted themselves an otherworldly blue for combat. It was a hue calculated to inspire complete terror in the enemy. To be sure, if the color of the warriors' faces did not unnerve Suetonius' legionnaires, the sheer numbers Boudicca led must have been singularly impressive. But what the Romans had going for them was superb conditioning, rigorous training, and precise military discipline. They also had complete confidence in Suetonius, their commander.

Roman soldiers were accustomed to defending themselves while attacking fortified positions by forming up in a tight phalanx formation, the men arrayed shoulder to shoulder, their shields creating one great, continuous shield, a mobile walled fortification. Boudicca's spear throwers, hurling their weapons uphill, were wholly ineffective. Those spears that made contact with the legionnaires glanced harmlessly off the impenetrable shield barrier. When Suetonius calculated that the first few waves of spear throwers had exhausted their supply of projectiles, he ordered his men to re-form into a great wedge, from which they let fly a hail of stout Roman javelins.

The effect of the volley was devastating. Boudicca's hordes, fierce but undrilled in the arts of disciplined combat, panicked under the thoroughly coordinated attack. They broke ranks at the very moment that Suetonius capitalized on his javelin assault with a mixed infantry-cavalry charge, storming downhill to envelop the queen's warriors on the front as well as both flanks. This maneuver—a double envelopment, which, by the first century, was already a classic battle tactic—resulted in the deaths of an estimated 80,000 of Boudicca's followers. The loss of so many warriors in a single movement demoralized all survivors and brought Boudicca's rebellion to an immediate end.

OUTGENERALED

Whether inspired or enraged, Boudicca achieved stunningly lethal early success, only to be fatally outgeneraled by Suetonius. Legend has it that, after suffering her crushing defeat, she groped her way home and there swallowed poison. Some historians have been quick to cite the dearth of Anglo-Roman archaeological artifacts in Norfolk as compelling evidence of the scope of the punishment Suetonius visited upon the surviving rebels. Modern scholars believe that the destruction was virtually total and was followed up by a nearly genocidal campaign of slaughter. Yet others point to an unmistakable change in the way Rome governed Britain after Boudicca's rebellion. Policy and practices became more tolerant and even enlightened.

In the long run, Boudicca appears to have succeeded in improving the lot of Celts under Roman rule. More important, Roman policy throughout the imperial provinces became markedly more liberal after her rampage. The rebellion she led helped transform Roman rule from a coercive tyranny into a kind of commonwealth. In many provinces, imperial subjects were even offered a variety of routes to full Roman citizenship, a status that put the rule of law on the side of the citizen, who thereby enjoyed the protection of civil authorities as well as the expectation of justice at their hands.

Thus, out of one of the bloodiest provincial episodes that ever confronted Roman settlers and soldiers—the Romans and their Briton allies lost some 70,000 men, not including the untold numbers of noncombatants killed in the destruction of towns—came a positive step toward enlightened government, which even into the modern era would influence leaders who sought empire and would provide models for shaping policy and local governments.

In a fierce tribal conflict may be found the seeds of the nineteenth- and twentieth-century British Empire, which strove to achieve dominion over a far-flung realm through varying combinations of enlightened, culturally tolerant government and harsh military rule.

THE FIRST HOLOCAUST:
A MESSIAH REBELS AGAINST ROME
132–135

Simon bar Kokhba's rebellion rocked the Roman Empire and provoked
in response a genocidal war against the Jews, which proved to be
the first of several that have marked history, both ancient and modern

O f the terrible year 135 in Judea, the Jerusalem Talmud records that the Romans "went on killing until their horses were submerged in blood to their nostrils." The Talmud, a combined record of rabbinical Torah analysis, Jewish law, and early Jewish history, claims that millions of Jews were slaughtered. This, surely, is an exaggeration, because the Jewish population of second-century Judea did not reach into the millions, but it is an exaggeration born of a horror all too real. The Roman Cassius Dio, who wrote an eighty-volume history of the empire, estimated that the legions killed 580,000 Jews, destroyed 50 fortified towns, and leveled 985 smaller villages.

It is a butcher's bill that seems compatible only with modern methods of organized genocidal warfare: the Turkish slaughter of Armenians at the beginning of the twentieth century, during and just after World War I (possibly more than a million dead); of the Cambodian "Killing Fields" of the dictator Pol Pot during 1975–1979 (perhaps more than 2 million killed in a population of 7 million); and, between these, the Holocaust, in which 6 million Jews were murdered at the behest of Adolf Hitler. As the end of the Bar Kokhba Revolt (132–135) proves, the ancients also possessed both the capacity and the will to commit genocide.

Yet the Bar Kokhba Revolt was not merely a 2,000-year-old historical precedent for the Holocaust. It made two millennia of Jewish persecution and the Holocaust possible. The devastation of the year 135 marked the true beginning of the Diaspora—the dispersion of the Jews and the enduring loss of their homeland, of any homeland. Stateless through the middle of the twentieth century, Jewish people everywhere were at the mercy of every people and every state.

◄

Polish-born American artist Arthur Szyk (1894–1951) prospered as a popular illustrator and during World War II earned fame for his anti-Nazi political illustrations. A Jew, he was also noted for his depictions of episodes from the history of the Jewish people, such as this 1927 miniature depicting Simon bar Kokhba's rebellion against Roman oppression.

ENLIGHTENED PERSECUTOR

More than a few monsters ruled the Roman Empire, but—until the Jewish revolt of 132–135—Hadrian (76–139) was not among them. He came to the imperial throne at the height of the Pax Romana, the first two centuries after the birth of Christ, during which Rome's influence on the realms it had either conquered or subdued was largely beneficial; much of the world enjoyed a previously unknown degree of peace and prosperity. A man of learning and cultivation, Hadrian for the most part ruled both wisely and well. As a contrast to his predecessors' rapacious

PUB. ÆL. ADRIAN.

urge to expand the empire at all costs, he devoted his reign to consolidating the empire and achieving productive control over all that was already within Rome's grasp.

No sooner was Hadrian crowned on August 11, 117, than he abandoned the ill-starred, costly, and vexing conquests the Emperor Trajan (53–117) had made east of the Euphrates and now extended an offer of peace to the powerful Parthians, who controlled most of Mesopotamia. He retained only Armenia, which Parthia did not contest. At the other end of the Roman Empire, in Britain, the new emperor personally oversaw construction of the great wall that today bears his name, traversing the waist of northern England, from modern Newcastle upon Tyne on the North Sea coast west to Bowness-on-Solway on the Solway Firth. It was conceived as a stone and turf alternative to continually battling the Picts and other ungovernable tribes of Britain's wild north country.

A ruler of seemingly inexhaustible energy, Hadrian personally led legions to Mauretania (modern western Algeria and northern Morocco) to suppress an insurrection there before turning northeast to meet with the Parthian ruler Osroes I (reigned c. 109–129) to avert the renewed outbreak of war with Parthia.

▲

Publius Aelius Hadrianus, the Emperor Hadrian, lived from 76 to 138 and reigned from 117 until his death. He is depicted here as he appeared about the year 100, when he was a high-ranking Roman legion commander.

RESTORING JUDEA, REBUILDING JERUSALEM

On his return from peace negotiations in Parthia, Hadrian visited the Roman province of Judea, pausing to survey the ruins of Jerusalem. The holiest city of the Jews had been destroyed in the year 70 by Rome's legions during the failed Great Jewish Revolt, after which the Emperor Vespasian (reigned 69–79) sought to suppress the still-rebellious Jews by replacing Marcus Antonius Julianus, a mere procurator (civil administrator) with a praetor (legion commander), Tineius Rufus, who served in the full capacity as military governor, backed by his legion, the X Fretensis.

The sight of Jerusalem's ruin sincerely moved Hadrian, who promised that he would rebuild the city. But Jewish gratitude proved short-lived, when it was learned that Hadrian intended to rebuild the holy Jewish city as a Roman metropolis, raising upon the ruins of the Second Temple a new temple dedicated to the chief Roman deity, Jupiter.

It was not that Hadrian sought to offend or incite the Jews, but that he believed reincarnating Jerusalem in the image of Rome, embodying both Roman culture and religion, would transform the Jews into good provincial Romans without the necessity of war. As with the wall he built in Britain, Hadrian intended to substitute construction for combat. That Hadrian himself was not entirely convinced his strategy would succeed peacefully, however, is suggested by the fact that to the Legion X Fretensis he added another, the VI Ferrata, with the objective of enforcing order as the great reconstruction got under way in 131. In that year, he also gave Jerusalem its new, Roman name: Aelia Capitolina.

THE SIGHT OF JERUSALEM'S RUIN SINCERELY MOVED EMPEROR HADRIAN, WHO PROMISED THAT HE WOULD REBUILD THE CITY. BUT JEWISH GRATITUDE PROVED SHORT-LIVED, WHEN IT WAS LEARNED THAT HADRIAN INTENDED TO REBUILD THE HOLY JEWISH CITY AS A ROMAN METROPOLIS.

Doubtless many Judeans were happy to see their chief city rebuilt, even under a Roman name, but no Jew could become reconciled to the heinous sin of plowing up the Temple. At this point, Hadrian—who, for all his political savvy, apparently did not appreciate the power of religious belief—added fuel to the fires of rebellion the Jupiter temple had kindled. While he showed much sympathy toward the Jews and their suffering at the

Last Stand of Sicarii

The Great Revolt (also called the First Jewish–Roman War, 66–73) culminated in 73 with the siege of Masada.

The first-century Jewish Roman historian Josephus records that Herod the Great (73 BCE–4 BCE), Roman Judea's first client king, fortified Masada, an isolated rock mesa on the eastern fringe of the Judean Desert overlooking the Dead Sea, between 37 and 31 BCE. He intended to use it as a last-ditch refuge in the event of a rebellion.

At the start of the Great Revolt in 66 CE, the Sicarii—an extremist faction of the Jewish rebels known as Zealots—overwhelmed the Roman garrison stationed at Masada and seized the fortification, which became a stronghold sheltering the Jewish Sicarii and their families who fled Jerusalem. These warriors did not merely hole up at Masada; they used it as an advance base from which they raided and harassed Roman settlements.

Josephus records that in 70 the Sicarii—who opposed not only the Romans, but other Jewish groups—under Elazar ben Ya'ir occupied Masada, transforming it into a fortified town, complete with synagogue and mikvahs (ritual baths). Two years later, Judea's Roman governor, Lucius Flavius Silva, led the X Fretensis legion against Masada. After failing to breach the stronghold's wall, Silva laid siege to Masada by building a wall around it and then raising a rampart against the western face of the mesa—a massive construction project, probably involving the labor of Jewish slaves, which required moving tens of thousands of tons of stones and earth.

The result was a 375-foot (114 m)-high assault ramp completed in the spring of 73. By this time Masada had been held under siege for about three months. The Romans stormed the fortress and were surprised to be met with no resistance. When they breached the wall with a battering ram on April 15, 73, and entered Masada, they were stunned by a spectacle of death. The 936 Sicarii had put all buildings and food caches to the torch, and then committed mass suicide rather than face capture and Roman enslavement.

hands of earlier Romans, he could not reconcile himself to one custom in particular, which he considered a hideous mutilation. Hadrian promulgated a law barring the sacred practice of circumcision. For the Jews of Judea, it was the final straw.

A MESSIAH RISES

Simon ben Kosba believed himself descended from the House of David, the second—and greatest—king of Israel (c.1000–967 BCE). At the time of Hadrian's decrees, Rabbi Akiva, who is celebrated in the Talmud as the "Head of all Sages," anointed Simon, bestowing upon him a new surname, Bar Kokhba. It meant, in Aramaic, Son of a Star, a reference to the star prophecy found in Numbers 24:17: "A star has shot off Jacob." By this name, Rabbi Akiva identified Simon bar Kokhba as the Messiah, the savior of the Jews.

The surviving historical record does not indicate whether Simon bar Kokhba himself claimed to be the Messiah, but even the suggestion of such a claim was enough to alienate a small Jewish sect that followed a "rabbi" whom the Romans had crucified almost exactly a hundred years earlier. The foundation of their faith in this rabbi—Jesus of Nazareth by name—was that he and only he had been the true Messiah. Thus, on the eve of a second Jewish revolt against Rome, the Christians definitively split from the other Jews, so that Bar Kokhba's Revolt may be said to mark the emergence of Christianity as a new religion separate from that of the Jews, rather than a sect within Judaism.

THE STRATEGY OF REBELLION

Simon bar Kokhba was careful to plan a rebellion that would not repeat the errors of the revolt of 70 CE. He understood that the Romans were foreign occupiers and as with all occupiers, they were most vulnerable at their lines of supply and communication. Sever these, and they could not hold out for very long.

The first Jewish revolt had been fierce, but uncoordinated—a popular uprising rather than a well-thought-out military campaign. The Roman–Jewish historian Josephus recorded that in 70 three independent Jewish armies actually fought each other to decide who would occupy the Temple Mount. While they battled in this way, the Roman legions, unresisted, broke through the walls of Jerusalem and advanced toward the temple. Incredibly, according to Josephus, the Jewish forces continued to contend with one another throughout the three weeks from the time the walls were breached to the final Roman assault on the temple. Determined that nothing like this would happen again, Bar Kokhba assumed absolute authority over all Jewish forces.

His first move, in 132, was to rise up in Modi'in in central Judea, and from here methodically coordinate the spread of the rebellion throughout the countryside. The Jewish forces avoided directly attacking the greatest Roman stronghold, Jerusalem, and instead isolated the garrison there, cutting it off from supply and communication. The Romans were stunned by the Jews' unity and military discipline. The Jerusalem garrison was soon defeated, and by early 134, Bar Kokhba's forces had wiped out one entire legion and its auxiliaries.

JERUSALEM LIBERATED

The defeat of the Jerusalem garrison emboldened Bar Kokhba to mint coins in his name. The first batch struck was proudly dated "Year 1 of the liberty of Jerusalem" and the second "Year 2 of the liberty of Jerusalem." In the Roman world, nothing proclaimed the legitimacy of a ruler and state more boldly than coinage.

For most of 133, Simon bar Kokhba ruled a relatively peaceful realm, but by the early summer of 134, Hadrian, in Rome, was apprised of the seriousness of the rebellion. As he had done before in times of trouble, he set out to personally inspect the scene of battle.

Judging the situation to be dire, he summoned Sextus Julius Severus, governor of Britain. Knowing that Severus was a commander accustomed to dealing with ungovernable tribal peoples, Hadrian assigned him to lead a force of 35,000 legionnaires against bar Kokhba. Before the Severus counteroffensive was concluded, Hadrian would commit to the reconquest of Judea a dozen legions, a total of 60,000 men, at the time between one-third and one-half of the entire Roman army.

ROMAN GOVERNOR SEVERUS WAGED WAR NOT AGAINST OTHER WARRIORS, BUT AGAINST THE CIVILIAN POPULATION OF JUDEA, INCLUDING OLD MEN, WOMEN, AND CHILDREN. HIS OBJECTIVE WAS TO GRIND AWAY THE JEWS' WILL TO CONTINUE THE FIGHT.

Even after all twelve legions had been deployed, the Romans were outnumbered in every engagement, and they absorbed heavy losses. After he finally succeeded in retaking Jerusalem, Severus established his headquarters there and decided to avoid any more open battles, which had proven too costly, even in victory. Instead, operating from his Jerusalem base, he waged war not against other warriors, but against the civilian population of Judea, including old men, women, and children. His objective was to grind away the Jews' will to continue the fight. That will, he discovered, did not break easily.

With his people dying around him, with towns, villages, farms, and all sources and stores of food destroyed by the legions, Bar Kokhba retreated to the fortress town of Betar, located southwest of Jerusalem, in the modern Palestinian village of Battir. Now it was he who was outnumbered, and the Romans pounded against his stronghold until they breached it.

Each legionnaire was equipped to serve as an arsenal unto himself. He wielded the *gladius*, the Roman short sword that was as well suited to hacking as to thrusting. He carried a stout shield, used both defensively and offensively as a bludgeon. Most legionnaires also carried the *pilum*, a javelin. Superbly organized, disciplined, conditioned, and equipped, the legionnaires fought through to Bar Kokhba and killed him and then, to a man, killed all the army that remained to him.

HADRIAN ATTEMPTS TO ERASE A PEOPLE

By the time Bar Kokhba was defeated, the Romans had taken a genocidal toll—580,000 Jews killed, according to Roman sources, many more according to the Talmud.

Severus set about mopping up the few remaining pockets of Jewish resistance, and Hadrian, the formerly enlightened Roman ruler, expanded these mop-up operations into a policy of oppressive occupation intended to wipe out Judaism, which he deemed incompatible with Roman rule, once and for all. Those few Jewish Judeans who survived the suppression of the rebellion and the oppression that followed it were exiled—first from Jerusalem and then from all Judea. Thus the Jews were cast to the four corners of the ancient world.

In this horrific way did Hadrian regain Judea for the Roman Empire. But Hadrian's own losses were so heavy that he took little satisfaction in the victory. The emperor had been accustomed to reporting triumphs to the Senate by beginning each report with the formulaic pronouncement, "If you and your children are well, all is well. For I and the army are all in good health." In his report on the reconquest of Judea, however, he dispensed with this customary formula and simply narrated the costly facts. He even refused the triumphal entrance into Rome, an honor traditionally accorded military conquerors.

Hadrian did not content himself with killing the Jews of Judea. He sought to expunge all trace of the Jewish homeland from the world's memory. Henceforth, the name "Judea" was scratched out from all Roman maps, and "Syria Palaestina" substituted. The choice was deliberate, assigning to all Judea the name of the Jews' ancient enemies, the Philistines. In this way, Judea became known to the ancient and modern worlds as Palestine. As for Jerusalem, it was now Aelia Capitolina, from which Jews were forever barred.

Beyond altering geography, Hadrian did what he could to eradicate the Jewish religion. He outlawed the Torah and Torah law, as well as the Hebrew calendar. Those Judaic scholars who had survived the suppression of the revolt he rounded up and summarily executed. The sacred Torah scroll that had been housed in the Second Temple was seized and burned on the Temple Mount. As he had promised, he raised a new Roman temple on the Mount, installing within it two statues: one of Jupiter and the other of himself.

SURVIVING GENOCIDE

Nearly a century and a half after the suppression of Bar Kokhba's Revolt, Constantine I, the first Christian emperor of Rome (reigned 306–312), allowed Jews to return to Jerusalem on Tisha B'Av so that they might weep in mourning of their destruction at the surviving Western Wall of the Second Temple—the structure today known as the Wailing Wall.

But, of course, the Jews had not been destroyed. Babylonia became the center of Judaism in the ancient world, even though some Jews began returning to the former Judea and Jerusalem throughout the second through fourth centuries. Wherever they took up new lives, the Jews adapted, and Hadrian's apocalyptic response to the revolt against Rome, intended to wipe Jews and Judaism from the world, in the end only proved the extraordinary resilience of the people and their faith.

▶

This map depicts the southern part of the region that became known as Palestine as it existed in Biblical times. Judea is identified on the map, although Hadrian purged the name from all Roman records and designated it Syria Palestinia, Palestine.

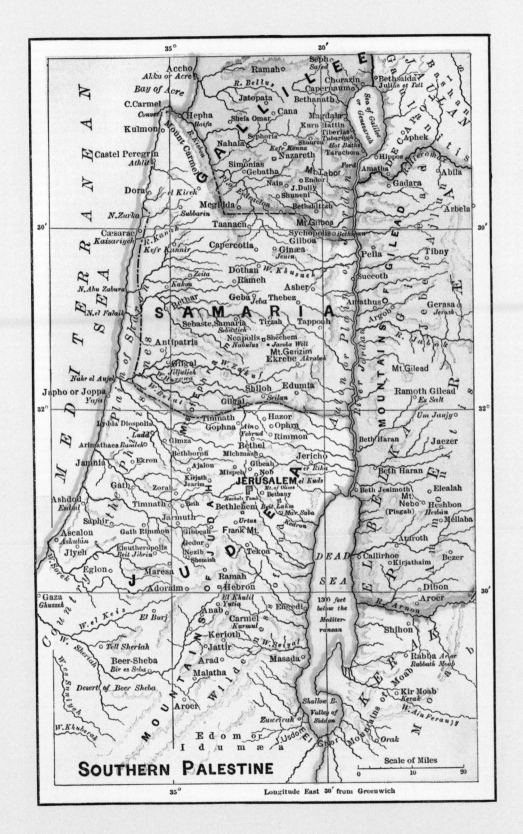

SOUTHERN PALESTINE

Longitude East 30′ from Greenwich

TRIUMPH OF THE CALIPHATE: ISLAM CONQUERS SPAIN

711–718

The Islamic conquest of Spain shortly after Islam came into being was the catalyst

that created a religious and continental identity among the disparate people of Europe,

beginning the transformation of many different tribes into kingdoms, empires,

and ultimately the nations we now know

Conquest can wipe out a people—or it can define them. When the Umayyad Muslims stormed into Spain and conquered the ruling Christian Visigoths, the result was not mere devastation, but the creation of something entirely new in the world. Call it Europe.

The conflict between Islam and Christianity has consumed centuries, and its end has yet to be reached, but the beginning clearly came when Tarik ibn-Ziyad led a Berber army from Morocco across the Strait of Gibraltar, onto Iberia—the Spanish peninsula—and on July 9, 711, into battle at the Guadalete River. Up to that moment, the landmass we call Europe was peopled by a collection of tribes and tribal kingdoms. In the 500 years that followed, the struggle between the faithful of two religions created among those tribal Christians a new common identity that was unprecedented in history because it was continental in scope. The half-millennium of religious war that began on a Spanish summer day in the eighth century would make them Europeans.

TARIK'S ARMY

After the death of the Prophet Mohammad in 632, the forces of Islam exploded out of Arabia, broadcasting the new religion in every direction. Within three decades, Arab armies defeated and partially conquered two empires north of Arabia, each founded on a different religion: the Christian Byzantine Empire (at the time encompassing much of modern Turkey and the Balkans) and the Zoroastrian empire of Persia, which extended through Central Asia, reaching to India.

The Umayyad family—according to tradition descended with the Prophet Mohammad from a common ancestor, Abd Manaf ibn Qusai—took control of Islam in 661 after defeating the rival Hashimite clan. Their dynasty established, the Umayyads sought to spread Islam further, but this time turned west, into North Africa, as well as east, into Central Asia. Al-Walid I was the sixth Umayyad caliph—literally "commander of the faithful"—who reigned from 705 to 715. After retaking parts of Egypt from the Byzantines, he advanced into Carthage and then moved to western North Africa. Simultaneously with these conquests, Al-Walid, revered to this day as both wise and mighty, not only expanded and modernized his armies, but built a powerful navy. This enabled him, early in 711, to send his most brilliant general, Tarik Ibn-Ziyad, to lead an

Having led a Berber army from Morocco across the Strait of Gibraltar to Iberia—the Spanish peninsula—Tarik ibn-Ziyad clashed with Spanish forces at the Guadalete River on July 9, 711, in a battle that brought Islam to Christian Spain.

army across the Strait of Gibraltar into Spain. The soldiers were Berbers, indigenous people of North Africa.

Few details are known about Tarik's life, but three facts speak volumes about his character as a warrior and leader of warriors. First, his name has come down through Spanish legend as Taric el Tuerto—Tarik the One-Eyed—which suggests that this commander of armies came up through the hard-fighting warrior ranks as a hands-on combatant. Second, the very place from which he embarked his army to conquer Spain, Gibraltar, is named for him: The Arabic *Gibr Tariq* means "Rock of Tarik."

But most telling is what he did after his warriors set foot on Iberian soil. According to the Arab historian Al Maggari, he put all of his ships to the torch, then turned his back on the blazing fleet and addressed his 7,000 soldiers, their eyes, one imagines, wide with horror, reflecting the flames:

Oh my warriors, whither would you flee? Behind you is the sea, before you, the enemy. You have left now only the hope of your courage and your constancy. Remember that in this country you are more unfortunate than the orphan seated at the table of the avaricious master. Your enemy is before you, protected by an innumerable army; he has men in abundance, but you, as your only aid, have your own swords, and, as your only chance for life, such chance as you can snatch from the hands of your enemy. If the absolute want to which you are reduced is prolonged ever so little, if you delay to seize immediate success, your good fortune will vanish, and your enemies, whom your very presence has filled with fear, will take courage. Put far from you the disgrace from which you flee in dreams, and attack this monarch who has left his strongly fortified city to meet you. Here is a splendid opportunity to defeat him, if you will consent to expose yourselves freely to death.

▶

This chalk-colored lithograph by Theodor Hosemann (1807–1875) depicting Tarik ibn-Ziyad was an illustration intended for a mid-nineteenth-century German history of the Middle Ages. Hosemann imagined Tarik in garb more typical of a European warrior leader than of an Arab tribesman.

Tarik.

The Zoroastrians

Before it was extensively marginalized by Islam, Zoroastrianism was one of the great religions of the world and the primary faith of ancient Iran. It is based on the teachings of the Iranian poet-prophet Zoroaster (also called Zarathushtra), whose life is dated variously to about 100 BCE, the sixth century BCE, or even 6000 BCE.

The religion is centered on a belief in a single god, Ahura Mazda, who created *asha*, truth and order, which exists as the antithesis of druj, the falsehood and disorder that is chaos. The universe embodies a conflict between order and chaos, which human beings are obliged to contend with. Living a moral life is a shield against chaos until the day breaks in which Ahura Mazda will triumph once and for all over druj, bringing into being the end of time and the union of all with the creator.

It will not be a quiet event. A tsunami of molten metal will purge the earth of evil even as a titanic battle above purges it from heaven. At this millennium, the physical self of the living and of the dead will melt away into a spiritualized self contained within eternally rejuvenated bodies requiring no physical sustenance. These beings—of so airy a substance as to cast no shadow—will live in a world without tribes, race, or nations and in which all speak a single language.

Zoroastrianism doubtless had hundreds of thousands of adherents in ancient Iran. Today, some 70,000 Zoroastrians live in northern India and parts of Pakistan. While the religion is also still practiced by small numbers in Iran, it is done so more or less covertly, since it is blasphemous in the eyes of Muslims.

The prophet Zoroaster is shown bearing the light of truth and goodness, the element of Ahura Mazda, the god who battles the darkness of *druj*, the force of chaos and falsehood.

Then the most important words of all: "Do not believe that I desire to incite you to face dangers which I shall refuse to share with you. In the attack I myself will be in the fore, where the chance of life is always least. . . . Do not imagine that your fate can be separated from mine, and rest assured that if you fall, I shall perish with you, or avenge you."

Tarik's is a most remarkable lesson in command. After ensuring that his warriors had no alternative to victory but death or enslavement, he laid his own life on the line. He continued by telling them that their mission was to "establish the true religion" in Iberia, but he also reminded the soldiers of what they had long heard tell, "that in this country there are a large number of ravishingly beautiful Greek maidens, their graceful forms are draped in sumptuous gowns on which gleam pearls, coral, and purest gold, and they live in the palaces of royal kings. The Commander of True Believers [Al-Walid] has chosen you for this attack from among all his Arab warriors; and he promises that you shall become his comrades and shall hold the rank of kings in this country. . . . The one fruit which he desires . . . is that the word of God shall be exalted in this country . . . The spoils will belong to yourselves."

ON THE FACE OF IT, THE ARABS BEHAVED MORE AS A BAND OF WARRIORS THAN AS A COHESIVE ARMY. AND YET, FACING MUCH BETTER ORGANIZED FORCES, THEY USUALLY WON.

TARIK'S TACTICS

Military historians have long marveled at the remarkable success of the Arab armies, which during the first two centuries of Islam were primitive by comparison to the armies of the kingdoms, empires, and peoples over which they triumphed. In the seventh century, the armies of Persia and Byzantium were larger, more disciplined, better organized, and equipped with more modern weapons. In the eighth century, the Visigoth forces, having learned much from their contact with Rome, were far more advanced in the military art than those who came to conquer them.

It is known, for example, that the Arab warriors fought in an ad hoc manner, taking advantage—individually rather than en masse—of whatever physical features the battlefield terrain happened to present and exhibiting a tendency to attack and retreat, then attack again, rather than form up in the style of a Roman legion to make a single-minded advance.

On the face of it, the Arabs behaved more as a band of warriors than as a cohesive army. And yet, facing much better organized forces, they usually won. John Keegan, dean of modern military historians, has speculated that "'Primitive' tactics become effective if the warrior is inspired by a belief in the certainty of victory and is always willing to return to the struggle, however often he disengages when a particular fight goes against him."

The warriors of early Islam fought with such inspiration, which Tarik reinforced by giving them a grim choice between death on the one hand and belief in victory on the other.

THE RISE AND FALL OF KING RODERIC

The armies Tarik knew he would face in Iberia were those of the Visigoth king, Roderic, who had, through a violent but obscure coup d'état in 710—a year before the Battle at the Guadalete River—seized the throne of a kingdom verging on disintegration brought on by dissension among the nobles and a string of inept kings. Three centuries earlier, Alaric I—his name meant "king of all"—had led the Visigoths out of the Balkans, defeated the legions of a decadent Roman Empire, and then descended on Rome itself, sacking the great city in 410, the first Germanic leader to do so.

Through a series of events still poorly understood by historians, the Visigoths eventually came to settle in southern Gaul (the modern south of France) as *foederati* (clients) of the Roman Empire, but then proclaimed their own kingdom, independent of Rome, centered in Toulouse. From here, Visigoth armies advanced across the Pyrenees and into Hispania (Iberia, or Spain), where they defeated both the Vandals and Alans, two other great Barbarian tribes. In 507, the Visigoths were in turn defeated north of the Pyrenees by a Frankish army under the Franks' first acknowledged king, Clovis I. The Franks' victory confined the Visigoths for the most part to Hispania.

It seems that the Visigoths were never very content walled in by the mountains, and the Visigoth government in Spain became fragmented, torn among competing members of a small governing elite, the people clinging together only by virtue of their common Christian faith. By the coup of 710, Roderic secured control of southern Hispania, and no sooner had he usurped the throne than he recruited a powerful force to oppose the Muslims who had landed and begun raiding the far southern Iberian peninsula.

The armies of Roderic and Tarik met at a small stream, the Guadalete River, near Medina Sidonia. The resulting battle is sketchily described in unreliable records and legends. Most historians believe that Tarik had landed with 7,000 troops and immediately requested 5,000 reinforcements from the caliph. Assuming these arrived—and did so in timely fashion—Tarik may have commanded an invading force of 12,000; however, most historians believe that fewer than 2,000 had advanced with him to the Guadalete. These were almost all elite Berber cavalrymen under Arab officers. They were mounted on Arabian steeds, pampered, high-spirited animal athletes capable of outperforming the far humbler horses of the Visigoth cavalry.

Arabic sources record that Tarik was vastly outnumbered by some 100,000 troops under Roderic, but all modern historians believe this figure was wildly exaggerated and the consensus is that the Visigoth king actually had with him only about 2,500 men.

The strategy and tactics by which Tarik defeated Roderic are not recorded, but a contemporary chronicler wrote that the Visigoth forces rapidly collapsed because a number of the commanders whom Roderic had hastily recruited coveted his throne and when Tarik attacked they took flight with the warriors they led. If their plan had been to leave Roderic in the lurch, to be slain by the Muslims, they were successful. But if they also

The Birth of Islam

Mohammad ibn 'Abdullāh, Mohammad the Prophet, was born about 570 in the Arabian city of Mecca and died in Medina on June 8, 632. He was orphaned early in his life and raised by his uncle. When he came of age, he made his living as a merchant and a shepherd, but by his middle years he suffered a restless spiritual discontent that sent him into the solitude of a mountain cave not far from Mecca. Here, at the age of forty, during the month of Ramadan, God revealed himself to Mohammad. Three years later, Mohammad took his revelation to the people, proclaiming—among other things—two major doctrines of faith: that "God is One" and that he requires of the faithful total surrender to him. Mohammad further announced himself as a prophet and messenger of God, claiming a place among other prophets, including Adam, Noah, Abraham, Moses, David, and Jesus, all of whom continued to be revered in Islam.

Initially met with scorn and persecution, Mohammad and his small band of followers retreated to Medina in 622—an event commemorated as the Hijra, the commencement of the Islamic calendar. Working from the city, Mohammad, a brilliant diplomat, orator, and military commander, was able to unite the discordant Medinan tribes and with them formed an army of 10,000, which after winning several victories, he led in the almost bloodless conquest of Mecca in 629. By the time of the Prophet's death just three years later, Islam had spread across most of the Arabian Peninsula and had given the disparate tribes of the region a common religious identity. Today, it is estimated that between one and nearly two billion people are Muslims.

believed that this would make room for their own rise, they were mistaken. After defeating and killing Roderic, Tarik's warriors fanned out in search of the king's rivals, ran them to ground, and killed them to a man.

The force of Tarik's personality was apparently so compelling that those of Roderic's men who survived the battle eagerly joined the Berbers in completing the conquest of Spain. In company with these men, Tarik swept through southern Spain, defeating another Visigoth force at the Battle of Ecija, capturing Córdoba, and then in early 712 taking the Visigoth capital, Toledo.

The Battle of Guadalete—as imagined some 1,200 years later by the Spanish painter Salvador Martinez Cubells (1845–1914). This detail depicts the commencement of the Goths' retreat in the face of Tarik's Berber cavalry.

THE ARRIVAL OF MUSA

Learning of Tarik's conquests, Musa ibn-Nusayr, governor of Ifriqiya (Muslim North Africa) and conqueror of Tangiers and all of the territory corresponding to modern Morocco, recruited an army of his own, which consisted of 18,000 Arabs, and led them to Spain, landing at Algeciras in June 712.

From here, they advanced to Medina Sidonia and quickly took it. Seville was next to fall, followed by Merida, which had been the center of Roman Hispania since its founding by the Romans in 25 BCE. The city fell to Musa on June 30, 713, after which Musa joined his army to that of Tarik, who had by this time acquired new allies—the Jews of Spain, persecuted beginning in 587 by the Visigoth King Recared, who had converted from Arian Christianity (which was tolerant of the Jews) to Catholicism (which was not).

Musa and Tarik campaigned together for a time before Tarik launched a separate effort against northwest Spain, where he conquered Léon and Astorga. At this time, as it became apparent to the new Umayyad caliph, Sulayman bin Abd al-Malik, that the conquest of Spain was virtually complete, he suddenly recalled both Tarik and Musa to Damascus, Syria. Before leaving Spain, Musa installed his son, Abd al-Aziz, as governor of Muslim Spain, now called al-Andalus. Why the new caliph summoned the two conquerors of al-Andalus is not known; however, while Tarik was apparently honored in the Damascus court, Musa ibn-Nusayr fell into disfavor with caliph and ended his days not in Damascus, but in Medina Sidonia, Spain, where he was regarded as an "old and broken man."

A Legend of Revenge

Although the historical details of the Battle of the Guadalete are few, the legends concerning it are many. The most pervasive is that one of Roderic's unreliable subordinate commanders, a Count Julian, furnished Tarik with the ships he used to transport his invaders from Gibraltar to the Spanish mainland. This act of betrayal, according to the legend, was revenge for Roderic's having raped Julian's daughter Florinda years earlier, when both the king and the girl were little more than children.

The legend, which is Christian and not Muslim, attests to the Christians' unwillingness to believe that a champion of their faith could have been defeated by an Islamic army without some act of treachery. Among the few historical facts known about the battle, however, is that the Arabs possessed a navy before the invasion.

"Julian" cannot be specifically accounted for in the historical record, although some historians believe that he was a North African Catholic named Urban, who is mentioned in a chronicle compiled in 754 as a figure who accompanied the governor of Muslim North Africa, Musa ibn-Nusayr, across the Strait of Gibraltar.

THE GOVERNORSHIP OF ABD AL-AZIZ

Musa had bequeathed to his governor-son a vast realm that had been quite thoroughly subdued. With great intelligence, al-Aziz negotiated peace with the Visigoths at Murcia, transforming the remaining Visigoths throughout southern Spain into compliant vassals. In the meantime, two additional Visigoth strongholds had yet to be conquered. Al-Aziz took Saragossa in 714 and Barcelona in 717.

Under al-Aziz, the Umayyads were lenient to the Christians they conquered. Although they encouraged conversion to Islam, they did not force it and were, in fact, highly tolerant of the practice of Christianity as well as Judaism, provided that the adherents of these religions neither said nor did anything derogatory to Islam. By 718, many Spanish Christians were living prosperously under the al-Aziz government, and those who refused to make an accommodation were pushed into the Pyrenees frontier, isolated from the rest of al-Andalus.

THE ADVENT OF CHARLEMAGNE

For many years, there was much cultural exchange between the Moors—as the Spanish Muslims were now called—and the Christians. Al-Andalus became a rich and vital source of Islamic learning, especially in mathematics and medicine, and it was a source on which the Christians drew, disseminating the knowledge northward into Europe. However, the recalcitrant Christians who occupied the extreme northern reaches of Spain periodically waged war against the Moors. They made of the mountainous frontier between Islamic Spain and Christian Europe a no-man's land, through which the Frankish emperor Charlemagne advanced in 778 with a 25,000-man army composed of Franks, Bavarians, Burgundians, Lombards, and others, intent on conquering al-Andalus.

It was the first attempt by people who leagued together as European Christians to conquer Muslims—and yet, even in this, the separation between Christians and Muslims was never absolute. Whereas Christian and European identity was starting to coalesce around the charismatic Charlemagne, the Islamic world—at least in Spain—was beginning to fragment. By 777, Abd al-Rahman, founder of the Umayyad Emirate of Córdoba, which would rule much of the Iberian peninsula for almost three centuries, had extended his personal control over about two-thirds of Spain. For some, namely the emir of Barcelona and the Muslim governors of Saragossa and Huesca, this situation bespoke a monopoly of power they were not prepared to tolerate. Accordingly, the three Muslim leaders made an overland journey of almost 1000 miles (1609 km) to Saxony for the purpose of conspiring with Charlemagne in what they hoped would be the defeat of Abd al-Rahman.

Yet when the Frankish king actually invaded in 778, the governor of Saragossa who had conspired with him suddenly feared being overwhelmed by the forces of Christianity and instead of opening his town to Charlemagne and his army as promised, he barred its gates. In the meantime, without the charismatic Charlemagne to keep them in line, the Saxons had risen in revolt, so that the Frankish conqueror found himself trapped between the realm of Islam and rebels of his own religion. Accordingly, he sought refuge for himself and his men in Pamplona, a city of Catholic Basques. To his stunned surprise, these people resisted him, and instead of using his army as he had planned, against a Spanish Muslim emirate, Charlemagne turned it loose on Pamplona, razing this Christian city.

Charlemagne withdrew northward through the Pyrenees, repeatedly attacked by vengeful Basques. At Roncesvalles, a mountain pass, his rear guard fell under heavy attack and was annihilated. Among the dead was one "Roland, Lord of the Breton Marches," a figure who became the hero, three centuries later, of the *Chanson de Roland (The Song of Roland)*, the earliest surviving work of French literature. What had been in reality a complex intermingling of two great cultures, religions, and regions—a blend of intellectual influence, civil accommodation, prosperous commerce, military enmity, military alliance, and betrayal on all sides—was transformed in this epic poem into a simplified and utterly distorted myth in which Christianity clashes with Islam.

The *Chanson de Roland* disseminated a pervasive mythologized view of the relationship between Christian Europe and the Muslim world. As a result of the long struggle over Spain, European Christianity largely defined itself in opposition to the Muslim realm as it existed in al-Andalus. Yet that very struggle demonstrates that the vision of the *Chanson* was a fiction—more bluntly, a lie. What had taken place in 711 was not just a battle on the bank of a Spanish river, but an intellectual, cultural, political, and spiritual synthesis in which, sometimes violently, sometimes collaboratively, sometimes merely tolerantly, Christians, Jews, and Muslims variously borrowed, stole, and spurned what each had to offer the other. From this process, modern Europe emerged.

SHOGUNS RISING: THE GENPEI WAR

1180–1185

A desire to reclaim a birthright and avenge a religious outrage began
the Genpei War, which would have a profound and long-lasting
impact on Japan, culminating on the attack on Pearl Harbor in 1941

In 1180, four clans—the Fujiwara, Tachibana, Minamoto, and Taira—dominated medieval Japan. More powerful than the emperor as direct governors of the people, the clans nevertheless competed for his approving smile to legitimize their claim to authority. For his part, the emperor would send to each clan he favored a son who had been deemed ineligible to inherit the throne. This young man would marry into the clan and thereby come to control it. The result was a complicated, fragile system of government that virtually assured war as a way of life.

In 1180, among the four clans, the Taira, as ruled by Taira no Kiyomori, was the most powerful. Kiyomori had parlayed conquest and a shrewd political marriage to establish Japan's first samurai—that is, military—government. He gave his daughter Taira no Tokuko in marriage to the Emperor Takakura in 1171, the union producing a son, Prince Tokuhito, in 1178. The very next year, Kiyomori led a coup d'etat that forced all of his rivals out of power.

Kiyomori filled the now-vacant government posts with his family and allies, taking the precaution of imprisoning the most important supporter of the rival Minamoto clan, Go-Shirakawa, who held a position unique in Japanese feudal government. He was a "cloistered emperor," a ruler who had abdicated—Go-Shirakawa had done so in 1158—but who still wielded powerful influence. With Go-Shirakawa confined, Kiyomori forced Emperor Takakura to step down in 1180 in favor of Prince Tokuhito, who thus became the Emperor Antoku.

While it was one thing to lock up Go-Shirakawa, it was quite another to control his family. In May 1180, the imprisoned ruler's son, Prince Mochihito, humiliated by the ascension of the infant Tokuhito over him and further outraged by reports that Kiyomori was defiling ancestral graves and defying Buddhist law, called on all of the Minamoto clan to rise against Kiyomori and the Taira. Thus, from a desire to reclaim a birthright and avenge a religious outrage, began the Genpei War, which would have a profound and long-lasting impact on Japan and in the mid-twentieth century most of the rest of the world.

◀

This woodblock print from the late 1850s by the Japanese artist Yoshitora (fl. 1850–1880) depicts Minamoto Yorimasa seated and attired in full court regalia.

OPENING BATTLE

Uji, a village of temples on the southern outskirts of Kyoto, a city of temples, was surrounded by wilderness in the twelfth century. Mists rose from the glassy, slow-flowing river, wreathing

The Way of the Warriors

The one feature of medieval Japan familiar to all Westerners is the samurai. In Japanese, the word denotes a class of person who serves the nobility—with the added connotation of rendering intimate, trusted service. This does not mean that the samurai were a servant class. On the contrary, they were themselves the military nobility.

By the era of the Genpei War, the twelfth century, the word samurai had become a synonym for *bushi*, which more narrowly described the middle and upper ranks of warrior nobility. The term *bushido* ("The Way of the Warrior") describes the code of conduct to which the samurai aspired and is often loosely compared to the Western medieval concept of chivalry. *Bushido* took on a distinctly sinister connotation during World War II, when it was revived in the code of conduct that justified war crimes and crimes against humanity.

Because most Westerners think of samurai as warriors, they believe their exclusive weapon was the samurai sword. It was indeed the preeminent samurai weapon and symbol, literally and metaphorically a cutting-edge weapon, the product of sublime craft and a high level of metallurgical knowledge. Samurai blades combine a soft steel leading edge that is razor-sharp with a hard steel body that gives the blade extraordinary strength. Although the samurai were master swordsmen with superb swords, they also used all the weapons of medieval warfare, including bows and arrows, spears, and, later, firearms. As a result of the Genpei War, the samurai became the chief governing and administrative authorities throughout Japan.

A traditional Japanese woodblock print depicting a scene from the Genpei War. Among the many martial skills the samurai mastered was fighting on horseback with swords and bows. While these weapons are universally familiar, the fearsome *naginata* was unique to the samurai; it is the curved blade attached to the pole that is carried by the warrior pictured in the lower right of the print.

the wooden bridge over which Prince Mochihito spurred his horse one day early in 1180, trying desperately to outrun the pursuing Taira. He found refuge in Uji's Miidera temple, where he awaited rescue by the Minamoto army. A warrior monk who had sided with the Taira led a brilliant delaying action against the Minamoto force, which thus arrived too late to save the temple, but did retrieve Mochihito. He rode with the Minamoto samurai, now joined by a group of warrior monks, toward Nara, due south of Uji. Enfolded deep within a primeval forest, Nara was a place of ancient shrines that three centuries earlier had been the capital of Japan.

The Minamoto army was led by Minamoto no Yorimasa. A figure renowned more as a poet than as a general, he had tried to stay out of the conflict between the clans and had even left military service to enter the Buddhist priesthood. But he found himself unable to ignore Mochihito's call to arms, and he in turn recruited his Minamoto kinsmen while also rallying warrior monks to meet the Taira army of Kiyomori. On the march to Nara, Yorimasa overtook the Taira army at Uji and led the defense of the Byōdō-in temple there. In an effort to foil the Taira attack, Yorimasa's warrior monks demolished the graceful yellow-brown wooden bridge leading to the temple, but Kiyomori's men nevertheless stormed the temple and prepared to capture it.

Sensing imminent defeat, Yorimasa composed a death poem, part of the ritual prelude to *seppuku*—literally, "belly cutting"—for the samurai, the only honorable alternative to surrender. The poem reads:

> Like an old tree
> From which we gather no flowers
> Sad has been my life
> Fated no fruit to produce.

Although he had time to write the poem, it is doubtful that he also enjoyed sufficient leisure to indulge in the rest of the ritual—a cleansing bath, the donning of pure white robes, and the eating of a final meal. He did summon a *kaishakunin*, a second, who laid the *tantō* (knife) before him. After opening his white kimono, Yorimasa plunged it, hard, into his left upper abdomen, dragging the blade from left to right.

Now it fell to the second to perform *dakikubi*, inflicting a deep sword cut in the neck. Yorimasa's seppuku is the first recorded instance of the samurai's ritual suicide. His second, however, did not strictly observe ritual. In performing the *dakikubi*, seconds were to avoid inflicting total decapitation by leaving a thin band of flesh to hold head to body. In this instance, however, the faithful second, fearful that the enemy would seize Yorimasa's head as a trophy, severed it completely, tied it a rock, and cast it into the river. As for Mochihito, because he was not a samurai, he did not commit suicide. Captured, he was duly executed.

FIRES OF WAR

By way of revenge against the warrior monks who had opposed them, the Taira victors at Uji soon returned to the Miidera temple—the "Temple of the Three Wells"—and put the splendid eighth-century structure to the torch before they moved on to Nara. Warrior monks poured out from that town's many monasteries and temples to resist the attack.

The Nara monks fought exclusively on foot, their weapons consisting of bows and arrows and the samurai's *naginata*, a strong, slender pole on which a curved blade was mounted, shaft and blade together providing the warrior a reach of seven feet (2 m) or more. Formidable as the *naginata* was, the Taira came as cavalry, and their mobility, combined with their *nihontō* swords—the edged weapon most closely associated with the samurai—gave them a great advantage even over the defenders' superior numbers. After a brief siege, the Taira broke through the defenders' lines and burned all but one of Nara's major temples. The conflagration killed some 3,500.

A LEADER RISES

Among others who responded to the prince's call to rise against the Taira was Minamoto no Yoritomo, third-eldest son of Minamoto no Yoshitomo, the heir apparent of the Minamoto clan. Exiled in 1160 to Izu in the remote and rugged eastern Japanese province of Kantō after his father was killed in an abortive uprising against the Taira, Yoritomo was forced even out of this place of exile by his jailer after he impregnated the man's daughter. While wandering the wilds of Kantō, Yoritomo encountered Hojo Tokimasa, warlord of the Kantō plains. Yoritomo conspired with him to undermine the Taira at every opportunity. When Tokimasa discovered in 1179 that Yoritomo had been carrying on an affair with his daughter, Hojo Masako, he did not respond as the Izu jailer had. Instead, in 1180, he assassinated Masako's fiancé, the pro-Taira governor of Kantō, which allowed Yoritomo to marry Masako, cementing the alliance.

With a large army now at his disposal, Yoritomo established his headquarters at Kamakura, little more than 30 miles (48 km) southwest of modern Tokyo. On September 14, 1180, Yoritomo fought the Battle of Ishibashiyama, in the Hakone Mountains, near Mount Fuji. Hearing that his enemy was marching toward the Hakone Pass, Taira no Kiyomori dispatched one of his best commanders, Oba Kagechika, to stop him. Kagechika led a surprise attack by night, and the bloody fight checked Yoritomo's advance before it had fairly begun.

This is Japan during the epoch of the shoguns, 1185–1867.

Despite the defeat, Yoritomo not only retained his army intact, he grew it. Later in the year, he recruited the Takeda clan—considered a branch of the Minamoto—and members of other families throughout the provinces of Kai and Kozuke in the region north of Mount Fuji. These new allies joined Yoritomo's forces at Fujigawa in the nick of time to fend off the onslaught of the Taira army, which was always hot on Yoritomo's heels. Semi-legendary history records that the Taira warriors mistook the flapping of a rising flock of birds for the commencement of a Minamoto surprise attack. Panicked, they broke and ran, without even offering battle.

By the spring of 1181, Yoritomo had won the support of most of the prominent families in the Kantō domain. For a time, he contented himself with consolidating his hold here rather than attempting to spread his rebellion far and wide.

A SETBACK

In the meantime, also in 1181, another Minamoto general, Minamoto no Yukiie by name, attempted a nighttime surprise attack against Taira no Tomomori and his army at Sunomatagawa (modern Sunomata, Gifu Prefecture) after he stumbled upon this force deployed along the opposing bank of the Sunomata River. Wasting no time, Yukiie ordered his men to wade across, only to lose the vital element of surprise because the defending Taira found it very easy, in hand-to-hand combat, to tell friend from foe even in the pitch black of a moonless night. The Taira were dry, the Minamoto soaked.

After suffering severe losses, Yukiie and his surviving cohorts withdrew back across the river, the hunters having become the hunted. At Yahagigawa, Yukiie made his stand, sending his samurai to dismantle the bridge over the Yahagi River and to erect a defensive wall with the scavenged lumber. Despite these measures, the Taira onslaught forced him to resume his retreat. In the end, it was sickness that halted the Taira, who turned back after Tomomori was stricken with a fever.

YORITOMO MAKES HIS MOVE

In 1183, having decided that his forces were now powerful enough to drive the Taira entirely out of Kantō, Yoritomo ordered an advance on the enemy clan's capital, Kyoto. He put the attacking forces under the co-command of his younger brother Minamoto no Yoshitsune and their cousin Yoshinaka, who built a fortress at Hiuchiyama (in Echizen Province). In April–May 1183, another of the clan's commanders, Taira no Koremori, attacked the fortress—a move that would seem to have been foolhardy, since the fortress was built atop high rocky crags and was to all appearances unassailable. Yoshinaka had even built a dam to flood a moat below the fortress. Warriors who ventured to cross the moat for an attack could be swept away in a flood.

But Koremori was no fool. He had secured the services of a turncoat among the Minamoto fortress garrison, who tied a message to an arrow and loosed it into the Taira camp. The note provided instructions for breaching the dam, draining the water, and attacking straight across the moat. The "impregnable" fortress at Hiuchiyama fell quickly—though Yoshinaka escaped with most of his samurai.

YOSHINAKA EMBRACES HIS COUSIN

Despite scattered victories such as that at Hiuchiyama, by the late spring of 1183, the armies of the Taira clan were wasting away, as much by famine as by battle. To make up their losses, Taira commanders gathered recruits from all over the countryside. Although they may have recruited as many as 100,000 new troops (This is according to contemporary sources; modern historians believe the total was fewer than half this number.), the effort was self-defeating. The newcomers were peasant farmers, who left their fields unharvested to join the Taira ranks, thereby deepening the famine.

Yoshinaka knew that the next Taira attack would be massive. He had clashed with his cousin Yoritomo earlier in the year, in March, when Yoritomo threatened to fight him for control of the Minamoto clan. Refusing to take the bait, Yoshinaka persuaded Yoritomo that only a fully united front could resist the Taira. To demonstrate his own good faith, he sent his son Yoshitaka as a voluntary hostage to Yoritomo's Kamakura headquarters.

The Samurai's Samurai

Oba Kagechika (d. 1180) was among the most famous of samurai during the Heian Period (794–1185), the epoch that saw the rise of the samurai and created the model that subsequent generations of samurai emulated. Oba achieved legendary fame for the valor he displayed in the Hōgen Rebellion of 1156, a civil war contesting both the imperial succession and control of the Taira-allied Fujiwara clan.

He challenged Minamoto no Tametomo to combat by calling out to him, "Lord Hachiman! During the Three Years War, in the attack upon the stockade at Kanazawa, Kamakura Gongorō Kagemasa, then only sixteen years of age, went to the front of the battle, and when his left eye was pierced by an arrow through his visor he loosed a shaft in return and took his assailant. I am the youngest descendant of that Gongorō, Oba Heita Kageyoshi's son, Oba Sabur Kagechika. Come on and fight!"

His was the perfect blend of respect, defiance, boast, and courage that marked the ideal of samurai conduct.

The Sun Flag

The starkly simple national flag of Japan, a large red circle on a field of white, is familiarly called the Hinomaru, literally "sun disk," although its official name is Nissh ki, "sun flag." While it is universally acknowledged that the flag represents the rising sun, an image that has always resonated powerfully in Japanese religion and culture, little is known about the historical origin of the flag, except that its colors are those of the Minamoto clan. There is a widely revered legend that the modern Hinomaru was presented to the samurai Minamoto no Yoshimitsu by Emperor Reizei. Tradition holds that the flag today enshrined at the Unpo-ji temple in Yamanashi Prefecture is that very treasure.

The Hinomaru was used on military pennants throughout the fifteenth and sixteenth centuries, but it was not until 1870 that the Emperor Meiji officially adopted the Hinomaru as the "civil ensign" of the nation. During World War II, the Hinomaru became for the Allied nations, especially the United States, a hated symbol of Japanese imperial militarism, and its use was suppressed for a time during the postwar U.S. occupation of the country. It came back into favor, however, but was not legally and universally adopted until legislative passage of the Law Concerning the National Flag and Anthem in 1999.

SHOWDOWN AT KURIKARA

The alliance was solidified in the nick of time. Shortly after the reversal at Hiuchiyama, Yoshinaka learned that Koremori's large Taira army was advancing along the western coast of Honsh u. Yoshinaka saw an opportunity to intercept this force, and with his uncle Minamoto no Yukiie and his own *shitenn o* (cadre of loyal lieutenants: Imai Kanehira, Higuchi Kanemitsu, Tate Chikatada, and Nenoi Yukichika), he made the long march toward the narrow mountain passes connecting western Honsh u with the eastern portion of the island.

As Koremori approached the passes, he divided his army, one wing taking the Kurikara Pass up the slope of a mountain called Tonamiyama and the other descending on Etchu Province. Yoshinaka observed the twisting snake of Taira warriors threading its way through the pass. Aware that Koremori's army far outnumbered his own, Yoshinaka set out a great many white banners—the emblematic color of his clan—on a hill he knew Koremori could see. By giving the impression of possessing a much greater force than he actually commanded, Yoshinaka prompted Koremori's advance to halt at the crest of the pass until nightfall.

While Koremori paused and pondered, Yoshinaka deployed one cohort to hit the Taira from the rear, another to lie in ambush at the foot of the pass, and a third—under his personal leadership—to present itself to the enemy front and center. The great commanders have always been those who possess the imagination to put themselves in the mind of their adversary and then to conduct their own strategy and tactics accordingly. According to Japanese chronicles, the Taira had a reputation for effete refinement that disinclined them to undertake the conventional brutalities of war as practiced by the Minamoto clan. It is likely that Yoshinaka sought to exploit this reputation by offering the Taira the opportunity for ritualized single combat as an alternative to all-out war. This ploy would buy him additional time until dark and misdirect Koremori's commanders, preventing them from seeing his movements.

YOSHINAKA INITIATED THE EXCHANGE BY LETTING LOOSE A FUSILLADE OF ARROWS TIPPED WITH DRIED LILY BULBS INTO WHICH SLITS HAD BEEN CUT SO THAT THEY WOULD WHISTLE EERILY IN FLIGHT.

Moving his central force into position, Yoshinaka initiated the exchange by letting loose a fusillade of arrows tipped with dried lily bulbs into which slits had been cut so that they would whistle eerily in flight. It was the traditional challenge to individual combat, resembling the European knightly joust. As Yoshinaka knew they would, the Taira eagerly accepted the challenge and descended from the crest of the pass. Thus Yoshinaka coaxed the cream of Koremori's army from its advantageous high-ground position.

While the Taira were entirely absorbed in the jousts, Yoshinaka and his lieutenants took up attack positions. No sooner had darkness fallen and the single combats come to an end than the Taira samurai turned about to discover a large Minamoto force approaching them from behind. Yoshinaka had furnished these men with more than the requisite number of clan banners, again to give the illusion of superior numbers. Simultaneously with the attack on the Taira rear, Yoshinaka ordered the troops of his central force—who, in the darkness, had mounted to the top of the pass vacated by the Taira—to release a large herd of oxen they had rounded up. With flaming torches bound to their horns, the massive animals descended the pass, plodding directly into the Taira army.

Bewildered, the enemy warriors attempted to charge the herd. Single combat, man on man, is one thing, but man against 1,000 pounds (454 kg) of ox is quite another. Most of the Taira soldiers were trampled to death or knocked off the treacherous pass, falling to a bloody end on the jagged rocks below. Those who managed to get by the beasts were soon swallowed up in darkness and fell easy prey to the portion of the Minamoto army that had been lying in ambush, out of sight. The few survivors fled the field, and the Battle of Kurikara, June 2, 1183, was the turning point of the Genpei War, leading directly to the Taira abandonment of Kyoto, which soon fell to Yoshinaka.

For Yoshinaka's dazzling victory, Minamoto no Yoritomo delivered neither his congratulations nor his gratitude. Instead, he assumed that the ambition of the triumphant general would be uncontrollable; therefore, Yoritomo dispatched Yoshitsune and another brother, Nonyori, to do battle against him. A number of fights developed around Kyoto during 1184, from which Yoshitsune ultimately emerged victorious. Driven out of Kyoto, Yoshinaka was killed in combat at nearby Awazu.

VICTORY AT SEA

Throughout the rest of 1184, the Minamoto forces doggedly rolled up all remaining Taira resistance. On April 25, 1185, at Dan-no-ura in the Shimonoseki Strait off the southern tip of Honshū, a Minamoto fleet under the command of Yoshitsune fell upon the Taira fleet and defeated it in the course of some six hours.

By all accounts it was a spectacular sea battle. Although the Taira fleet was outnumbered, its commanders had the advantage of operating in home waters and had intimate knowledge of the treacherous tides of Shimonoseki Strait. Fancying themselves masters of naval tactics, the Taira divided their fleet into three squadrons, whereas the Minamoto ships hoved in together, all abreast, their decks lined with archers. The battle began with an exchange of arrows fired at long range.

Hoping to achieve quick victory, the divided Taira fleet took advantage of the tides to drive their ships into an envelopment of the enemy. They closed around the Minamoto, as a pair of hands might close round and strangle a throat. The long-range combat rapidly transitioned to fighting hand-to-hand with long and short swords as crews boarded one another's vessels. Had the Taira been able to bring this portion of the combat to a swift and decisive close, they would surely have carried the day, but the tide that had brought them in now flowed out, forcing the ships apart and returning the advantage to the large Minamoto fleet.

▲

The Dan-no-ura sea battle was the subject of many nineteenth-century Japanese woodblock prints. Believing drowning to be the only honorable alternative to capture, the imperial grandmother prepares to leap overboard with the child emperor Antoku.

Yoshitsune possessed another advantage as well. General Taguchi Shigeyoshi had betrayed his Taira employers and revealed to him which ship bore the six-year-old Emperor Antoku, together with the crown jewels. Armed with this intelligence, Yoshitsune ordered his archers to concentrate their arrows against the helmsman and oarsmen of Antoku's vessel. After it drifted out of control, he ordered fire against the oarsmen and helmsmen of every other enemy ship within range. Before long, the emperor's ship and those around it drifted aimlessly, creating panic among their crews. Sensing inevitable defeat, many of the enemy samurai leaped overboard, preferring suicide by drowning to surrender.

Before long, the emperor's ship and those around it drifted aimlessly, creating panic among their crews. Sensing inevitable defeat, many of the enemy samurai leaped overboard, preferring suicide by drowning to surrender.

Both six-year-old Emperor Antoku and his grandmother, the widow of Taira clan leader Taira no Kiyomori, were among the drowned. To this day, the Heike crabs, which are found in the Straits of Shimonoseki, are considered highly delectable—in no small part because they are believed to hold the spirits of the child emperor and the Taira warriors slain in his service.

The few Taira warriors who survived the battle were captured and for the most part executed. During the culminating moments of the exchange, in an ecstasy of despair, the Taira crews began heaving the crown jewels overboard rather than let them fall into Minamoto hands; however, only two items, a mirror and a great sword—said to have been carried from heaven by the first emperor of Japan—splashed into the sea before a boarding party captured the jewel ship. Divers soon recovered the mirror, but most historians believe the sacred sword was lost. Cherished Japanese custom differs from the opinion of the scholars and holds that the sword was found and that it is the weapon now housed at Atsuta Jingu, a much-visited Shinto shrine in Nagoya.

THE LEGACY OF DAN-NO-URA

The victory at Dan-no-ura put Yoritomo on the path to control of Japan. He had not merely defeated a rival clan, but had for the first time in Japanese history created an effective alliance among regional powers, building in the process a government and establishing policies and institutions that replaced aristocratic rule with the reign of the shoguns, the military rulers of civil government.

In 1191, Yoritomo visited the new emperor in Kyoto, who certified Yoritomo's authority by appointing him *sei-i-tai-shogun* ("barbarian-defeating generalissimo") for life. As the first of the shoguns, Yoritomo initiated a tradition of militarism in Japanese government, enshrining the identity of the samurai, along with the bushido code of warrior conduct and honor. These cultural elements would rise and ebb throughout Japanese history, but they would never entirely disappear, and by the late nineteenth century, they fed the flames of a militaristic imperialism, which increasingly shaped the conduct of Japanese foreign policy, first revealed to the Western world by the stunning Japanese victory against the Russian fleet in the Russo-Japanese War (1904–1905).

The military dictatorship the Genpei War created lasted a century and a half—from 1185 to 1333—but the tradition of Japanese militarism lasted much longer and was of far more than historical consequence. The chain of cause-and-effect from the attack on Pearl Harbor on December 7, 1941, ran straight back to the twelfth-century struggle between the Taira and Minamoto clans, which had created in Japan a collective national mythology and ethos that would be quenched only in the fires of the most destructive weapon ever used in warfare, the atomic bombs dropped on Hiroshima and Nagasaki in August 1945.

CHAPTER 5

REVOLT AND REACTION:
THE PEASANTS' WAR IN GERMANY

1524–1526

In Europe's biggest popular uprising prior to the French Revolution,

armies of German peasants marched across the northern reaches of the Holy Roman Empire

in a bloody struggle to transform medieval society forever

I

t seems to have begun like this. In August 1524, in the Black Forest of the Rhine Valley (a place of old-growth woods so lush that both the sun and the Renaissance were slow to penetrate), the Countess of Lupfen one day ordered the peasants living on her husband's fief to gather strawberries and snail shells. The first were for her table, the second to wind her skeins around after she had spun them from the wool of the peasants' sheep who grazed her husband's domain.

These were not especially burdensome demands for the lady of the manor to make of her tenants, but for some reason they sparked a flame. Perhaps it was because even the hamlets of the Black Forest were buzzing with tales of a priest in Wittenberg, Martin Luther by name, who was preaching that Christ had made everyone, peasant and countess alike, free and equal.

THE PEASANTS RISE

After spending his youth as a soldier of fortune, Hans Müller returned to his native village of Blugenbach, a place under both the shadow and heel of the monastery of St. Blasien. Sensing the anger all about him, he recruited some 1,200 peasants who no longer wanted to gather strawberries and snail shells at the behest of the countess. On the feast day of St. Bartholomew, August 24, Müller marched them to Waldshut, easternmost of the so-called "forest towns," and proclaimed there a secret order, the Evangelical Brotherhood, whose members sent riders throughout Germany, each bearing a dispatch from him, inciting the peasants of one village after another to rise.

From Baden in the Black Forest, to the Alsace in the west and throughout the Rhineland and Mosel territories, as far as Thuringia in the east, the message of the Brotherhood was carried. The order made two demands: that there should be no lord but the Holy Roman emperor, to whom the peasantry would gladly render just tribute in return for a guarantee of what they deemed their rights as free Christian men; and to ensure that the lords would be gone, together with their church allies, the Brotherhood also demanded that all castles and monasteries be destroyed.

Müller's message kindled what would be called the Peasants' War, which would become the biggest popular uprising in European history until the French Revolution. By the time German nobles of the Swabian League brought an end to it about two years after it had

This 1879 painting depicts the attack peasant leader Jäcklein Rohrbach conducted against the town of Weinsberg on April 16, 1525. Jäcklein's peasant forces killed the garrison defending the town and forced the local nobleman, Count Ludwig von Helfenstein, together with sixteen of his knights, to run a gauntlet of men armed with pikes and long knives.

begun, 130,000 peasants were dead. Yet, when this orgy of death and destruction had ended, so did most memory of it. For more than three centuries no one seemed to care about the Peasants' War, at least not until 1850, when Friedrich Engels—with Karl Marx, the cofounder of communism—wrote about it in an effort to explain the failure of the revolutions that swept Europe in 1848–1849. Class warfare of the bloodiest sort, Engels wanted to show, was nothing new.

THE PEASANTS' WAR WOULD BECOME THE BIGGEST POPULAR UPRISING IN EUROPEAN HISTORY UNTIL THE FRENCH REVOLUTION.

PRINCES' JUSTICE

By mid-October 1524, Müller had about 5,000 followers, armed with pitchforks, scythes, and axes, but with winter not far off, he decided to accept an offer from the chancellor of the Bishop of Constanz to open negotiations with the nobility at a court convened in Stockach, in Baden-Württemberg, at what is now the southern border of Germany. Müller and his peasant army moderated their original demand for an end to the rule of the lords and the destruction of their castles and instead presented sixteen articles: modest demands that included the abolition of the lords' exclusive hunting rights, an end to serf labor, a reduction in taxes, protection against arbitrary arrest, and guarantees of fair trials.

◄

After discovering that he had become an unwitting instigator of the Peasants' War, Martin Luther, architect of the Protestant Reformation, called for the suppression of the uprising by the harshest possible means.

Hierarchy: The Way It Was in 1524

German society at the outbreak of the Peasants' War was strictly divided into the following classes:

The Princes

Theoretically, these territorial rulers were subordinate only to the Holy Roman emperor, but he was so far away and so weak that most German princes were absolute monarchs of all they surveyed. The lesser nobility and the clergy paid no taxes, so the burden of supporting the princes fell wholly and heavily upon the peasants.

The Lesser Nobility

By the early sixteenth century, the spread of mercenary armies and the growing use of gunpowder and foot soldiers (infantry) were beginning to make the role of knights obsolete. Still, these nobles sought to support their luxurious lives in hereditary castles, and so demanded a great deal of the peasants who were tenants on their domains.

The Clergy

Like the knights, the clergy were also under threat by the sixteenth century. The development of printing spread literacy and new ideas, wresting from the church its long monopoly on learning. Bishops, abbots, and local priests were often corrupt, selling indulgences (forgiveness for sins) and levying taxes on the peasants within their parishes. It was against such corruption that Martin Luther protested in 1517.

The Patricians

In towns, the families of hereditary wealth constituted the patrician class, whose members dominated the town councils and held other key administrative posts. By the sixteenth century, this class was also under assault from the rising middle class of merchants and tradespeople. The patricians maintained their wealth by levying various duties and tolls.

The Burghers

The burghers were the emerging upper middle class, well-established tradespeople who, with their self-acquired wealth, were a notch below the patricians, whose wealth was hereditary. This class was now making increasing demands for power and influence.

The Plebeians

The upper level of the lowest class of sixteenth-century society were called the plebeians. They were urban laborers and journeymen craftspeople. Some were former burghers who had fallen on hard times. Landless, the plebeians had no real rights under law.

The Peasants

At the bottom of the lowest class were the peasants, who were the rural agricultural workers and tenant farmers. Peasants owned nothing and were themselves, in effect, the property of some member of the upper classes, a prince, a lesser noble, an urban patrician, or even a bishop. They were obliged to render whatever service was demanded of them and pay often exorbitant taxes that kept them at or just below a level of barest subsistence.

Having presented their case, the peasants withdrew to their homes, whereupon the nobles at Stockach demanded that they not remain idle in their villages, but resume rendering all the traditional services and paying all the regular taxes until the court had issued its decision. The peasants indignantly refused, and the revolt spread farther, engulfing Swabia, Franconia, and Alsace.

THE STUFF OF REVOLUTION

Had the nobles bargained with the peasants in good faith, the revolt might have been contained, maybe even ended, before it fairly began. Their strategic error was of course the product of a selfish desire to preserve the status quo, but its ultimate source went even deeper. The refusal of the nobles to negotiate was a failure of vision.

Whereas the nobles saw the peasants trying to take something away from them, the peasants saw themselves fighting for nothing less than their rightful place in society.

Those nobles who took the proceedings at Stockach so lightly failed to acknowledge that the social reality they shared with the peasants had changed. Both peasant and noble had been born into a universe headed by a Holy Roman emperor (whose reach extended from Germany in the north, to Italy in the south, and from the Russian and Turk borderlands in the east to France and the Low Countries in the west) and by a pope (whose realm, in theory, was nothing less than the human soul). But neither emperor nor pope dealt directly with prince or peasant. For noble and peasant, the immediate reality was the relationship that existed between them. It was a relationship of landlord to tenant and master to servant, a relationship nevertheless ratified by empire and church, which were held to be the manifestations of God's kingdom on Earth.

A Sixteenth-Century Armory

Peasants armed themselves with whatever came to hand. Since the thirteenth century, feudal laws had barred them from owning weapons. They all had pitchforks, however, as well as long butchering knives. Many had scythes, rakes, and boar spears—long pointed weapons for killing wild boars. In some places, peasants had been formed into militia companies at the behest of their lords. Among these groups, polearms—a combination battleaxe/spear mounted on stout wooden poles about eight feet (2.4 m) long—were available, as were rudimentary articles of armor, such as breastplates and helmets.

The armies of the nobles, both local and mercenary, were equipped with polearms, armor, swords, battleaxes, and arquebuses (an early form of musket)—so heavy that they had to be fired from a forked rest—and field artillery, capable of firing three- or four-pound (1.3 or 1.8 kg) cannonballs.

All of these weapons gave the forces of the nobility major advantages; however, the two most important "weapons" they possessed were horses and castles. The peasants had almost no cavalry, whereas the forces of the nobles were mounted in large numbers. This gave them greater speed and range. Tactically, cavalry permitted swift and devastating hit-and-run attacks that were difficult to defend against. As for castles, these provided fortified bases from which armed units could operate, whereas the peasants were mostly in exposed encampments, which were much more difficult to defend.

Then came Luther, who protested church corruption and, in so doing, challenged the church itself, including the right of pope and priests to stand between the people and their God. Those who followed Luther's teachings to their ultimate conclusion came to believe that every Christian was equal in the eyes of God. The more moderate among these believers were still willing to accept the authority of the Holy Roman emperor and even the pope, but not the lesser lords and priests who hovered between these figures and themselves.

At Stockach, the nobles failed to grasp the magnitude of the stakes in this "Peasants' War." They could not—or they refused to—understand that *they*, princes and lords, had to justify *their* rightful place in the universe.

Those who incited and led the peasants, not just soldiers like Müller, but radical theologians, such as renegade Lutheran Thomas Müntzer, were motivated by an understanding of the grandest implications of Martin Luther's protests—the very basis and structure of society had to change.

THE PITCHFORK-ARMED FORCES OF THE PEASANTS RESEMBLED ARMIES FAR LESS THAN WHAT THEY REALLY WERE: MOBS.

The peasants themselves, however, glimpsed this dimly, if at all. Their immediate experience of right and wrong, of justice and injustice, was the treatment they received at the hands of their landlord. If a capricious demand for strawberries and snail shells really could ignite a revolution, a sincere demonstration of fair treatment really could end one. Instead, the nobles used the loose alliance that had long existed among them, the Swabian League, to hire a mercenary army under one of their own, Georg III Truchsess von Waldburg, to put down the rebellion at any cost.

GERMANY IN FLAMES

At first, vastly outnumbered, Truchsess could do little but watch, attacking isolated peasant bands whenever the opportunity presented itself, but taking no truly decisive action. When the Stockach court reconvened in December 1524, it consisted exclusively of noblemen, and the peasants began to understand they had no hope of justice. Nevertheless, guided by Thomas Müntzer, they issued a new set of demands, twelve articles this time, reduced from the earlier sixteen. The articles included reduction of interest rates and an end to compulsory service to feudal lords; mitigation of legal penalties for certain offenses; restoration of former fishing, hunting, and grazing rights; the abolition of serfdom on the grounds that Christ had made all men free (in return, the articles promised obedience to authorities legitimately appointed by God's representatives on Earth); and the right of the people to choose their own pastors.

The twelve articles were moderate and reasonable, but the nobles refused to take them seriously and, truth to tell, the articles meant nothing to most of the peasants. By this point, the peasant forces, loosely organized, were beyond the control of a scrap of parchment stained with writing they could not read. Their pitchfork-armed forces resembled armies far less than what they really were: mobs.

Across the region, separate peasant mobs, each several thousand strong, were commanded by the likes of George Metzler, a tavern-keeper, and others, including Wendel Hipler and Jäcklein Rohrbach. Florian Geyer, a Franconian nobleman, and Götz von Berlichingen, a mercenary knight, also led peasant units with the aim of eliminating rivals among fellow nobles and acquiring their property.

There were battles in the Peasants' War, but for the most part, there were rampages. Armies did not square off against one another; instead, the peasants knocked down castles and churches and murdered all who were unfortunate enough not to run away. By the spring of 1525, destruction was general throughout Germany.

On April 16, Jäcklein Rohrbach led rebels against Weinsberg, killed the men-at-arms assigned to defend the town, and forced the local nobleman, Count Ludwig von Helfenstein, together with sixteen of his knights, to run a gauntlet of peasants armed with pikes and long knives. They were butchered alive.

PEASANTS VICTORIOUS

By early May, peasant forces numbered perhaps 30,000 or more. Everywhere, they were victorious over the nobility, and the bishops of Bamberg and Speyer, the abbots of Hersfeld and Fulda, and even the elector (elected ruler) of the Palatinate made concessions to whatever the peasants demanded.

At this point, led by the burghers, several cities joined in the uprising, which became increasingly well coordinated by a board of peasants. The board planned to reshape the uprising into a genuine revolution. It wanted to establish a "chancery" at Heilbronn (in the southwest of modern Germany), from which the rebel bands would be commanded and coordinated and at which a peasant government was to be created.

Once it accomplished this, it would send most of the peasants under arms home and maintain only a select group of the best warriors in the field while the Heilbronn leaders focused on bringing permanent political change by overthrowing the territorial princes. After they were removed, the next step was to reorganize the Holy Roman Empire itself to give the peasant class a full voice in the government and to greatly strengthen the empire at the expense of the local princes. As for church property, it would be secularized and given to the feudal lords in exchange for the cancellation of the peasants' obligations to them.

Noble Justice

After Würzburg surrendered to him, Truchsess convened what he called a "court of justice" in the heart of the town. But he did not grant his peasant captives the dignity of a trial. The verdict on each was summary, and the executioner Truchsess nominated was Hans, his court jester, who nimbly struck off heads one after the other to the applause and laughter of the knights and mercenaries.

Typically, Truchsess asked the accused two questions. *Can you read?* And if the answer was yes, the next question was *Have you read the Bible?* Those who answered yes to one or both of these questions were beheaded without another word.

In haste, errors were made. The gout-afflicted old priest of Schipf, a stalwart enemy of the peasants, was borne on a litter by four of his men to receive thanks from Truchsess for his services. The zealous Hans, mistaking the old man for a peasant, sneaked behind him and lopped off his head.

"I seriously reproved my good Hans for his untoward jest," Truchsess later remarked.

Alarmed by the agitation at Heilbronn and the murder of Helfenstein and his knights, the petty sovereigns of the Swabian League came together with the intention of crushing the rebellion once and for all. Even Martin Luther himself, who had earlier appealed to the nobility to distinguish between justifiable and unjustifiable peasant demands, was now appalled by a violence that for him did not betoken liberation, but chaos and anarchy. Indiscriminately he now condemned all of the rebels, urging, on May 6, the princes of ravaged Thuringia and the Harz district to join in the extermination of the "murdering and robbing band of the peasants"

COUNTERATTACK

The Swabian League sent Truchsess more troops, whom he led in a campaign to recapture the towns that had fallen to the peasants and to put down the uprising with utmost brutality. At the head of some 10,000 men, he swept through Alsace, slaughtering perhaps 20,000

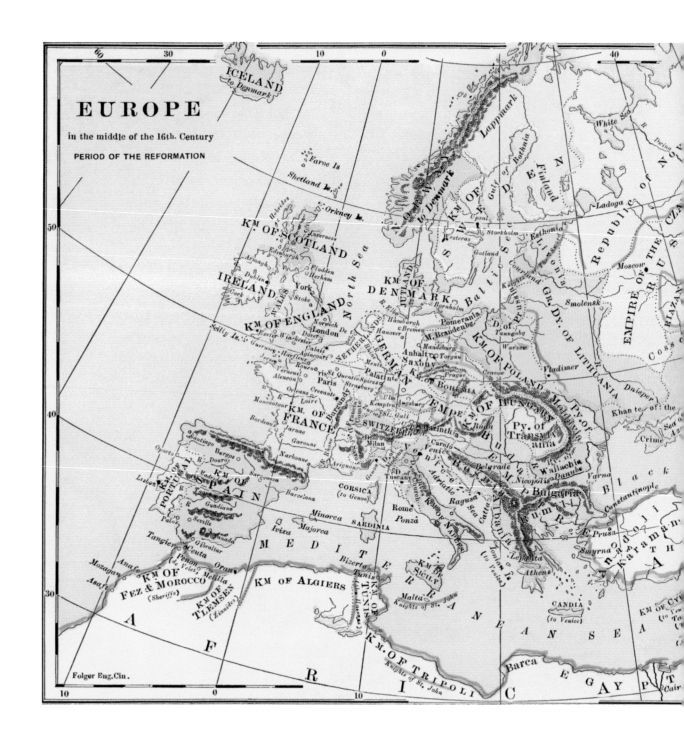

This is Europe as it existed during the early Protestant Reformation—the era of Germany's Peasants' War.

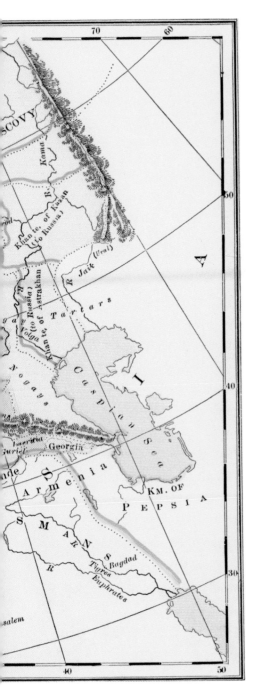

rebels. While he operated in the west, other noble armies formed in Hesse and Saxony under Georg, Duke of Saxony, Landgraf Philipp I of Hesse, and Frederick III, Elector of Saxony, to do battle with about 8,000 peasants under their fiery leader, Thomas Müntzer, whose radical battle cry was now *Omnia sunt communia!* (All things are in common).

The forces clashed at Frankenhausen on May 15, 1525. The nobles were handsomely equipped, their knights and mercenaries well trained and well mounted. The peasants were poorly armed and had neither training nor cavalry horses. Their losses have been estimated at between 3,000 and 10,000, whereas the noblemen suffered (by report) no more than a half-dozen casualties: two killed and four wounded. Taken prisoner, Müntzer recanted his heresies under torture and accepted the Roman Catholic mass—just before he was beheaded on May 27, 1525. His head and body were displayed as a warning to all those who might again preach treasonous doctrines.

By the time of Müntzer's execution, all of southern Germany had been pacified. In Alsace, on May 17, the united armies of Duke Anton of Lorraine and the Governor of Mörsperg defeated the last peasant armies. Swabian League forces next ended all resistance at Würtemberg, and in June, peasant mobs at Odenwald and Rothenburg were crushed. The town of Würzburg surrendered on June 7.

Fighting persisted sporadically in Austria, but the organized rebellion was over before the beginning of summer 1525. This did not stop marauding bands of noblemen and their mercenaries from punishing whatever peasant groups appeared to them to be hostile, either in act or intent. It is estimated that by the end of 1526 no fewer than 130,000 peasants were killed, either in battle, by random slaughter, or by more or less formal execution.

A REVOLUTION THAT MIGHT HAVE BEEN

What is perhaps most remarkable about the Peasants' War is how little known it was. Had Friedrich Engels not encountered a little-read history by Wilhelm Zimmermann and then used it to write his own book in 1850, the Peasants' War would be even more obscure today. Engels believed that the history of the Peasants' War had been deliberately suppressed, first by the Catholic Church (with the connivance of Martin Luther, who opposed the church, but was hardly an advocate of the mob or even of genuine political equality) and then by one European regime after another, all the way through modern times.

The last thing the ruling classes wanted was to exhibit a popular rebellion that came perilously close to leveling the social order. The peasants, precisely because they were peasants, vastly outnumbered the noble forces arrayed against them, and it does not take much imagination to see that the only reason they did not prevail was their failure to organize effectively under the Heilbronn leadership. Had they done so, they would have ceased to be a mob and become instead first an army and then a sociopolitical class to be reckoned with: powerful in number and united in cause.

The peasants of sixteenth-century Germany did not possess the degree of class consciousness required to effect enduring change. The laboring peoples of Europe would have more opportunities to alter their place in the scheme of things—in the French Revolution at the end of the eighteenth century, in the abortive but widespread revolts of 1848–1849, and in the Russian and Bolshevik Revolutions of 1917—each time with much hope and yet with even more death and destruction in an elusive quest for the finality of universal justice and liberty.

▲

A contingent of knights lead the men of the defeated Swabian peasant army to their doom—imprisonment, forced labor, mutilation, or execution. This colored woodcut was created in 1525, the year of the event depicted.

"THE THIRD ROME": IVAN THE TERRIBLE AND THE BOYARS' REVOLT

1547–1572

Russia's first czar transforms personal madness into an enduring and catastrophically influential

model of totalitarian rule based on fear and enforced by terroristic violence

orn into privilege on August 25, 1530, the son of Vasili III, powerful grand prince of Moscow, Ivan might just as well have been an orphan. It is not that Vasili hadn't longed for a son and heir, a desire so strong in him that when his wife of twenty years, Solomoniya Saburova, proved barren, he not only divorced her, but denounced her as a sorceress and had her locked away as a nun for the rest of her life. By doing this, Vasili hoped to escape the stigma of adultery when he married the young Serbo-Russian beauty Elena Glinskaya. She bore him the long-hoped-for son, but when Ivan was just three years old, a painful boil appeared on his father's leg. It would not heal, and soon the entire limb putrefied with infection, blood poisoning followed, and Vasili III, writhing on his deathbed, enjoined Elena to rule in Ivan's name until he was old enough to rule on his own.

At the time of Ivan's birth, Russia was not a kingdom, but a collection of principalities and fiefdoms centered on Moscow and bounded roughly by Kiev in the south, the Ural Mountains to the west and northwest, Archangel on the northeast, the Baltic Sea to east, and Smolensk on the southeast. This region was loosely governed by a class of noblemen called the boyars, among whom the late Vasili III had been the most powerful. Two boyars, Elena's brothers-in-law, Yuri of Dmitrov and Andrei of Staritsa, challenged her regency over Ivan and commenced a bitter struggle accompanied by backstabbing that was both figurative and literal. It ended only when Elena engineered the imprisonment of Yuri in 1524 and Andrei three years later.

Elena, however, continued to raise the temperature of palace intrigue by her liaison with a handsome young boyar named Ivan Feodorovich Ovchina-Telepnev-Obolensky and her secretive dealings with Daniel, the powerful metropolitan (Russian Orthodox bishop) of Moscow. At the height of the discord, in 1538, Elena suddenly died, almost certainly poisoned by boyars of the Shuisky family, who usurped the regency. Ivan was eight years old.

EARLY LESSONS

The boy had already known heavy loss and chronic terror. He had seen family members, both kind and cruel, simply disappear—here one day and gone the next. He had felt the anger and fear that perpetually billowed through the Kremlin palaces like smoke. With his mother dead, the Shuisky boyars assumed control of him and his young brother Yuri.

The Shuisky men contended with other boyar families for dominion over Muscovy, the struggle for power making anything

◄

Czar Ivan the Terrible, on horseback, accepts the surrender of the ruling khan of Kazan. He added the realm to his Russia in 1552.

resembling good government impossible. The people suffered, and the young princes saw nothing but violence and the threat of violence within the Kremlin walls. Beyond those walls, they could see little but general want. In all this, both Ivan and his younger brother were utterly neglected, sometimes even to the point of semi-starvation. They were allowed to go about in filth and rags until some public occasion or formal ceremony required their being scrubbed and properly clothed.

IVAN PASSED THE TIME HURLING DOGS FROM THE TOP OF THE KREMLIN WALL AND SPENT HOURS ABSORBED IN OBSERVING THEIR PAINFUL DEATHS.

Ivan observed, endured, and learned. Seeing men tortured under his own eyes, he learned to take pleasure in torturing small animals. He passed the time hurling dogs from the top of the Kremlin wall and spent hours absorbed in observing their painful deaths. It is said that this behavior attracted the notice of the otherwise neglectful boyar regents, who looked on admiringly in the belief that such cruelty was appropriate training for one destined to rule.

And rule Ivan would, bringing about the transformation of medieval Muscovy into an empire over which he would claim the imperial title of Czar of All Russia. The people would call him Ivan Grozny—literally Ivan the Awesome—but the conduct of his reign would bequeath to history a different translation, Ivan the Terrible. It also brought the homage of a much later ruler, Joseph Stalin, a man not given to reverence, but who saw in Ivan the Terrible a brother in the history of Russian rule.

IVAN THE ENLIGHTENED

On January 16, 1547, at the Cathedral of the Dormition in Moscow, Ivan was crowned with a skullcap worked in gold filigree, bejeweled, trimmed in sable, and surmounted by a gold cross. For some two hundred years, Monomakh's Cap had been the crown of Muscovy's grand princes, but on this occasion, the sixteen-year-old Ivan, having learned that the surest way to acquire power was to seize it, proclaimed himself no mere prince of Muscovy, but emperor—czar—of Russia, the first ruler to claim that title.

Ivan commenced what looked to be an enlightened reign, marked by swift reforms and modernization, intended both to improve the lot of the Russian people and to diminish the power of the boyars. The new czar revised, rationalized, and liberalized the law code; established the streltsy, a standing army that would reduce reliance on mercenaries and forces loyal to individual boyars; created the Zemsky Sobor, a rudimentary popular assembly; and established the Chosen Council, an assembly of nobles directly answerable to him. He also set about standardizing and unifying the rituals of the Orthodox Church throughout Russia. To increase the efficiency of the government, Ivan even introduced a degree of local self-administration, especially in the northeast, and in the boldest step of all, he brought the first printing press into the country.

In the face of these reforms, the boyars were worried—and well they should have been. The title Ivan had assumed, *czar*, was a Russian derivation of the Latin *caesar*. Under the tutelage of the new Orthodox metropolitan, Macarius, Ivan formulated the doctrine of "Moscow—the Third Rome," a term and concept first broached by Ivan's father, Vasili III. He intended to become the absolute ruler of a unified and greatly expanded Russian empire, with Moscow at its center, much as the city of Rome had served as the nucleus of the vast Roman Empire. And the boyars, who had poisoned his mother and abused him, would have little or no part in it.

Before the boyars could rise effectively against Ivan, a fire broke out in Moscow on June 24, 1547. It tore through the wooden city with frightening speed, the flames leaping

Ivan the Good?

Worldwide, Ivan the Terrible is the embodiment of tyrannical misrule. Outside of Russia, the excesses of Joseph Stalin—the political paranoia that fueled mass exiles and executions, the proliferation of gulags, the creation of a terror-driven police state—were compared to those of the czar. And it is true that Stalin looked to Ivan IV as a historical model of rule for Russia—not, however, to justify tyranny, but to validate what he considered a necessary course of strong leadership.

Far from being a perverse interpretation of the career of Ivan the Terrible, Stalin's point of view was straight out of the great body of Russian folklore. For in contrast to the rest of the world, the Russian people had traditionally pictured Ivan as a friend to the common folk precisely because he was the enemy of the boyars. Many Russian folktales depict Ivan as befriending peasants and defending them against boyars as well as the rising merchant (middle) class. In one well-known tale, Ivan even partners with a common thief to rob a boyar.

In place of the "mad" czar capable of limitless cruelty—the image portrayed in novels, operas, plays, and even films worldwide—Russian folktales depict Ivan IV as a kind of combination Robin Hood and stern but loving father to the people. The pervasiveness of such folkloric depictions suggests the power of the ideal image of any czar as the protector and benefactor of the people. Even the compelling reality of Ivan's extreme misrule could not trump this ideal, which was firmly fixed in the popular imagination of the Russian people.

Fortress, Palace, Seat of Power

At the heart of Moscow, the Kremlin is today the official residence of the Russian president and has been a center of government since at least the fourteenth century; however, it is believed that the site has been inhabited since about 2000 BCE and early in its history became a fortified complex of secular and religious structures. During much of the medieval period, the Kremlin was known simply as the *grad*—town—of Moscow. Grandly extended by Prince Yuri Dolgoruky in 1156, it was largely destroyed by the Mongols in 1237 and then rebuilt mostly in oak in 1339. The Grand Duke Ivan I had ordered the first stone structures built during the early 1300s, and when Peter, metropolitan of Rus, moved his seat from Kiev to Moscow, the Kremlin became an ecclesiastical capital. Great churches and cathedrals were built. Only one, the Savior Cathedral, survived into the twentieth century, but was demolished on orders of Stalin in 1933.

Grand Prince Dmitri Donskoi tore down the Kremlin's oak walls and replaced them with stone during 1366–1368. It was from these that young Ivan, learning the cruel ways of Russian czarist rule, hurled dogs to their deaths.

Another Kremlin structure that played an important role in the life of Ivan the Terrible was the Cathedral of the Dormition, site of his coronation. Construction of the original cathedral began in 1326. This building was torn down in 1472 and was to be replaced by a new cathedral designed by Russian architects, but in 1474, just as the structure was nearing completion, it was shaken to its foundation by a rare Moscow earthquake. Grand Prince Ivan III asked the Italian architect Aristotele Fioravanti to build an entirely new cathedral, which was completed and consecrated in 1479.

Ivan the Terrible commissioned a great cathedral of his own, officially known as the Cathedral of Intercession of the Virgin on the Moat, but familiarly called Saint Basil's, which was completed in 1561. This exuberantly colorful multidomed church remains one of the most familiar sights and symbols of Moscow and is often mistaken for the Kremlin itself—though, in fact, the cathedral lies outside of the Kremlin walls on Red Square. It has been said that Ivan was so awed by the beauty of Saint Basil's that he rewarded the architect, Postnik Yakovlev, by blinding him so that he could never design a structure to rival it. Such was the legendary cruelty of Czar Ivan that the story was and remains widely believed. However, the fact is that Yakovlev went on to build several other churches after Saint Basil's, suggesting that even Ivan's brutality had a limit.

over the Kremlin walls and touching off the gunpowder stored in the magazines distributed throughout several of the compound's towers. Before it was over, the Great Fire of Moscow had killed nearly 4,000 and rendered homeless 80,000—virtually the entire population of the city.

So great a calamity at the opening of Ivan's reign might have doomed the czar; however, the people of Moscow did not blame him, but his maternal Glinski relatives. Displaced and bereft of all that they owned, a Muscovite mob rose up against the Glinski boyars. Yuri Glinksi was stoned to death inside the fire-damaged Cathedral of the Dormition, as Metropolitan Macarius looked on in horror. Yuri's brother, Mikhail, took flight for Lithuania, only to be caught and killed. Even Ivan's maternal grandmother, Anna Glinski, did not escape the wrath of the mob. She was accused of having kindled the fire with sorcery.

Czar Ivan was only too happy to see the fall of the Glinski boyars and may even have incited the popular rebellion against them. He did draw the line, however, at the mob's demand that he turn his grandmother over to them. She was family, after all—and besides, the old woman posed no threat to his power.

These are the cathedrals of Moscow's Kremlin, as depicted in a watercolor from 1819.

MADNESS AND TYRANNY

With the populace having turned against them, the boyar aristocracy reeled from what seemed a mortal wound. For his part, Ivan built up the Chosen Council as his assembly of non-boyar and thoroughly subjugated boyar advisers. With the help of the Council, he centralized the government in Moscow, ensuring that the newly created self-administrative bodies in the northeast were directly answerable to him, and for the next decade, the rule of Ivan was the most enlightened and modern Russia had ever known. The former bounds of old Muscovy expanded prodigiously, eventually encompassing through conquest the eastern khanates of Kazan, Astrakhan, and Siberia, creating a diverse but centrally governed empire of nearly a billion acres. The czar, it seemed, was well on his way to creating the Third Rome of which he dreamed.

Up to this point, all of the boyars who had been killed were victims of the Russian people. Ivan's own method of suppressing their power was to co-opt them, incorporating them into his government and even his inner circle, where they had a stake in his well-being and where he could keep an eye on them. Russia was on the very verge of unprecedented prosperity, power, and stability when, in 1560, suddenly gripped by terrors born in childhood, Czar Ivan summarily dissolved the Chosen Council. Looking upon its members, he no longer saw trusted advisers, but only a collection of potential rivals and assassins. At this time, he reversed the enlightened trend of his rule over the populace, promulgating the first of several laws that severely restricted the mobility of the peasants and laid the foundation for universal serfdom among this class.

MODERN HISTORIANS BELIEVE IVAN SUFFERED A PSYCHOTIC BREAK, SOME SUGGESTING THAT IT MAY HAVE BEEN THE RESULT OF A LATE-STAGE SYPHILITIC INFECTION.

A darkness seemed to engulf the czar's character and personality. Modern historians believe he suffered a psychotic break, some suggesting that it may have been the result of a late-stage syphilitic infection. In his own era, many of Ivan's courtiers believed the change, sudden though it appeared to be, was rooted in a nearly fatal illness he had suffered

in 1553. At that time, Ivan summoned to what he believed was his deathbed the remaining boyars of whose loyalty he was confident. He asked them to swear an oath of allegiance to his infant son, so that he would be assured of ascending the throne. Some complied, but many others, believing the czar's death imminent and feeling no urge to remain loyal, refused. Ivan was outraged and found in their refusal further reason to distrust them.

For the most part, after he unexpectedly recovered from his illness, the czar forbade any reprisals against the disloyal boyars. Then, just before he dissolved the Chosen Council, his first wife, Anastasia Romanovna, suddenly died. The czar assumed that some of the turncoat boyars had poisoned her—as they had poisoned his mother—in a plot to overthrow him and put in his place his cousin, Vladimir of Staritsa. With the Council dissolved, the reprisals and assassinations began.

Among the most prominent to fall was Prince Alexander Borisovich Gorbatyi-Shuisky. One of the last of the once-powerful Shuisky boyars, he had led the Ivan's armies in the conquest of the Khanate of Kazan in 1547–52. As a reward for his service, the czar appointed him the first Russian governor of Kazan, but soon growing jealous of Gorbatyi-Shuisky's tremendous popularity, Ivan accused him in 1564 of

▲

The Russian artist Vasili Vasilevich Vlaimirov (1880/81–1931) titled this illustration, "A Boyar's Execution during the Dreadful Reign of Tsar Ivan IV (1530–84)."

hatching an assassination plot and secretly supporting Andrey Kurbsky. One of Ivan's most trusted friends and advisers, Kurbsky had served in the conquest of Kazan and in a subsequent war against Livonia (modern Latvia and Estonia), but on April 30, 1564, after Ivan decided against renewing Kurbsky's imperial military commission, he defected to Lithuania. Ivan sent manhunters to fetch Alexander Gorbatyi-Shuisky, together with his seventeen-year-old son Peter, and return them to Moscow, where they were both beheaded.

THE RISE OF THE BOYARS

The executions of a popular general and his son incited many of the boyars to open rebellion, which Ivan countered with a reign of terror in which thousands were rounded up, tortured, and killed at his behest. The czar kept a meticulous tally of his victims—surviving documents include some 4,000 names—and piously donated money to churches and monasteries to secure prayers for their departed souls.

Even in the frenzy of his bloodlust, Czar Ivan remained a politician of uncanny skill. The boyars might view him as a madman, but he understood that his persecution of this hated class earned him the loyalty of the Russian people. He resolved to manipulate this sentiment by taking his leave of Moscow and settling in the nearby hamlet of Aleksandrovskaia Sloboda. Here, from what to all appearances seemed his retirement, he announced his intention to abdicate. As Ivan knew it would, the announcement galvanized the people of Russia, who vastly preferred the rule of a "mad" czar to that of the greedy and ruthless boyars. They begged Ivan to remain on the throne.

With a feigned but effective demonstration of reluctance, he agreed—on condition that the people put together a payment to him of a large indemnity and that the metropolitan give his blessing to the purge, by eviction or death, of the principal boyars from an *oprichnina*, a royal domain to be put under his direct, exclusive, and absolute control. When both conditions were agreed to, Ivan recruited a band of *oprichniki*, a secret police force charged with clearing the royal domain of all the landed aristocracy. To ensure the loyalty of these men, Ivan gave them a portion of the property and wealth of those they evicted or killed.

◄

This map illustrates five hundred years of Russian growth, from 1300–1796. Ivan the Terrible, who was responsible for much of the expansion, was the first Russian ruler to proclaim himself czar-emperor.

The Knout

Thanks to Ivan the Terrible and many of the czars who succeeded him, Russia became for the rest of Europe a symbol of the brutality of absolute tyranny, and Russian tyranny was, in turn, distilled into a single emblematic object, the knout.

It was a heavy whip that came in at least three varieties. The ordinary knout had a sixteen-inch (41 cm) rawhide lash attached to a wooden handle. At the end of the lash was a metal ring on which a lash of harder leather was attached, terminating in a beak-shaped hook. A variation on this instrument was a knout consisting of numerous thongs interwoven with wire, each thong ending in a wired end. The third type was the "great knout," which had a handle about two feet (61 cm) long, to which a four-foot (1.2 m) flat leather thong was attached. At the end of this was a metal ring, to which a two-foot (0.6 m)-long hide strip was tied, sharply pointed at the end. Before punishment was administered, this strip was soaked in milk and dried in the sun to make it hard.

From the time of Ivan III (1462–1505) until Czar Nicholas I abolished it in 1845, the knout was the universal means of corporal punishment for virtually all criminal and political offenses in Russia. At the whim of the prince, the czar, or the judge, the corporal punishment could easily become capital punishment. A hundred lashes with the regular knout usually resulted in death. Just twenty lashes with the "great knout" were almost invariably fatal.

The oprichnina encompassed about a third of Russia as it existed at the time, taking in much of the country's most fertile land and most of the large central cities, including parts of Moscow. All that lay outside of the oprichnina was denominated the Zemshchina and was given over to the boyars. Ivan enjoyed absolute control over the oprichnina, the government of which he modeled on the Orthodox Church, but whereas church officials were answerable to God, Ivan answered to no one.

After purging the boyars, Ivan's oprichniki continued to wield the most extreme violence against anyone who offered the least resistance to the will of the czar, nobles and peasants included. All learned to fear this terroristic secret police force, whose uniform was a black cowl and whose saddle-bows were decorated with brooms and heads of dogs fixed in perpetual snarl, for it was the mission of the oprichniki to sweep the country clean of treason and hound out the traitors.

The price of Ivan's absolute dominion over the oprichnina was heavy. Control, after all, was equated with devastation, some of it by way of reprisal for resistance, but most of it preemptive, in anticipation of a rebellion that never came. When, for instance, in 1570, Ivan feared that the ancient city of Novgorod would be seized by the knights of the Teutonic Order and Sweden, which were at war with him, he sent the oprichniki to eliminate that possibility by destroying the city. Some accounts record casualties in excess of 30,000.

A MODEL FOR TERROR

If government is defined as a means of promoting the welfare of a people, the oprichnina was a catastrophic failure. Tax revenues declined instead of increased, and Ivan's war to acquire territory in Livonia foundered and failed. On the other hand, the oprichniki eliminated the most powerful of the boyars, and an attitude of quaking, abject submission to the czar was permanently instilled throughout Russia, even in the Zemshchina, outside of the oprichnina. Ivan abolished the oprichnina and disbanded the oprichniki in 1572, but by this time, the power of the boyars had been fatally reduced, and the Boyars' Revolt crushed, never to rise again.

The approach Ivan the Terrible took to the Boyars' Revolt was to wage a war of political intrigue and outright terror. It provided a model for many subsequent czars, who believed that fear created a stronger national bond than loyalty. The end of the czars in the Russian Revolution of 1917 did not mean the end of this calculus of ruling power. Joseph Stalin resurrected the government of Ivan in the twentieth century, bringing to bear the lessons of the czar upon modern totalitarianism in a police state. Stalin so admired Ivan that during World War II he approved director Sergei Eisenstein's project of making a film about the czar precisely because the Soviet dictator recognized in Ivan the kind of bold and decisive leadership he saw—or wanted to see—in himself. (Stalin loved the first part, completed in 1944, of what Eisenstein planned as a biographical trilogy, but when the director showed him the second part in 1946, the dictator ordered it banned because Ivan was portrayed more as an unbalanced tyrant than an unmitigated hero.)

The use of terror, assassination, and a dedicated secret police force, plus the creation around the czar of a cult of personality that pitted the people against the nobility for the purpose of fostering absolute allegiance to an absolute dictator, provided an archetype not only for Soviet dictatorship, but for the rise of Mussolini, Hitler, and the others who came to power between the twentieth century's two world wars. After World War II, Ivan's dream of expanding Russia into a "Third Rome" was reincarnated in Stalin's plans for the Soviet Union, which came to dominate all of eastern and much of central Europe through fifty years of Cold War.

THE BEAVER WARS: "NO INK BLACK ENOUGH TO DESCRIBE THE FURY OF THE IROQUOIS"

1638–1684

Driven by fashionable Europe's demand for North American beaver fur,

the Iroquois tribes sought to corner the trade in pelts by literally killing their competition

in an obscure series of wars that resulted in the annihilation of at least one rival tribe

and shaped all colonial wars to come, including the American Revolution

Through the winter silence of the Iroquois woodland comes the muffled crunch of moccasin boots in the snow. A lone figure covered in fur—a robe of animal pelts loosely draped from his shoulders—crunches to the river bank and eases down to the frozen river. He steps on the ice, stopping at what would be midstream in a warmer season, looks upstream toward a snow-covered beaver dam, then down at his feet.

From his shoulder, he lowers an iron axe, takes it in both hands, lifts it high over his head, then brings it down heavily into the thick river ice. He strikes blow after blow, chipping out a hole perhaps a foot and a half (0.5 m) in diameter. The sound of the flowing river comes up through it. The Iroquois lays the axe beside the hole, reaches into his robe, and withdraws a thick wooden club. He drops to his haunches, lays the club across his thighs, looks into the hole, and waits.

There are few sounds: the purling stream and the occasional crack of a branch or bough weighted heavily with snow and ice. Marked by the course of the pale winter sun, hours pass. The Iroquois, resting on his haunches the whole time, waits and watches.

At length he hears a faint splashing. He kneels, placing the club beside him. Suddenly, a buck-toothed, furry face appears above the rim. Plunging his hands into the icy water, the man seizes both of the chubby animal's short forepaws in his fists.

It is a beaver, eyes wide with fright.

Holding fast to the animal's paws and the Iroquois springs to his feet, swinging sixty pounds (27 kg) of living wet fur in front of him, over his head, then down very hard, onto the ice. The stunned creature is motionless. The man takes up his club and brings it down sharply onto the beaver's skull, once, twice. The snow-dusted river ice is splashed red with blood.

◄

Native Americans are shown carrying beaver pelts to trade with Europeans in this seventeenth-century engraving. Europeans clamored for beaver fur to use to trim collars, cuffs, and the tops of boots, but mostly, for hats. A hat of beaver fur was worn less for warmth than to proclaim socioeconomic status.

NEW WORLD, NEW SOCIETY

As the Dutch traders reckoned these things, it was early in the second third of the seventeenth century. For the Iroquois hunter, it was nothing more or less than a late winter morning. He would wait for another beaver or two to emerge through the hole he had cut, kill them as he had the first, and then carry his heavy load back to his village, where he could warm himself by the longhouse fire. He knew more beaver would come to him. He knew that they swam well under the ice, but like everything else, beavers have to breathe, and so they cannot resist a patch of blue sky through the ice.

Some Iroquois brought their pelts to the trading town of Fort Orange (today Albany, New York), but the most aggressive Dutch traders made the long trudge from that town to the most remote Native American villages to have their pick of the best pelts. This meant not only risking the hazards of the wilderness, but doing so loaded down with trade goods that marked a man as a prime target for thieves. Most trading, therefore, was done in those Native American villages located closest to the white settlements.

The typical Iroquois village was a bustling place, a forest refuge surrounded by a stockade consisting of upright logs driven into the earth and interlaced with saplings—as if a giant woven basket enclosed the settlement. The centerpieces of the village were the longhouses—there were at least two—about twenty feet (6 m) wide, twenty feet (6 m) high, and often more than 200 feet (61 m) long. Like the stockade, the walls were built of upright logs in between which saplings were woven. The roof was an arch created of saplings and was pierced by five or six holes for ventilation and to let out smoke from cooking and heating fires. Except for a hide-covered doorway at one end, these were the only full-time openings to the outside. Traders and missionaries who visited the villages always remarked on the perpetual darkness in the longhouses.

Each longhouse provided communal shelter for upward of twenty families. Thus a trader who had spent weeks tramping alone in the forest was typically overwhelmed by what seemed a mass of humanity when he entered the village to trade, offering guns and metal goods of all kinds, especially knives and iron axes, in exchange for pelts. Not that the traders' visit was all business. Indeed, many took wives from the villages, in part because they were available, but also to cement cordial relations with the tribe. Trade created a vibrant interracial culture on the frontier.

EXTINCTION AND GENOCIDE

Generations of Americans have grown up reading first- or second-hand the romantic historians of the nineteenth and early twentieth centuries, who portrayed the relationship between Europeans and native North American peoples as that of invader to invaded. In this view, the Native Americans were at once noble savages too innocent to live in a white world and an inferior race destined—naturally and inevitably—to be conquered by a superior race. In truth, as the lively trade in beaver pelts demonstrates, white–Indian relations were often based on economics and sometimes resulted in the creation of a culture that harmoniously blended both ways of life.

Such was the case in the seventeenth century, in the vast forest region centered on the Dutch trading settlement of Fort Orange, which after the English nudged the Dutch out of New Netherland in 1664 became Albany in a colony rechristened New York. Long after the late fifteenth century's promise of instant wealth from New World "gold and spices" had faded, tobacco remained the product of greatest value in the southern portion of the continent, and in the north, it was beaver fur. The American Indians found that Europeans would trade almost anything for it, and so they hunted, trapped, and traded until the beaver was all but extinct throughout the lands of the five Iroquois tribes—Mohawk, Oneida, Onondaga, Cayuga, and Seneca—that occupied a great swath of what today is upstate New York, from the Mohawk River in the east to Seneca Lake and the Genesee River, along the southern shore of Lake Ontario, in the west.

The scarcity of "product" compelled the Iroquois to expand their western range, and as they pushed into the territory of the Hurons and tribes associated with them, they found it, quite simply, most convenient to kill their competition in a fierce campaign of tribal genocide.

Old Hat

Trappers and traders were at the source end of a supply chain serving a market that by the close of the Renaissance, with the rapid rise of a European middle class, was exploding. Gentlemen—and to a lesser extent, gentlewomen—throughout Europe, but especially in England and France, clamored for fur, an economic and cultural symbol of newly won status and prosperity.

Fur was used to trim collars, cuffs, and the tops of boots, but mostly it was used for hats. For the men of Western Europe, from the sixteenth through the mid-nineteenth centuries, the hat functioned less to warm the head than to proclaim socioeconomic status, political orientation, cultural attitude, and even religious persuasion. During this period, upscale male headgear evolved into elaborately architectural creations that demanded a fur rich in appearance, highly durable, sufficiently stiff to maintain an often flamboyant structure, yet readily malleable into whatever shape fashion might dictate. The ideal material for building such a culturally charged article of clothing was beaver fur, and the ideal supplier of this material was the North American Indian.

In addition to trapping beaver for trade with Euro-American merchants, the Native American tribes wore robes made of several pelts stitched together. Throughout most of the seventeenth century, these second-hand garments were even more valuable than pelts from freshly trapped animals. Beaver fur consists of an outer layer of rough, coarse "guard hairs" and an inner layer of soft fur highly suitable for processing into felt for hats. In the case of the beaver robes, the friction of wear, combined with the action of human sweat and skin oils, removed the coarse guard hairs, rendering the beaver fur smooth, soft, durable, comfortable, and lustrous. The rich and powerful of Europe clamored for it. The European appetite for fur, once whetted, would not be sated for more than 300 years.

WARS UNREMEMBERED

That genocidal campaign would be known as the Beaver Wars. Spanning 1638–1684, they were brutally destructive in themselves, decimating entire tribes, but also momentous in their enduring effect on the destiny of what would become the United States. The Beaver Wars created the patterns of white–Indian relations that would profoundly influence the course of all the colonial wars that followed, including the French and Indian War and the American Revolution. Even after the United States became a nation, these alliances and enmities would influence the outcome of the War of 1812 and then go on to create the cultural and political climate in which the later nineteenth-century Indian Wars of the Plains and the Far West were fought.

If the Beaver Wars are little known today outside of academic circles, it is largely because traditional popular historians have created the impression that almost all warfare involving Native Americans was against whites. In large part, the impression is due to the scarcity of first-hand written records of Indian-on-Indian conflict. Unrecorded history is by definition unremembered history. Beyond this, we have been led to believe that the relatively few intertribal wars, Indian-on-Indian conflicts, were largely symbolic contests to resolve disputes or ritual diversions, activities verging on sport, much like the joust of medieval Europe.

▶

This is a map of the Great Lakes from 1755. The five Iroquois nations were the dominant economic, military, and political force around the Great Lakes in the seventeenth century. Their control of trade extended as far east as the interior of Maine and as far west as Lake Ontario.

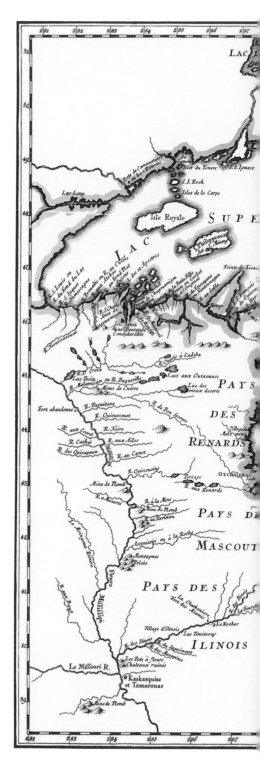

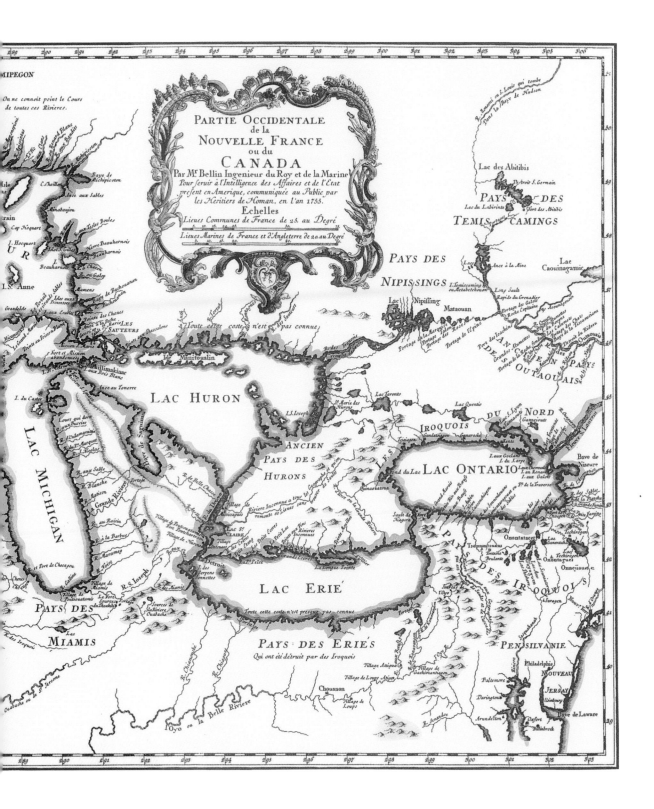

MIPEGON

On ne connoit point le Cours
de toutes ces Rivieres.

PARTIE OCCIDENTALE
de la
NOUVELLE FRANCE
ou du
CANADA
Par M.r Bellin Ingenieur du Roy et de la Marine
Pour servir à l'Intelligence des Affaires et de l'Etat
present en Amerique, communiquée au Public par
les Heritiers de Homan, en l'an 1755.
Echelles
Lieues Communes de France de 25. au Degré
Lieues Marines de France et d'Angleterre de 20. au Degré

PAYS DES
TEMIS CAMINGS

PAYS DES
NIPISSINGS

LAC HURON

ANCIEN
PAYS DES
HURONS

LAC ONTARIO

IROQUOIS DU NORD

LAC MICHIGAN

LAC ERIE

PAYS DES IROQUOIS

PAYS DES
MIAMIS

PAYS DES ERIE'S
Qui ont été détruit par des Iroquois

PENSILVANIE

NOUVEAU
JERSAY

Philadelphie

The Beaver Wars are evidence that intertribal warfare could be waged for keeps, not merely to defeat the enemy, but to wipe him out. The motive for the scale of destruction in the Beaver Wars was to cultivate, preserve, and increase profitable trading relations with the Euro-American colonists.

HIGHEST STAKES

In early America, trade was power—not just a matter of survival, but a means of mastery. In the seventeenth century, the Iroquois tribes cast their lot with the Dutch and then the English; whereas, west and north of the Iroquois, the Hurons became trading partners of the French, who were rivals of the English.

Several other western tribes allied to the Hurons also established commercial relations with the French—and therefore doomed themselves to being swallowed up in the Beaver Wars. The most important of these tribes were the Tobaccos (also called the Petuns or Tionantati) and the Eries (or Cat People). All that we know about the Beaver Wars comes from scattered reports by missionaries and traders and a body of traditional stories of the Iroquois themselves, so it is not possible to construct a detailed narrative of all the wars. We do know that, cumulatively, fifty years of these wars took a nearly genocidal toll on the western tribes.

THE MARTYRDOM OF THE MISSION TOWNS

For its first decade, the Beaver Wars consisted not of major battles, but of ambushes and murders, albeit multiplied many times, so that they became a terrible fixture of life on the fringes of Huronia, as the French called the territory of the Hurons. For the Europeans who sought control of the forest and all it had to offer, the continual presence of violence became just another commodity to exploit.

Recognizing an opportunity to usurp trade from the French, the directors of the Dutch West India Company at Fort Orange reversed their long-standing policy against arming the Indians, trading to the Mohawks some 400 rifles on April 7, 1648. They knew that the warriors would use them against the French-backed Hurons, and in this way the Dutch West India Company employed the Mohawks as proxy troops against the French and the tribe that traded with them.

On July 4, 1648, a thousand Mohawks, their hair cut for war—the scalp bare save for a strip down the middle, three finger widths across, running from forehead to nape, descended on the Huron village of Saint Joseph (present-day Port Huron, Michigan).

When Père Antoine Daniel, the Jesuit missionary of the village, heard the warriors scaling the stockade, he ran to the chapel, where the women, children, and old men had sought refuge. He pronounced a general absolution and baptized those who now begged for the sacrament, and then urging each to save him or herself, the priest went out to meet the warriors as they clambered over the stockade. Hoping, perhaps, to create a diversion that would buy time for more of the village to escape, he seized a cross and walked toward the enemy. The attackers froze—but only for a moment. Several of the Dutch guns were leveled at the Jesuit, who was shot many times while other warriors killed or captured everyone they found, pausing only to put each building to the torch. As the chapel began to blaze, they flung the priest's lifeless body through its open door.

Leaving Saint Joseph in flames, the raiders stalked off with some 700 prisoners and then struck the nearby mission village of Saint Ignace, home mostly to women, children, and old men, who found themselves trapped within their own stockade fortifications. After a few terrible minutes of slaughter and fire, the Mohawks moved on to Saint Louis, about three miles (5 km) away. The warriors attacked as if they were a force of nature, but their hit-and-run tactics had a strategic downside. Haste left survivors. Three Huron refugees from the Saint Ignace raid outran the Mohawks, reaching Saint Louis in time to alert most of its 700 inhabitants. Only about eighty warriors stayed behind, together with those too old or too sick to move. Awaiting the onslaught with them were the two Jesuit missionaries who had come from Saint Ignace, Jean de Brébeuf and Gabriel Lallemant.

A thousand to eighty is an overwhelming superiority of numbers. Nevertheless, the small band of Huron warriors twice turned back the Iroquois, killing perhaps thirty of the enemy. In their third assault, the Iroquois attacked the stockade from several directions, hacking at the woven walls with their hatchets, breaking through in many places. Once inside, it was soon over.

Those few defenders who survived, together with the two Jesuits, were taken captive and the town set ablaze behind them. The prisoners were sent back to Saint Ignace, now occupied by the Iroquois. All were tortured to death, but the most intense brutality was reserved for Brébeuf and Lallemant, who were bound to stakes, scalped alive, "baptized" with boiling water, and made to wear necklaces of red-hot hatchets. It was said that fifty-five-year-old Brébeuf remained perfectly silent throughout the ordeal, at the end of which the warriors cut out his heart and ate it—a singular tribute accorded only to the bravest of adversaries. The Indians believed that by eating the heart of a courageous enemy they would partake of his courage.

Using Saint Ignace as their base of operations, the Iroquois raked the smaller villages of the region, including, on March 17, Sainte Marie (present-day Sault Sainte Marie, Michigan), a fortress town defended by a garrison of forty well-armed Frenchmen who were augmented by as many as 300 Huron warriors. This time, the Hurons launched a preemptive ambush on the Iroquois advance guard as it approached the town. The Iroquois fought back, forcing the Huron detachment into retreat until the main body of Huron warriors rushed to their rescue, routing the Iroquois, who regrouped and mounted a new assault against Sainte Marie. By this time, the Huron defenders had been reduced to about 150 warriors, half their original number. They fought fiercely, killing (by French estimate) a hundred of the Iroquois and suffering the loss of all but twenty of their own number.

Yet their sacrifice had not been in vain. So shaken were the attackers that instead of exploiting their costly victory they retreated to Saint Ignace, where they tied to stakes a large number of the prisoners they held—men, women, and children—and then put the village to the torch, burning Saint Ignace together with the helpless prisoners.

◄

In this fanciful oil painting entitled "The Martyrdom of Three Jesuit Priests," Fathers Brébeuf and Lallemant are shown at the stakes, while Father Isaac Jogues is shown kneeling after being captured by the Iroquois. In reality, Brébeuf and Lallemant were tortured to death in 1649 and Jogues three years earlier.

By the end of March 1649, the Hurons had abandoned fifteen principal towns. For all practical purposes, the Huron nation ceased to exist as an organized community. Some individuals blended into allied tribes, many finding refuge with the Tobaccos. As for the French Jesuit missions, without Indians to convert, many were simply abandoned. That the French suffered defeat alongside their Huron allies was most satisfactory to the Dutch traders.

OF TERROR AND TOTAL WAR

In November and December 1649, the Mohawks and Senecas punished the Tobaccos for harboring enemy refugees. As the Iroquois approached the Tobacco mission town of Saint Jean, its warriors prepared for combat. Yet day after day passed without an attack. Unable to endure the suspense, the Huron warriors sortied out of their fortified town to engage the enemy in the open.

At two o'clock on the afternoon of December 17, 1649, Mohawk and Seneca warriors fell upon the now undefended town of Saint Jean. Even as the attackers opened fire, Charles Garnier, one of the missionaries there, moved from Indian to Indian, hastily performing the requisite baptisms and absolutions up to the moment that he was cut down by three musket balls. Paralyzed by his wounds, Garnier was helpless to defend himself against a warrior's hatchet. He was found later with his brains beaten out. The few survivors of the raid wandered westward. After the passage of half a century, during the first years of the eighteenth century, these refugees mingled with the surviving Hurons to become the Wyandots of the Detroit and Sandusky region.

The Beaver Wars were marked by spasms of unspeakable terror, some episodes recorded, most not. These attacks killed many, but their long-term impact was even worse. They disrupted Huron society, transforming what had been a tribe into a collection of refugees. Without the sustenance of a village, a community, life in the wilderness became insupportable. To destroy a tribe did not require killing every last man, woman, and child. Death on a genocidal scale followed dispossession—exile into the wilderness.

Early in 1650, for example, a band of Hurons holed up on Île Saint Joseph in Lake Huron. In March, after weeks on the island, the refugees were compelled to seek food and shelter on the mainland. In the struggle to get to shore across the softening ice, many fell through and drowned. Those who made it across survived by fishing, only to fall prey to marauding Iroquois war parties. That the refugees were near starvation did not diminish the ferocity of the attackers.

Even Jesuit missionary witnesses, who had seen all manner of torture and cruelty, were stunned. "My pen," wrote Père Paul Ragueneau, "has no ink black enough to describe the fury of the Iroquois . . . Our starving Hurons were driven out of a town which had become an abode of horror . . . These poor people fell into ambuscades of our Iroquois enemies. Some were killed on the spot; some were dragged into captivity; women and children were burned . . . Go where they would, they met with slaughter on all sides. Famine pursued them, or they encountered an enemy more cruel than cruelty itself."

A Fate Worse than Death

The prisoners taken by Indians in raids were often subjected to torture, in which the tormentors, including warriors, women, and children, exalted. Typical methods included cutting, flaying alive, dismemberment, piercing, beating, and burning. It was common among Mohawks to cut off an ear or a finger and force the captive to eat it.

Isaac Jogues, a French missionary captured by Mohawks during the Beaver Wars, suffered the amputation of his thumb. When the digit was presented to him, he later wrote: "I offered it to Thee, my true and living God, calling to mind the sacrifice which I had for seven years [as a priest administering the holy Eucharist] constantly offered Thee in Thy Church. At last, warned by one of my comrades to desist, since they might otherwise force it into my mouth and compel me to eat it as it was, I flung it from me on the scaffold and left it I know not where." Jogues was captured a second time—and tortured to death.

WAR WITHOUT END

Late in 1653, four of the five Iroquois tribes concluded a series of peace treaties at Montreal, breaking with the Mohawks in an effort to curb that tribe's domination of trade. As it was, the treaties did not stop the fighting. Warfare continued, culminating in the defeat of the French-allied Eries, who by 1656 could no longer call themselves a tribe. There were just too few of them left alive.

The defeat of the Hurons, the Tobaccos, and the Eries made the five Iroquois nations the dominant economic, military, and political force between the Ottawa River in the north and the Cumberland in the south. Their control of trade extended into Maine in the east and as far as Lake Ontario in the west. Yet even at this high point, the Iroquois continued to fight. Battle had become a way of life.

In 1663, a handful of serious defeats ended the Iroquois dream of a total monopoly on trapping and trade. Yet as one dream faded, another took shape, Iroquois economic ambition becoming imperial in its magnitude. The footholds the five tribes had gained in the

Scalping: The Bloody Truth

No feature of Native American warfare is more familiar or subject to more fantastic folklore and basic misunderstanding than scalping. Traditionally, whites have pointed to scalping as evidence of the American Indians' incorrigible barbarity. Others have attributed to it significance as a kind of religious favor to one's enemy, claiming that the act of taking a scalp was intended to release the "spirit" or "soul" of the slain.

A number of revisionist historians have claimed that scalping was unknown among Native American tribes before the arrival of Europeans, but there is ample evidence that scalping was, in fact, practiced among North American Indians before the advent of the Europeans. Jacques Cartier reported it in 1535, Hernando de Soto in 1540, Tristan de Luna in 1559, and others subsequently. It was not universal among Native Americans, however, and it spread generally from east to west with the migration of eastern tribes and contact with whites, who had adopted the custom from eastern Indians. Thus, while whites did not introduce scalping to the Indians of North America, they did contribute to the proliferation of the custom, both by pushing eastern tribes westward and by their own example.

There is no evidence that scalping was meant to be of spiritual benefit to the victim. Quite the contrary, the act of scalping seems to have been intended as an insult, and the scalp served as a battle trophy. Colonial and later authorities added a profit motive to the practice by offering "scalp bounties," rewards paid for the delivery of scalps taken from hostiles.

Tribes practiced various methods of actually taking the scalp. Some took the whole skin of the upper head, ears included; others removed only the crown. After Europeans introduced sharper, sturdier steel knives and hatchets among the American Indians, many tribes practiced a faster method of scalping, grasping the forelock, making a single gash in the front of the head, and popping out the "scalp lock" trophy with a sharp tug. As the "scalp lock" method was an abbreviated technique for taking scalps, so the practice of scalping seems itself to have originated as a substitute for decapitation. The scalp trophy stood for the head even as the head represented the entire person of the victim. In some tribes, particularly among certain Plains groups, decapitation persisted, and a severed head was considered an even greater trophy than a scalp or scalp lock.

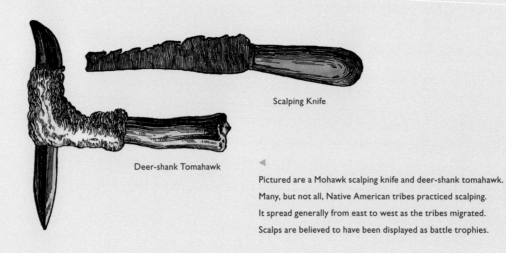

Scalping Knife

Deer-shank Tomahawk

Pictured are a Mohawk scalping knife and deer-shank tomahawk. Many, but not all, Native American tribes practiced scalping. It spread generally from east to west as the tribes migrated. Scalps are believed to have been displayed as battle trophies.

western beaver peltries were no longer sufficient to satisfy what had become a hunger for absolute dominion in the Northeast and Upper Midwest. Fighting continued sporadically through the 1670s until the Iroquois launched a new, concerted campaign in 1680 against French-allied Native Americans on the far western frontier, along the Illinois and Mississippi rivers. All that is known about what was almost certainly the biggest intertribal war of which any evidence exists is that the Iroquois achieved several early victories, only to be decisively defeated by 1684, mainly by the Shawnee and Miami tribes.

A LINGERING PRESENCE

Unlike the Hurons and other tribes the Iroquois fought through nearly a half-century, the Iroquois, even in defeat, remained a powerful presence. The Beaver Wars had set up the enmities and alliances that would shape all of the colonial wars that followed, through the American Revolution.

Although they would continue to find many Indian allies, the depletion of the Hurons deprived the French of what would have been the most powerful Native American ally of all. A French–Huron alliance might well have given France, not Britain, final victory in the French and Indian War. With that, U.S. history would have taken a profoundly different course. As it is, the Iroquois victories in the Beaver Wars helped determine that the lower colonies would remain English, and this in turn set the terms of the American Revolution to come.

Tradition claims even more. Many historians have observed that the framers of the Articles of Confederation and the Constitution that followed were inspired not only by European political philosophers and models of government, but also by the structure of the Iroquois Confederacy. In 2004, the U.S. Department of State officially acknowledged the influence of the Iroquois constitution. Irony is rarely among the many meanings evoked by genocide, but in the case of the Beaver Wars, those who live under the Constitution of the United States must accept the singular irony that a great concept of order and justice emerged from a tribal people who long ago waged total warfare for the sake of profit and power.

KING PHILIP'S WAR: AMERICA'S COSTLIEST CONFLICT

1675–1676

This war between New England colonists and some of their seventeenth-century American Indian neighbors created the genocidal pattern of "ethnic cleansing" that would mark the next two and a quarter centuries of white settlement on Native American lands. In proportion to both the white and Indian regional populations of the era, it remains the deadliest war Americans have ever fought.

W hat Columbus started when he arrived in the New World was not exactly an invasion or a conquest. It was a new civilization—call it Euro-America—and a host of European powers and American Indian tribes struggled for survival, prosperity, coexistence, and mastery of it.

Often, they fought. In the Southwest, during the 1500s, there were periodic revolts against brutal Spanish *conquistadors* (conquerors) and *encomienderos* (in effect, landowners). In the Northeast and Southeast, the wars were fought mainly to control trade and acquire land. From 1622 to 1644 in Virginia, the tribes of the Powhatan confederacy warred with their English neighbors over the expanding colony's incursions onto their lands, and in western Massachusetts and Connecticut, during 1637–1638, long-running land disputes led to a brief but terrible war between New England colonists and the Pequot tribe. The English colony had been established for scarcely a decade. Merest survival was a high-odds struggle. The war nearly wiped it out; but in the end it was the Pequots who all but ceased to exist as a people. Badly mauled, New England was nevertheless triumphant, for a time.

THE DEATH OF KINGS

For more than two decades following the Pequot War, an unsettled peace reigned between the Indians and colonists of New England. Then, in 1661, the death of Massasoit, chief of the Wampanoags of southeastern Massachusetts and Rhode Island, a longtime ally of the English, started a chain of violent events culminating in 1675 in a cataclysm the English called King Philip's War.

Wamsutta, whom the English called Alexander, succeeded his father Massasoit as the principal Wampanoag sachem and continued the tradition of alliance with the English as a hedge against the powerful rival Narragansett tribe. However, under Alexander, the Wampanoags divided their loyalty between two rival English colonies, Rhode Island and Plymouth, which fiercely competed for the purchase of American Indian lands. Both colonies sought to establish a protectorate over the Wampanoags to bolster the tenuous charters from which their legitimacy precariously dangled. The Plymouth charter was for all practical purposes void because the colony had been founded either in fraud or error. The settlers, including the celebrated Pilgrims, had been authorized to plant a colony in Virginia, but

◄

The Wampanoag chief Metacomet was mocked by the English colonists as "King Philip." This eighteenth-century English engraving dresses him in the fanciful garb the artist could only imagined a Wampanoag sachem would wear. The Brown Bess musket he leans on is from the era of the French and Indian War (1754–1763), not from the late seventeenth century.

whether by accident or design, landed far up the coast, well outside of the boundary of their charter, setting foot in 1620 (according to legend) on Plymouth Rock.

As for Rhode Island, which had been founded as a catch-all colony for those whose religious heterodoxy was unwelcome in the Puritan Massachusetts Bay and Plymouth colonies, its charter was now under assault by the Restoration government in England as well as the powerful leaders of Massachusetts Bay.

Accused by Plymouth Colony authorities of plotting war, Alexander was seized at gunpoint by Major Josiah Winslow (soon to become governor of the colony) and taken to Duxbury ostensibly to answer the charges. Actually, the arrest and imprisonment were tactics intended to intimidate Alexander into selling land to Plymouth instead of Rhode Island; however, during his captivity, Alexander fell ill. Anxious to avoid his dying in custody, Winslow released him, but Alexander did not survive the journey home.

Alexander's twenty-four-year-old brother, Metacom or Metacomet, whom the English called Philip, succeeded him as sachem. He charged that Winslow had poisoned his brother. Although Philip had no evidence for the accusation, it seemed plausible to many Wampanoags.

BAD BLOOD

Plymouth leaders responded to Philip's charges by accusing him of plotting against the colony and summoned him to Plymouth Town on August 6, 1664. He denied the accusations, but nevertheless pledged that he would seek permission from the colony before concluding any sale or exchange of land. With that, relations between colonists and Indians remained peaceful until the following year, when a land dispute between Massachusetts and the Narragansett tribe threatened to erupt into war. The intervention of a royal commission mollified both sides, but Philip tried to exploit the dispute to undermine the Narragansetts by telling New York colonial authorities that the tribe was plotting war against New York. Confronted with these charges, the Narragansett chief, Ninigret, accused Philip of hostile designs against Plymouth, and the next year, 1667, he was again summoned to a colonial court.

Little is known about Philip. His actions in war suggest that he was both a charismatic and skilled combat leader, who possessed the vision to unite the tribes of New England against the colonists. Throughout the long history of North American warfare between whites and American Indians, a few Native leaders, including the Shawnee Tecumseh, the Creek-Seminole Osceola, and the Lakota Sitting Bull, have tried to unify tribes for military and political purposes. Philip was perhaps the first in this line. As far as the colonists were concerned, he was neither charismatic nor visionary, but haughty, and for that reason they bestowed on him the mocking title "King Philip" and repeatedly harassed him with demands that he answer one charge after another.

A LONG FUSE LIT

Early in 1671, after the new Plymouth settlement of Swansea expanded into his land, King Philip led his warriors in an armed display meant to intimidate the town's citizens. This prompted colonial officials to summon him to Taunton on April 10, 1671, where he signed the humiliating Taunton agreement, apologizing for "plotting" and agreeing to surrender the Wampanoags' arms.

As Plymouth gloated over King Philip's latest act of submission, Philip quietly sowed dissension between the rival Plymouth and Massachusetts Bay colonies by hinting that his retroactive pledge of allegiance to Plymouth threatened the legitimacy of land titles

The Wampanoags and Their Allies

In the seventeenth century, the Wampanoags lived mainly in southeastern Massachusetts and Rhode Island, and in the area of modern Martha's Vineyard, Nantucket, and the Elizabeth Islands. Early in the century, their population stood at about 12,000, but epidemics and warfare with the northern New England Micmac tribe reduced their numbers greatly before their encounter with the Pilgrims in 1620.

Six years earlier, an English sea captain, Thomas Hunt, captured several Wampanoags, including Squanto (also known as Tisquantum) and sold them to the Spanish as slaves. Eventually freed, Squanto returned to New England in 1619 only to discover that his entire band and family had succumbed to an epidemic.

When the Pilgrims arrived the following year, Squanto (and other Wampanoags) taught them how to cultivate corn and other crops. Squanto also acted as an emissary between the colonists and the Wampanoag sachem Massasoit. With his tribe badly depleted

by war and disease, Massasoit sought an alliance with the English as an aid to resisting the aggression of the powerful Narragansetts. The alliance was concluded in March 1621 and involved the cession of some 12,000 acres to what was then called Plymouth Plantation.

The Narragansetts trace their origin back some 30,000 years and by the early seventeenth century, the tribe controlled the Narragansett Bay area in what is today Rhode Island. Their territory also extended into parts of Connecticut and eastern Massachusetts.

The Nipmuc (a name signifying "freshwater people") Indians ranged throughout central New England during much of the seventeenth century, from the borders of Vermont and New Hampshire, through Worcester County in Massachusetts, and into northern Rhode Island and northeastern Connecticut. Their population just before King Philip's War may have been as high as 10,000. After the war, fewer than a thousand survived.

Massachusetts had earlier secured from the Wampanoags. Yet again Philip's scheming backfired, only bringing the rival colonies closer together. The sachem was hauled into a Plymouth court in September, fined £100 for violating the Taunton agreement, forced to submit for colonial review any purchase or sale of land, and forbidden to wage war against other American Indians without colonial permission. For the next three years, Philip forged alliances with the Nipmucs and even the Narragansetts.

"KING PHILIP'S WAR" BEGINS

In January 1675 there came what the English believed was a new and brutal revelation of Wampanoag treachery. John Sassamon was described in colonial records as a "very cunning and plausible Indian, well skilled in the English Language, and bred up in the Possession of Christian Religion, imployed as a Schoolmaster at Natick [Massachusetts], the Indian Town," who apparently spied on Philip at the behest of Plymouth governor Josiah Winslow. After revealing that Philip was plotting a major war against the English, Sassamon was found dead on January 29, his body sprawled on a frozen pond.

Three associates of Philip, a Wampanoag called Tobias, his son Wampapaquan, and one Mattashunnamo, on the strength of biased testimony, were convicted of murder. At first all three protested their innocence, but Wampapaquan finally confessed that he induced his father and Mattashunnamo to kill Sassamon. Some sources claim that Wampapaquan turned state's evidence in the expectation of winning mercy from the court. Others hold that the confession was elicited only after the noose around his neck broke. Hoping for a reprieve, he now also accused Philip of complicity in the crime.

In the end, none of those convicted escaped hanging, but the accusation against Philip brought him into court again. He was released for lack of hard evidence, and on June 11, three days after the executions and almost immediately after King Philip was let go, the Wampanoags began arming near Swansea and Plymouth Town. Soon, cattle were being killed and homes looted throughout the outlying settlements. As settlers deserted the frontier towns, American Indians rushed in to fill the vacuum.

AN UNEASY ALLIANCE

Thirty-five-year-old Benjamin Church, Rhode Island carpenter by trade, soldier by inclination, paid a visit to his near neighbor, Awashonks, squaw-sachem (female chief) of the Sogkonate (Saconnet) Indians. One of the few extant likenesses of Church is a crude woodcut that looks to be from the untutored hand of a folk artist, yet it reveals the wide-eyed countenance of a curious and intelligent man. He was one of those exceptional Anglo-American frontiersmen who liked, respected, learned from, and clearly admired the American Indians near whom he lived.

Tradition has it that he and Awashonks were lovers. Perhaps they were. What is certain is that they were friends, and Awashonks was eager to tell Church that she knew King Philip to be planning an all-out war. She went on to relate the particulars, as she understood them, and Church passed the information to Governor Winslow, who alerted Governor John Leverett of the Massachusetts Bay Colony. In this way a fragile and mistrustful alliance among Rhode Island, Plymouth, and Massachusetts Bay, hitherto colonial rivals, emerged.

The leaders of the three colonies agreed to mobilize a common army, but they also intended to elbow one another aside for any territory that might fall to them as a result of the anticipated victory against King Philip.

THE BATTLE IS JOINED

The army mustered during June 21–23 at Miles's Garrison, opposite Philip's base of operations at Mount Hope Neck, Rhode Island, just across the line separating that colony from Plymouth. As the militia laboriously assembled, the Wampanoags raided Swansea, Plymouth, descending on the townsfolk as they made their way to church on Sunday.

The significance of the attack was unmistakable to Plymouth elders, who pronounced it the dreadful judgment of God against a generation that had fallen away from the absolute Puritan piety of the colony's founders. Plymouth accordingly declared a day of communal repentance, called "public humiliation" on June 24; but on this very day, Philip struck Swansea a second time, as the penitents returned from church. He burned half the town and killed nine.

Four days after the second attack on Swansea, Church's troops were ambushed near the beleaguered settlement at Miles's Bridge, which led into Mount Hope Neck. Captain Church was disgusted by the pathetic performance of the colonial forces in this first military engagement of the war. "The Lord have Mercy on us," he wrote.

On June 29, the Wampanoags stormed Rehoboth, Rhode Island, and Taunton, Massachusetts Bay, razing eight Rehoboth farmhouses and killing "eleven Men, two Maids, and two Youths" at Taunton. Militiamen gave chase, but Philip and his forces disappeared into the southern Rhode Island swamps of Pocasset country, congenial ground to the American Indians but impenetrable by the English.

The First "Ranger"

Throughout King Philip's War, Benjamin Church would find himself quite literally a voice crying in the wilderness as he repeatedly called for abandoning formal European battle tactics and instead emulating Indian fighting practices.

More than possessing knowledge of Indian tactics, Church had a deep understanding of Indian military culture. He recruited Indian soldiers and asked them how "they got such advantage often of the English in their Marches thro' the Woods." He learned that they avoided "set" battles and instead used stealth to launch fierce hit-and-run raids. Executing this style of warfare required the greatest of skill in woodcraft and the highest degree of endurance, and it was clear to Church that traditional European tactics were ineffective fighting American Indians in the woods. Church organized and trained small groups to scout the forest, providing early warning of hostile activity and to conduct Indian-style raids. Because reports typically mentioned "ranging" so many miles into the woods, the men were called rangers, and thus U.S. army historians give Church credit for having originated the "ranger" concept of fighting a war used by today's elite Special Forces and Army Rangers.

▲

Benjamin Church was New England's chief hero in King Philip's War. He emulated Native American fighting techniques, which often proved more effective against Indian warriors than conventional European-style tactics.

NEW ALLIES

On July 1, Connecticut sent troops to aid Massachusetts, Plymouth, and Rhode Island, bringing the colonial alliance to four. But King Philip was also forging an alliance at this time, with the Pocasset squaw-sachem Weetamoo (Weetamoe), a formidable female chief whom one of her captives, the colonist Mary Rowlandson, later characterized as a "proud hussy."

Four colonies were now united against the Indians, but Edmund Andros, the crafty and powerful governor of the Duke of York's patent territories (including New York)—a leader so unabashed that his ostentatious interference with Puritan religious customs in Boston touched off a riot there in 1689—had something else in mind. He dispatched troops to western Connecticut on July 4, declaring as his purpose the protection of settlements there against King Philip. In fact, his colony was embroiled in a territorial dispute with Connecticut, and he intended to exploit the war to grab some land. Connecticut Governor John Winthrop checkmated Andros by withdrawing soldiers from the Rhode Island front to garrison Fort Saybrook, Connecticut. Intimidated, the New Yorkers withdrew—but the campaign against Philip had been seriously compromised by this intercolonial distraction.

THE PEASE FIELD FIGHT

Back in Rhode Island, Benjamin Church recognized that intercolonial strife was siphoning resources desperately needed to deal with the very real menace at hand. Something had to be done and done fast. He persuaded a reluctant captain of a Rhode Island militia company, Matthew Fuller, to coordinate with him in a surprise attack on the Indian forces at Pocasset swamp. Fuller and Church deployed their men on a moonless night, obliging them to lie in wait, all night, in the dismal swamp. For some, it was just too much. Church wrote that Captain Fuller's "party being troubled with the Epidemical plague of lust after Tobacco, must needs strike fire to Smoke it." This alerted the Indians, who "fled with great precipitation."

Despite a critical shortage of provisions, Church cadged from Fuller twenty men and pursued the Indians to "Captain Almy's pease [pea] field." Here Church divided his forces, ordering his men to flatten themselves on the ground. The other contingent, however, was not so stealthy, and the element of surprise was lost. Church ordered his men to start marching "at double distance"—with extra space separating each man—a ploy intended to give the impression of a much larger force. But it was no good. The force of twenty was besieged for the next six hours by 300 Indians.

As the Puritan clergyman and historian Increase Mather wrote, "The Swamp was so Boggy and thick of Bushes . . . It could not there be descerned who were *English* and who the *Indians*." He complained that the jumpy militiamen could not "see a Bush stir" without firing, sometimes killing their own. Unable to tell friend from enemy, especially as night came on, they retreated from the swamp, then slipped away, sometimes walking at a crouch, sometimes crawling, toward an English river sloop, which had arrived in the proverbial nick of time.

DIGGING IN

Colonial leaders became so disheartened by the performance of the militia that despite church's protests they aborted the pursuit of Philip and instead built a fort at the edge of the swamp, intending to starve him out. But Indian warriors did not starve easily, as Mary Rowlandson, taken captive from Lancaster, Massachusetts, in February 1676, learned:

> It was thought, if their corn were cut down, they would starve and die with
> hunger: and all their corn . . . was destroyed . . . [but] I did not see (all the time
> I was among them) one man, woman, or child, die with hunger.

Though many times they would eat that, that a hog or a dog would hardly touch; yet by that God strengthened them to be a scourge to His people. . . . They would pick up old bones, and cut them to pieces at the joints, and if they were full of worms and maggots, they would scald them over the fire to make the vermin come out, and then boil them, and drink up the liquor, and then beat the great ends of them in a mortar, and so eat them. They would eat horse's guts, and ears, and all sorts of wild birds which they would catch: also bear, venison, beaver, tortoise, frogs, squirrels, dogs, skunks, rattlesnakes; yea, the very bark of trees . . .

While the colonists wasted time building a fort, Philip slipped away on July 29 and escaped with his warriors into Nipmuc country.

THE WAR SPREADS

By the end of August, the theater of war had broadened into the upper Connecticut Valley, Merrimac Valley, New Hampshire, and Maine. Colonial society—colonial civilization—was in chaos.

The Massachusetts Bay Colony towns of Hadley and Deerfield were attacked, "leaving most of the Houses in that new hopeful Plantation [Deerfield] in ruinous heaps."

◄

This engraving celebrates a popular tale about General William Goffe, an elderly officer who on September 1, 1675, during a fierce Indian attack on Hadley, Massachusetts, suddenly appeared, took command of the local militia, and turned the Indian attackers back. None of the locals had ever seen Goffe before. So runs the tale, and although Goffe was indeed a historical figure, Goffe never fought King Philip or his followers at Hadley or anyplace else.

Almost immediately after this came a devastating attack against another Bay Colony set-tlement, Northfield (Squakeag). Dispatched with thirty-six men to relieve the garrison there, militia captain Richard Beers was ambushed and slain, along with twenty of his party. A hundred militia reinforcements arrived near Northfield on September 5, but "were much daunted to see the heads of Captain Beers Souldiers upon poles by the way side"—so "daunted" that they abandoned the pursuit of the raiders, leaving Northfield, Deerfield, and Brookfield to join a growing list of towns devastated and abandoned.

Only after months of such bloodshed did the colonies enter wholeheartedly into a union, proclaiming themselves (for the first time in history) the "United Colonies" and jointly declaring war on September 9, 1675. An army of 1000 was levied, but the men were not actually mustered until November and December. By that time, King Philip's War had engulfed Massachusetts, Plymouth, Rhode Island, Connecticut, and the more remote and sparsely settled "Eastern Colonies"—Maine and New Hampshire.

THE GREAT SWAMP FIGHT

Against a lurid backdrop of blood and fire, colonial leaders repeatedly tried and failed to negotiate a truce. Finally, in October, the Narragansetts concluded a treaty in Bos-ton. It is a measure of the tragic inconsistency of relations between the colonists and the Americans Indians that a month after signing the treaty Connecticut's colonial council resolved on November 2 to make a peremptory strike against the Narragansetts. Astound-ingly, Plymouth and Massachusetts agreed, and on December 18, Winslow marched his army—including a full company under the redoubtable Benjamin Church—into a blind-ing snowstorm to attack the stronghold of the Narragansett sachem Canonchet (whom the English called Canonicus) in a frozen swamp at Kingston, Rhode Island.

When the army's vanguard reached the fort on December 19, the soldiers were stunned to find a stronghold formidable beyond what they assumed American Indians were capable of building. Still, noting that the palisade at one corner of the fort was incomplete, two company commanders decided to attack, even though the main body of troops had yet to arrive. The Indians cut the companies down with flintlock fire, kill-ing both captains. Even Church blundered. Impatient, he also led a premature assault against a gap in the palisade. Struck by three bullets, which drilled into hip and thigh, the only regret the frontiersman expressed was that one of the shots had "pierced . . . and wounded a pair of mittens that he had borrowed from Capt. Prentis."

Mary Rowlandson's Captivity

The first American best-seller was published in Boston in 1682. *The Soveraignty & Goodness of God . . . a Narrative of the Captivity and Restauration of Mrs. Mary Rowlandson* went through two more editions in Cambridge and London that same year and continued to be popular for the next century and a half:

On the tenth of February 1675, came the Indians with great numbers upon Lancaster: . . . At length they came and beset our own house, and quickly it was the dolefullest day that ever mine eyes saw. The house stood upon the edge of a hill; some of the Indians got behind the hill, others into the barn, and others behind any thing that could shelter them; from all which places they shot against the house, so that the bullets seemed to fly like hail; and quickly they wounded one man among us, then another, and then a third. About two hours they had been about the house before they prevailed to fire it . . . Now is the dreadful hour come, that I have often heard of but now mine eyes see it. Some in our house were fighting for their lives, others wallowing in their blood, the house on fire over our heads, and the bloody heathen ready to knock us on the head, if we stirred out. Now might we hear mothers and children crying out for themselves, and one another, 'Lord, what shall we do?' Then I took my children (and one of my sisters, hers) to go forth and leave the house: but as soon as we came to the door and appeared, the Indians shot so thick that the bullets rattled against the house, as if one had taken an handful of stones and threw them, so that we were fain to give back. . . . But out we must go, the fire increasing, and coming along behind us, roaring, and the Indians gaping before us with their guns, spears and hatchets to devour us. No sooner were we out of the house, but my brother-in-law (being before wounded, in defending the house, in or near the throat) fell down dead whereat the Indians scornfully shouted, and holloed, and were presently upon him, stripping off his clothes, the bullets flying thick, one went through my side, and the same (as would seem) through the bowels and hand of my dear child in my arms. One of my elder sister's children, named William, had then his leg broken, which the Indians perceiving, they knocked him on the head. Thus were we butchered by those merciless heathen, standing amazed, with the blood running down to our heels. . . ."

Once the rest of the army finally arrived, the battle exploded into the single biggest armed encounter fought in North America to that time. Eighty of Winslow's 1000-man army perished, including fourteen company commanders. The Narragansetts, however, fared much worse. Six hundred were killed—perhaps even more—half of that number women and children.

Having spilled so much blood, Winslow's men would settle for nothing short of wreaking total annihilation. Over the protests of the badly wounded Church, who pointed out that the English, battered and exhausted, desperately needed the shelter of the Indians' wigwams for the winter night to come, the soldiers torched the entire encampment. Increase Mather gloated: "The English Souldiers played the men wonderfully; the Indians

also fought stoutly, but were at last beat out of their Fort, which was taken by the English. There were hundreds of *Wigwams* within the Fort, which our Souldiers set on fire, in the which men, women and Children (no man knoweth how many hundreds of them) were burnt to death. Night coming on, a Retreat was sounded."

The Great Swamp Fight inflicted catastrophic losses on the Narragansetts and effectively cut them off from all sources of sustenance and supply. Mather wrote, "Concerning the number of Indians slain in this Battle, we are uncertain: only some Indians which afterwards were taken prisoners confessed that the next day they found three hundred of their fighting men dead in their Fort, and that many men, women and children were burned in their Wigwams, but they neither knew, nor could conjecture how many: it is supposed that not less then a thousand Indian Souls perished at that time." Yet instead of demoralizing the American Indians, it galvanized the desperate anti-English alliances among the Wampanoags, Nipmucs, and Narragansetts.

KING PHILIP SEEKS MORE ALLIES

With the new year, Philip set out to extend his alliances throughout New England and even into New York, where the ever-resourceful Governor Andros had made preemptive diplomatic overtures to the Mohawks, persuading them not only to spurn King Philip, but to attack him. Far more interested in preserving their profitable trade with the English than in uniting with another tribe, Mohawk warriors forced Philip to flee back to New England. King Philip had proposed nothing less than a great Indian confederacy. Had Andros failed to win over the Mohawks, the history of white–Indian relations on the eastern seaboard might have taken a very different course.

For their part, Winslow's forces were unprepared to take military advantage of Philip's rebuff at the hands of the Mohawks. Crippled by its losses in the Great Swamp

▲

Josiah Winslow was governor of Plymouth Colony from 1673–1681. A hands-on leader, he personally commanded the Plymouth militia against King Philip in the Great Swamp Fight of September 1675.

Fight, plagued by a shortage of provisions, and exhausted by the elements, the New England army was immobilized for more than a month until late in January 1676 an Indian raid on Pawtuxet (modern Warwick), Rhode Island, spurred Winslow to renewed action. He led his reinforced but inadequately provisioned men on what became known as the "Hungry March" deep into the country of the Nipmucs. By the time this army neared its objective, so many men had deserted that the expedition had to be aborted.

Seeing the colonial force in disarray, Philip renewed his offensive. On February 10, 1676, his warriors raided Lancaster, Massachusetts, for a second time in the war. Mary Rowlandson, wife of the settlement's minister, was captured from Rowlandson Garrison. Her account of her ordeal, published in 1682, became a colonial best-seller and is the most vivid first-hand document of King Philip's War.

THE COLONIES RALLY

On April 21, some 800 or 900 warriors attacked Sudbury, Massachusetts Bay Colony, but in a daylong battle were repelled by militia. Something had changed in the colonial psyche. English forces rejected their former hunker-down defensive tactics and by the end of April, Captain Daniel Henchman swept through eastern Massachusetts with such ferocity that a large body of Indian hostiles ransomed their captives, including Mary Rowlandson, on May 3.

In western Massachusetts, on the night of May 19, Captain William Turner attacked an Indian encampment at the Falls of the Connecticut River above Deerfield, Massachusetts, with 150 men. His troopers poked their flintlocks into the wigwams, and opened on sleeping Indians at point-blank range. Warriors, women, children, and old men were shot to death. Most never awoke.

ATTRITION

Those who survived Turner's attack fled, regrouped, turned, and counterattacked, killing about forty men, including Turner. Nevertheless, the loss of probably more than 100 warriors made the counterattack a pyrrhic victory. Colonial leaders altered their strategy again, waging a war of attrition by destroying Indian crops, livestock, and shelter. It was the kind of prolonged warfare alien to American Indian culture and for which the loosely organized tribes were unprepared. Inexorably, King Philip and his allies weakened even as the colonists became increasingly aggressive.

On the run, Philip fought on, launching a new assault against Hadley early on the morning of June 12. A force of Connecticut militia and friendly Mohegans, although outnumbered 500 to 700, used their European artillery to repel the attackers. Philip again attacked Taunton, Massachusetts, on July 11, only to find that the town was now well prepared to defend itself. Indeed, by now, most of the Indians were coming to see their cause as lost. Confident of the growing Indian disaffection with King Philip, Benjamin Church decided to recruit into his army many of the Native Americans that he captured at Taunton.

THE END OF PHILIP

The leaders of the United Colonies commissioned Church to raise 200 men, of which 140 were to be allied Indians, and use this army "to discover, pursue, fight, surprise, destroy, subdue our Indian enemies." They set out on July 30, following Philip's trail relentlessly. On July 31, they found and killed his uncle. On August 1, they captured the sachem's wife and son. It was reported that on hearing of the capture of his family King Philip declared: "My heart breaks; now I am ready to die." Church and his men intended to oblige him.

On August 3, Connecticut's Major Talcott pursued Indian forces retreating west to the Housatonic River in western Massachusetts. Three days later, the Pocasset

◀

The famed seventeenth-century cartographer Nicholas Visscher published a map of New England—the first to include New Amsterdam—in 1655. The edition shown here was published in 1685, about ten years after the end of King Philip's War.

squaw-sachem Weetamoo, kinswoman and ally of King Philip, was betrayed by one of her own people, who led a party of about twenty of Church's men to her encampment near Taunton. They captured the twenty-six Indians there, but Weetamoo attempted to escape across what eyewitnesses described as "a River or Arm of the Sea," either on a makeshift raft or by clinging to a piece of wood. Later, colonists found her body, naked and drowned. They severed the head from the corpse and set it atop a pole on Taunton's green.

A few days after this, a deserter from Philip's fold led Church and his men to the sachem's camp. Only seven men were with Philip when Church attacked. As Philip took flight, a militiaman and a Native American known as Alderman each opened fire. The militiaman missed, but Alderman's shot tore through Philip's heart.

Church ordered the corpse to be treated as the body of a traitor, drawn and quartered, each portion hung up "as a monument of revenging Justice, his head being cut off and carried away to Plymouth, his Hands were brought to Boston."

With Philip's death, the war was all but over. On September 11, Church captured the aged Annawon, identified as Philip's "chief captain." Before execution, Annawon fell upon his knees before Church and "speaking in plain English, said *Great Captain, you have killed Philip, and conquered his Country, for I believe, that I & my company are the last that War against the English, so suppose the War is ended by your means; and therefore these things belong unto you,*" whereupon the old Indian presented the Englishman with Philip's most prized possessions. Except for sporadic skirmishes during August, September, and October, the war ended with this symbolic gesture.

THE COSTS OF WAR

The war was a catastrophe for New England's colonists and Indians alike. During the years 1675–1676, half of the region's towns were badly damaged and a dozen were completely destroyed, requiring the work of a generation to rebuild them. The fragile colonial economy suffered devastating blows, because of the direct cost of the war—some £100,000—and the disruption of the fur trade with the American Indians and the virtual cessation of coastal fishing and the West Indies trade.

The war siphoned off the manpower customarily devoted to these industries. Indeed, many workers never returned to their peacetime trades, and one in sixteen men of military age was killed. Many others—men, women, children—were also killed, captured, or starved. In proportion to New England's population of 30,000, King Philip's War was the costliest in U.S. history, with at least 600 violent deaths and untold additional deaths from other causes (privation, starvation, exposure, and sickness) related to hardships created by the war. As for the Native Americans, at least 3,000 perished—Wampanoags, Narragansetts, and Nipmucs, mostly—and many of those who did not die were sold into slavery in the West Indies.

A Frenchman who visited the English colonies a decade after the war reported "Nothing to fear from the Savages, for they are few in Number. The last Wars they had with the English . . . have reduced them to a small Number, and consequently they are incapable of defending themselves." That view was shortsighted.

True, many of the war's American Indian survivors were left demoralized and abject in their submission to the English. Others, however, fled to Canada, New York, and the Delaware and Susquehanna valleys, where they nursed a vengeance that exploded in a long series of raids, skirmishes, and full-scale wilderness wars culminating in the French and Indian War, the North American theater of the Seven Years' War, which modern historians call the first "world" war.

King Philip's War set the fierce tone of white–Indian relations in the United States, a violent pattern that would endure until the very last decade of the nineteenth century. It also demonstrated that, to win control of the future of civilization in the New World, the rivals were prepared to destroy whatever civilization they possessed in the present. Assessing King Philip's War, Governor Andros wrote with acerbic understatement, "The advantages thereby were none, the disadvantages very greate."

OTTOMAN ECLIPSE:
THE AUSTRO-TURKISH WAR
1683–1699

A decisive battle in a fateful seventeenth-century war changes the balance of power in Europe,

creating enduring religious and national enmities that would be magnified in the two world wars of

the twentieth century and the genocidal Balkan conflicts that followed the Cold War

The first autumn chill—it was September 11, 1697—was carried with the wind across the River Tisza. It would be a hard winter in lower Hungary, the northern reaches of Serb territory. Prince Eugene of Savoy trained his spyglass toward the river and studied the camp of the Ottoman army, which was divided on either bank. The troops were just beginning to cross over on a bridge supported by boats used as pontoons in a withdrawal back to the territory controlled by the sultan.

Eugene was gaunt at thirty-four, his high forehead and receding hairline making his long face look even longer, his bony aquiline nose drooping sharply as if deliberately pointing to a pair of buck teeth that were not fully covered by his thin lips. He was never meant to be a soldier. Born in Paris in 1663 to Italian parents, he had been a scrawny, sickly child, apparently fit only for a life in the church, for which he began preparing at the age of ten.

It was a desperately lonely childhood: Eugene's father, Eugene Maurice, Prince of Savoy-Carignan, always away fighting some war or other, and his mother, Olympia Mancini, intriguing with whatever member of King Louis XIV's court she imagined could raise her station. Many even believed she was a mistress of the king. At length, Olympia went too far, and she made too many enemies. When her husband died suddenly at thirty-eight in 1673, rumors circulated throughout the court that she had poisoned him, and then those rumors blossomed into loud whispers of a plot against the king himself. Driven by the whispers, Olympia fled to Brussels, leaving Eugene in the care of his paternal grandmother and aunt, both of whom mostly ignored the unattractive child. At age nineteen, when he announced his intention of joining the army rather than the church, they were surprised, but did not much care.

Now, fifteen years after that decision, Eugene held his first major command, the 50,000 or so troops of the Hungarian Imperial Army, a proud but threadbare force, which Eugene managed to feed and shelter with money he borrowed personally to compensate for a royal Austrian war chest emptied by fourteen years of continuous combat against the Ottoman Turks. Those violent and costly years had followed a dozen earlier wars, stretching back more than two and a half centuries.

Always, with hardly any let-up, the Turks banged against the southeastern wall of Europe, invading across the vast Hungarian plain, withdrawing, invading again, and eating up both money

◄

Prince Eugene of Savoy's Austrian army routs an Ottoman force under Sultan Mustafa II at the Tisza River, September 11, 1697. Note the Ottoman troops retreating—in panic— into the river, where many drowned.

and men. Now Eugene, the unprepossessing product of parental neglect, left to carve out his own place in the precarious realms of the Hapsburgs (see "Hapsburgs and Hungarians" on p. 122), saw a chance to surprise the army of the sultan and drive it into the cold autumn waters of the River Tisza. The resulting battle would change the world.

VIENNA UNDER SIEGE

Lodged between Austria, the southern end of the fading Holy Roman Empire, and the still-powerful Ottoman Empire, Hungary was the perpetual no-man's land for which the armies

Sultans and Viziers

The Ottoman Dynasty—the Imperial House of Osman—was founded in 1299, and by the end of the sixteenth century, the Ottoman Empire, based in Constantinople, spanned three continents, holding sway over much of southeastern Europe as well as the Middle East and North Africa.

The empire was ruled by the sultan, who was both the titular head of state and the imperial government, although much of his actual power depended on his ability to enforce it through subordinate rulers and officials, the most important of whom was the grand vizier, a kind of prime minister who presided over an advisory cabinet known as the divan and who wielded total power of attorney in all state affairs. While strong sultans enjoyed absolute power, the weaker ones were at the mercy of their grand vizier and lesser officials.

Whereas the grand vizier was housed in a palace known as the Sublime Porte, the sultan lived in Topkapi Palace with his harem of wives. Ascension to the sultan's throne was hereditary; however, sultans were chosen from among the previous sultan's sons, at least theoretically based on ability as judged in part by the masters of the Topkapi Palace schools, which were intended to train sultans and other government officials. In practice, however, favoritism trumped judgment, and many sultans proved disastrously incompetent and corrupt.

Sultan Mehmed IV, who reigned from 1648–1687, made an alliance with the Hungarian Magyars against their common enemy, the Austrian throne.

of Christianity and Islam contested their claims the underbelly of Europe. Doomed by its geography to be a prize of war, Hungary was destined by its topography to be an ideal battlefield as well, its Great Plain sprawling in flat, open country east of the Danube, inviting cavalry charges and the mass movement of infantry.

On March 3, 1683, an Ottoman army of 200,000 (allied with a force of Transylvanians) invaded Hungary from Adrianople, Turkey. They had been invited to this action by Count Imre Thököly, a leader of Magyar (ethnic Hungarian) rebels whose Calvinist Christianity was so bitterly opposed to the Catholicism of their Austrian Hapsburg overlords that an alliance with the Muslim Ottoman Sultan Mehmed IV seemed a grim necessity. Thököly hoped to use the

Ottoman invasion to break the Austrian grip on his people, after which—somehow—he would come to terms with the Muslim invaders on the issue of religion.

While the Ottoman army under Grand Vizier Kara Mustafa poured in from Adrianople, Thököly's Magyars began their attack. The Hapsburgs hastily concluded a defensive pact with Poland's King John Sobieski and confronted Thököly's 25,000 Magyars at Pressburg (modern Bratislava, Slovakia), which straddled the Danube. Defeating the rebels, the Austro-Polish army turned now to the much larger menace presented by the Ottoman invaders, who closed in on Vienna in June and July 1683. The Holy Roman Emperor Leopold I and his court fled the city; his 33,000-man army, under Charles of

The Magyar leader Count Imre Thököly allied his Protestant Hungarians with the Muslim sultan Mehmed IV in a struggle to break Hungary free of the Catholic empire of Austria.

Lorraine, fell back on the Danube town of Linz, well east of Vienna, to await the arrival of Sobieski's 30,000 Poles.

This left just 11,000 Austrian regulars and 6,000 citizen volunteers remaining in Vienna to defend the Hapsburg capital, which fell under siege by 150,000 Turks on July 17. Despite the lopsided numbers, the city was formidably fortified. Yet while the Viennese garrison struggled to keep the invaders at bay after the Ottoman forces succeeded in capturing the capital's outer fortifications, Sobieski deliberately held his forces back while he drove a hard bargain with Pope Innocent XI in an effort to extract from the Church a large financial subsidy to cover campaign expenses. When the Pope's negotiations with King Louis XIV broke down and the French king declined to march to Leopold's aid, Innocent gave Sobieski all that he wanted. The Polish leader then joined forces with the idling army of Charles of Lorraine, who, in turn, combined his troops with those of the electors of Saxony and Bavaria as well as some thirty petty German princes.

THE SIEGE LIFTED

It was mid-September by the time a total of some 80,000 allied troops formed up in the heights of Kahlenberg above Vienna. Incredibly, the small Viennese garrison, many starving and sick, still held the city. On the morning of September 12, Sobieski and Charles attacked the Turks, commencing a fifteen-hour battle to drive the besiegers from the trenches they had dug around the city.

While the relief forces pounded the Turks from the outside, the Vienna garrison attacked from within. As the battle plainly turned against him, Vizier Mustafa took flight, leaving behind most of his army, which suffered that day 15,000 killed—among them six pashas—and 25,000 wounded. The Viennese garrison lost 5,000 regulars and 1,700 citizen volunteers were killed. Losses to the Austro-Polish were 1,800 killed and 3,200 wounded. Some chroniclers claim that it took the soldiers and the liberated Viennese nearly a week to loot the booty the Turks left behind, including 300 artillery pieces, 9,000 ammunition wagons, and 25,000 tents overflowing with food and other goods.

Mustafa did not stop running until he reached Constantinople (modern Istanbul), where the sultan ordered him to be executed by strangulation—specifying that a silken cord be employed, in deference to the vizier's high rank. Sobieski had a far more pleasant errand, which was to deliver the Ottoman battle standard of the Prophet Mohammad

into the hands of Pope Innocent XI. The victory prompted Venice to join Austria and Poland in signing the Treaty of Linz on March 31, 1684, creating a Holy League against Turkey. Two years later, Russia signed on as well.

AN OTTOMAN ROUT

The Ottoman troops who managed to escape the siege trenches pounded across a boat bridge set up over the Danube. With the Austro-Polish army in pursuit, the Ottoman column piled onto the frail span, the sudden collapse of which added 7,000 more fatalities to the Turkish toll.

▲

This is a map of the Turkish Empire, as published in a 1606 Amsterdam atlas by Jodocus Hondius (1563–1612).

Hapsburgs and Hungarians

The Holy Roman Empire, a loose union of Central European territories, came together in 962 under Otto the Great, the first Holy Roman emperor. At its greatest extent late in the Middle Ages, it encompassed the kingdoms of Germany, Italy, and Burgundy, in addition to a region corresponding to most of modern Germany and Austria, as well as Liechtenstein, Switzerland, Belgium, the Netherlands, Luxembourg, the Czech Republic, Slovenia, and parts of France, Italy, and Poland.

In 1521, the most powerful ruling dynasty within the Holy Roman Empire, the Hapsburgs, split into Austrian and Spanish branches, the Austrian Hapsburg rulers acquiring the title of Holy Roman emperor in 1558. In addition to Austria, the Austrian Hapsburgs nominally ruled Hungary, which was mostly occupied by the Ottoman Turks.

During the sixteenth century, the rise of Protestantism prompted many local dukes and other rulers within the Holy Roman Empire to rebel against the Catholic emperor. The northern German region became mostly Protestant, while the south, including Austria, remained Catholic. In Hungary, some Protestant Magyar (ethnic Hungarian) groups united with Muslim Ottomans to oppose the rule of Catholic Austria, and in the seventeenth century the conflict between Protestants and Catholics continued to spread throughout the territories of the Holy Roman Empire, culminating in the Thirty Years' War, which ended with the Peace of Westphalia in 1648. This treaty assigned most of the territories virtually total sovereignty, thereby reducing the Holy Roman Empire to a shell. With this development, the Hapsburg emperors turned their attention entirely to the lands they still firmly controlled in Austria and sought to regain from Ottoman rule their Hungarian holdings.

The Ottomans had taken over most of Hungary after a decisive victory at the Battle of Mohács in 1526; however, the sultans never created an effective government for the territory, which remained a chaotic, nearly anarchic battlefield on which the Christian Hapsburgs continued to challenge the Muslim Ottomans. The Turks conquered the Danubian city of Buda in 1541, resulting in the division of Hungary into three parts: "Royal Hungary" in the northwest, controlled by the Hapsburgs ruling as kings of Hungary; Transylvania in the east, under Ottoman suzerainty; and central Hungary (encompassing most of modern Hungary), which became known as the Pashalik of Buda and was the region most frequently torn by warfare between the Catholic Hapsburgs and the Muslim Ottomans—with the Protestant Magyars sometimes allying themselves with one side or the other.

The Treaty of Karlowitz, which ended the Austro-Turkish War of 1683–1699, ultimately led to the annexation of the entire kingdom of Hungary from the Ottomans; however, it left the entire Balkan region seething with unresolved enmities among Catholics, Protestants, and Muslims as well as between Austro-Hungarian imperialists, passionate nationalists from Hungary, and many of the neighboring provinces under Hapsburg rule.

Yet the war did not end.

In 1684 Charles of Lorraine attempted to take the ancient Danubian town of Buda, which the Ottomans had held for 145 years. Driven by the momentum of the victory at Vienna, it had been a rash attack, which failed disastrously, at the cost of half of Charles's 34,000-man army. After regrouping, Charles mounted a second siege, which resulted in victory on September 2, 1686, but at the staggering cost of 20,000 Austrians killed or wounded.

At the time of Buda's fall, a Venetian army under General Francesco Morosini overran the Peloponnesus (in modern Greece). Squeezed everywhere, the Turks fell back into southern Hungary, where Charles of Lorraine attacked them on August 12, 1687, at Harkány, southwest of Mohács, the site of Suleiman the Magnificent's overwhelming victory over the Hungarians in 1526. This time, it was the Ottomans who suffered rout— some 20,000 casualties. Thoroughly demoralized and reduced to panic, the survivors of the Turkish army fled across the Danube and did not stop running until they were in Constantinople, where in a coup d'etat they promptly deposed Sultan Mehmed IV, who had sent them into battle. Croatia had been liberated from the Ottoman Empire.

THE RUSSIAN FRONT

Independently of the action on the war's western front, Czar Peter the Great of Russia conducted two military campaigns against the mighty Ottoman-held fortress of Azov on the Don River near the Sea of Azov in what is today southwestern Russia. The Ottoman fortress blocked Russia's access via the Azov Sea to the Black Sea, greatly limiting communication with the rest of Europe.

In the first Azov campaign, begun in the spring of 1695, Czar Peter ordered 31,000 men with 170 siege guns against the fortress while another Russian army of 120,000 men, including many Ukrainian Cossacks, fought diversionary battles to prevent the Ottomans from coming to the relief of the Azov garrison. Although the Russians cut off the fortress, its garrison of just 7,000 held out and twice repelled attempts to storm the fortress walls.

In September, the siege was lifted, but in the spring of the following year, the second Azov campaign was commenced, this time combining an ocean and river assault by the specially built Azov Flotilla with a land assault, the two forces comprising a total of 75,000 men. Simultaneously, about 70,000 cavalrymen made a diversionary attack along the Dnieper River, again to block reinforcements from the south.

On May 27, the seagoing portion of the Russian fleet blocked Azov and defeated the Turkish fleet on June 14. The fortress was bombarded from the sea, the river, and the land from the end of May until July 17, when Ukrainian and Don Cossacks stormed the fortress, whose walls had been partially breached. The garrison surrendered on July 19. The Russian victory helped to ensure total Ottoman defeat in the war.

DECISION AT ZENTA

Sultan Mehmed IV's successor, Suleyman II, wearily renewed the struggle against the Austrians and their allies. He defeated Holy League forces at Zernyest, Transylvania—at the time ruled by Calvinist princes under Ottoman suzerainty—in August 1690, which allowed the Ottomans to take Belgrade and most of Serbia by October 8. In response, the German elector Louis of Baden led a Holy League counteroffensive, which defeated a combined Ottoman–Transylvanian force at the Battle of Szalankemën in southern Hungary on August 19, 1691, inflicting some 20,000 casualties on the 80,000-man army. With this Austrian victory, Transylvania fell into Hapsburg hands.

After Szalankemën, the war sputtered into a series of sporadic skirmishes until yet another new sultan, Mustafa II led 50,000 troops in a new invasion in 1967. Eugene

A Warrior's Résumé

The Austro-Turkish War of 1683–1699 was only the first episode of Prince Eugene's brilliant military career. The priests who were his first mentors called him "le petit abbé" (the little cleric) because of his delicate frame and chronic ill health; yet it seems that through sheer willpower, he built a strong body and conditioned himself for life on the march and the field of battle.

In 1701, during the War of the Spanish Succession (1701–1714), he led an army of 32,000 men across the Alps to seize the Spanish lands in Italy. After Eugene's victory at Carpi on July 9, France's Louis XIV wrote to the commander whom the prince had defeated: "I have warned you, that you are dealing with an enterprising young prince: he does not tie himself down to the rules of war."

Eugene's brilliance led to his elevation as president of the Imperial War Council and responsibility for formulating the strategy of Austria and its allies throughout most of the War of the Spanish Succession. His careful planning culminated in the momentous victory at the Battle of Blenheim (1704), the credit for which he shared with Winston Churchill's most illustrious ancestor, the Duke of Marlborough.

After the War of the Spanish Succession, Eugene led a brilliant campaign once again against the Ottoman Turks in the Austro-Turkish War of 1716–1718, an achievement that Pope Clement XI acknowledged with the gift of a papal hat and jewel-encrusted sword.

In his own day, Eugene was universally recognized as a great commander, whose tactical imagination and inexhaustible energy were rare among the genteel and noble generals of the eighteenth century. As a child marked for a career in the church, he applied to the military the dedication of the most committed priest. He never married, and he had such little interest in women and the pleasures of the flesh that contemporaries dubbed him "a Mars without a Venus." He was, in fact, a hard, single-minded, and unbending man, whose willingness to risk—and to spend—the lives of his soldiers did not earn him the affection of those who served under him; however, his own personal bravery, which drove him to expose his own life to continual peril in the front lines of every major action (he was seriously wounded no fewer than thirteen times by 1717), won their grudging admiration.

of Savoy followed the invading Ottoman column with a Holy League army consisting of German, Austrian, and Hungarian infantry and cavalry, plus a small number of Serbian light cavalrymen—between 50,000 and 55,000 men in all. During August, Eugene repeatedly attempted to maneuver the Ottomans into a battle near Petrovaradin, a magnificent fortress later known as the "Gibraltar of the Danube," in what is today northern Serbia. Each time, however, the sultan managed to slip the noose, finally marching north in September to mount a siege against the fortress of Szeged in southeastern Hungary. Eugene pursued, sending his cavalry in an attack that made a prisoner of Dschaafer Pasha. The loss of this key commander prompted the sultan to abandon his plan of laying siege to Szeged. Instead, he decided to withdraw into winter quarters near TimiÐoara, in present-day western Romania.

In 1718, Eugene was called to command in the War of the Quadruple Alliance (1718–1720), but achieved disappointing results that radically reduced his influence over the affairs of the house of the Hapsburgs. Eugene served for a time as governor-general of the Netherlands before leading, at the age of seventy, Austrian forces in the War of the Polish Succession (1733–1738). Burdened by insufficient numbers of troops—and poorly trained troops at that—Eugene found himself frequently on the defensive, a situation that went against his naturally aggressive instincts. Even worse, age had sapped his legendary drive and blunted the mental edge that had made him so formidable a tactician. Fortunately, diplomacy prevailed over combat, ending the war before Eugene had suffered any serious defeat. He died in 1736, less than a year after departing the field.

This is Prince Eugene of Savoy, painted in 1754. A sickly, neglected child, Eugene became one of the premier military strategists of his day. He was universally recognized as a great commander, whose tactical imagination and inexhaustible energy were rare among the genteel and noble generals of the eighteenth century.

Making skillful use of small cavalry detachments to serve as his eyes and ears, Eugene quickly surmised the sultan's intentions and resolved to force a decisive battle before the Turks could hole up in camp.

Eugene led his army well behind his cavalry scouts, waiting for his opportunity to attack. On September 11, 1697, he observed the Ottoman army attempting to ford the river Tisza near Zenta. Clearly, they had no idea that nearly 32,000 Imperial troops were lying in wait. Eugene understood that an enemy army was most vulnerable when it was divided by some natural obstacle, such as a broad river. To ford the Tisza, the sultan had thrown a modest boat bridge across the water. It would take a very long time for 50,000 men to cross.

Eugene held his forces in silent hiding until the enemy was neatly divided on either side of the river. Then he opened up a massed artillery bombardment directly onto the Ottoman camp. Exploiting the panic created by the barrage, Eugene deployed his Imperial Dragoons—troops trained to ride to battle, but (unlike cavalry) to fight dismounted, as infantry. The dragoons rode up to the protective moat that encircled the Ottoman camp, tied their horses, and began a musket fusillade.

Reeling under the artillery bombardment and terrorized by the surrounding musketry, the Ottoman defenders leaped out of their entrenchments and scrambled toward the boat bridge. Quickly overloaded, this narrow passage was jammed. As more and more men bunched up at the bridgehead, Eugene redirected his artillery against the bridge and the army-turned-mob, pounding the retreating troops as they waited to cross.

He then sent his left infantry flank forward. They fought into position between the Ottoman left and the bridge, completely cutting off this avenue of retreat. Simultaneously, he hurled his center forces in a head-on attack, even as a portion of his left forces broke through the Ottoman lines and took up a position on a sand bank in the middle of the Tisza. From this small island, they poured musket fire on the boat bridge. To lay down fire perpendicular to an enemy column is to "enfilade" it, hitting the enemy from the flank, so that his men are unable to return fire efficiently. Enfilading fire is slaughter.

As the routed enemy continued to pile up at the bridge, Eugene's center engaged in hand-to-hand combat with swords and bayonets, thrusting through the defensive trenches that surrounded the Ottoman camp. Once inside the camp grounds, they found many soldiers cowering for cover behind the camp supply wagons, which were arrayed head-to-tail in an arc that began and ended at the river. As Eugene's center forces filtered in between the parked wagons, they slashed and bayoneted the helpless enemy.

More than 10,000 Turks drowned in the Tisza and twice that number lay dead on the ground of what had been their camp. No more than 1,000 made good their withdrawal across the boat bridge and back into Ottoman territory. The cost to the Imperial Army has been variously estimated at between 50 and 500 men, killed or wounded. In addition to the 30,000 Ottoman warriors slain, Eugene captured the sultan's harem, 87 cannons, the sultan's treasure chest, and even the royal state seal of the Ottoman Empire.

THE TREATY

For the sultan, defeat and humiliation were total. On January 26, 1699, in Karlowitz—today the Serbian town of Sremski Karlovci—his representatives and those of the Holy League signed the Treaty of Karlowitz, by which the Ottomans ceded most of Hungary and all of Transylvania and Slavonia to Austria. Podolia (the west-central and southwest portion of modern Ukraine) was restored to Poland, and the greater part of Dalmatia became a Venetian possession, as did the Peloponnesus.

With this treaty, the Ottoman Empire slipped into a long decline that would, by the nineteenth century, reduce what had been a mighty Muslim caliphate to a backward country that was disdainfully called the "sick man of Europe"—weak, corrupt, and vulnerable to the revolution that created the modern republic of Turkey in 1923. As Ottoman control in Europe receded, the power of Austria's Hapsburg monarchy rose proportionately until the Austro-Hungarian Empire became dominant in Central Europe.

Yet while the Muslim Ottomans had been evicted from a vast portion of Southern and Central Europe, the lines of religious conflict hardened between Muslims and Christians in the border regions that vaguely separated the Balkans from Asia Minor. And while the Hapsburgs came to dominate the region for a long time, they never succeeded in transforming it into anything resembling a true nation-state or even a successful imperial province. This failure ensured that the Balkans would remain a no-man's land. Indeed, it would become a seething cauldron of religious, nationalist, and even quasi-tribal violence, destined repeatedly to boil over into war, chronically destabilizing all of Europe. In the early and mid-twentieth century, conflict here would trigger one world war and contribute to the genesis of another. At the close of that century, the hereditary enmities born in the waning years of the seventeenth century would spark intensely bitter warfare in Bosnia and Kosovo, shattering the peace that fleetingly followed the end of the Cold War.

COLD AMBITION:
THE GREAT NORTHERN WAR

1700—1721

The warrior grandson of a warrior king set out to conquer Poland, Prussia, Saxony, Hanover, Denmark, and Russia in a monomaniacal and massively destructive campaign to make Sweden dominant over the Baltic and beyond. In the end, the Great Northern War of Charles XII Gustav debilitated Sweden and made Czar Peter the Great the most powerful monarch on Europe's vast eastern frontier.

C harles X Gustav (1622–1660) was not born to war but from a very early age he had been educated to it. The principal tutor of his youth was the most important military figure in Sweden, Field Marshal Lennart Torstenson, a generalissimo of such importance that the kingdom's 1643–1645 war with Denmark-Norway was named for him: "Torstenson's War." So, when King John II Casimir (1609–1672) of Poland was insolent enough to reject Charles's claim as "Protector of Poland," the king did what he had been taught to do—he personally led a large army of invasion, which seized Warsaw after a three-day battle in 1656. Having conquered Poland, Charles X marched into territory that is modern Lithuania, brushed aside all resistance there, and occupied it by the end of the year.

Think of war, and the country of Sweden does not come readily to mind. But in the seventeenth and eighteenth centuries, Charles X Gustav, who ascended the Swedish throne in 1654, sought to dissolve his kingdom's domestic discord in a heady brew of international conquest. His political stratagem transformed what had been an isolated realm into a relentless war machine, which attempted to draw the center of European power from the south to the north.

OBJECTIVE: DENMARK

While the Swedish monarch campaigned, his Prussian ally, Frederick William (1620–1688), finally negotiated Polish acquiescence to Charles's role as Protector of Poland. This freed Charles to advance westward to fight Denmark—now without the support of its ally Poland—for possession of the duchies of Holstein and Schleswig, as well as most of the territory of Jutland (the Danish mainland). Having secured these by early autumn 1657, the Swedish king led a spectacular assault from Jutland east to the island of Fünen in central Denmark, with the object of continuing on to Zealand, the principal Danish island, and capturing Copenhagen, the capital.

◄

With a face full of confidence and a fist firmly clenched around the handle of his sword, Charles XII Gustav presented himself to the German painter David von Krafft as what he undeniably was: the bold warrior king of Sweden.

In the meantime, however, the Danes sued for peace in February 1658, and Charles paused on Fünen, awaiting the results of treaty negotiations. Dissatisfied with the outcome, he resumed his advance on Copenhagen and laid the capital under siege in July, including a maritime blockade. This drew the aid of the fleet of Holland, Denmark's ally, which forced Charles to lift the blockade following the Battle of the Sound on October 29, 1658.

Worse, because Charles's land forces were spread thin between the Copenhagen siege and the occupation of Schleswig and Holstein, south of Jutland, Polish forces were able to drive out the Swedes there. A combination of Danes and Norwegians—Norway was Sweden's traditional rival—bested the Swedes on the Danish island of Bornholm and the Norwegian coastal town of Trondheim. These defeats extracted from Charles X a bid for peace in 1659.

SWEDISH SETBACK

But the Swedish king had not quite played out his string. He dragged his feet during negotiations, looking for a way to renew the fight. In November 1659, a Danish victory at the Battle of Nyborg, on Fünen, cost Charles his best soldiers, who were all made prisoners of war. This reversal became an outright catastrophe when less than four months after the battle the king died of a fever, leaving Sweden in the hands of his widow, Hedvig Eleonora of Holstein-Gottorp, who chaired the group of regents that hastily concluded the Treaty of Oliva in 1660. By terms of the treaty, Sweden held on to Livonia—modern Latvia, at the time claimed by Poland—but yielded Bornholm and Trondheim as well as East Prussia.

Thus the First Northern War of 1655–1660 ended in Swedish defeat—yet nevertheless in a net gain of Polish territory, which put Sweden in position to expand its hold over the Baltic coast. Before the end of the seventeenth century, Sweden—ostensibly the loser—came to control Finland, the Gulf of Finland, Riga, Pomerania, the vicinity of Bremen, and all of Livonia, making it the most powerful country in Northern Europe. Understandably, this situation galled the Russians, whose access to the Baltic was blocked; and the leaders of Denmark-Norway were frustrated by a Swedish alliance

scale 1:21 000 000

0   600 km
0   400 mi

Shetland Islands

Orkney Islands

ATLANTIC OCEAN

NOR SE

IRELAND

GREAT BRITAIN

PRO
Zaandam
Aug 1697–
Jan 169

Deptford, London
Jan–May 1698

Paris

FRANCE
Loire
Seine

● place visited by Great Embassy, 1697–98
◇ shipbuilding center of Peter I
▢ Russian territory, 1697
▢ Swedish territory, 1697
– · – international boundary, 1721

Great Northern Wa
✗ battle with
→ Swedish c
▨ Russian ga

with Holstein-Gottorp (part of Schleswig-Holstein ruled at the time by the dukes of Schleswig-Holstein-Gottorp). Because Holstein-Gottorp was located at the southern base of Jutland, the alliance had the effect of holding Denmark-Norway in check from the south, preventing the Danes from achieving control of Schleswig and Holstein.

As for the German states, the house of Brandenburg had won in the First Northern War control of East Prussia, but it now lusted after Swedish Pomerania, which provided access to the Baltic Sea, and also fretted over the influential role Sweden played in the Holy Roman

This map of Europe was in the process of being redrawn by the rapacious Charles XII.

Empire. The Poles, of course, continued to mourn the loss of Livonia, to which they never became reconciled.

HOSTILE CLIMATE

The actions of Charles X charged the climate of Northern Europe with a hostility that endured after his death in 1660 as well as after the death of his son and successor, Charles XI Gustav, in 1697. Thus fifteen-year-old Charles XII Gustav ascended the Swedish throne in a time of grave danger. The coronation of a callow king was often a clarion call to war, and Denmark-Norway was quick to cobble together an anti-Swedish coalition, almost immediately confronting the teenaged monarch with three major assaults. The first was a Danish invasion of Holstein-Gottrop. The second was an attack by Poland's King Augustus II (Augustus II, also known as Augustus the Strong, ruled from 1670 to 1733 and was elector of Saxony, which is modern-day eastern Germany) against Livonia at the key Baltic port city of Riga. The third was a siege against Narva, a Swedish-held city in modern Estonia, near the Gulf of Finland, led by Peter the Great (1672–1725) of Russia.

Even at age fifteen, however, Charles XII was no ordinary leader. After only a few months as the youth's principal regent, his grandmother, Hedvig Eleonora of Holstein-Gottorp, concluded that Charles XII was possessed of such prodigious abilities that she and the committee of regents she chaired voluntarily stepped down. Though the boy king had succeeded in impressing his grandmother, the rulers of Denmark-Norway, Russia, and Poland were hardly intimidated, and thus the Second "Great" Northern War commenced.

THE YOUNG WARRIOR

Donning the warrior mantle of his grandfather, Charles personally led initial operations against the Danes, driving the invaders out of Holstein-Gottorp, and then he seized the initiative by leading his troops in the conquest of Zealand on August 4, the very heart of Danish territory. This campaign revealed the young man's strategic brilliance. By concentrating his forces first on Denmark, menacing Copenhagen, Charles was able to force King Frederick IV to withdraw Denmark-Norway from the anti-Swedish coalition. Moreover, he signed the Treaty of Traventhal on August 28, 1700, restoring the *status quo ante bellum*, which favored Sweden.

With the Danish-Norwegian element deftly neutralized and out of the coalition, Charles turned next to Czar Peter the Great's army at Narva. On November 30, the young Swede landed an army of 8,000 near the port town and staged a surprise assault on some 40,000 Russian defenders, who were well dug into trench works. Even if he had been equally matched with the defenders, an older, wiser commander would have hesitated to attack a well-fortified position. Outnumbered more than four to one, no experienced commander would dare to launch such an attack.

Charles, however, made an ally of the elements. He used the cover of a heavy snowstorm to cloak his movements so that he was able to get his forces past the Russian outposts undetected, bringing all of his men into the center of the defenders' lines. The panic this caused among the Russians was electric. In a three-hour battle—some sources report it as a mere 15 minutes—the greatly outnumbered Swedes routed the czar's forces, forcing them to flee after they had left behind more than 10,000 dead. Swedish casualties were fewer than 1,000 killed or wounded. The battle was vintage Charles XII. In the eighteenth century, senior commanders had virtually no contact with their army's rank and file. Soldiers were inspired above all by a single quality in a general: his ability to bring victory. Success in one campaign inspired throughout the army a level of performance that virtually ensured victory in the next campaign. If a commander's name was attached to a record of triumph, little else mattered to the officers and men he led.

From this remarkable victory, Charles marched southwest, to the relief of Riga, against the Russians, Poles, and Saxons fleeing at the Swedes' approach. Charles pursued the enemy through Livonia, invading Poland proper. Flushed with these signal victories, Charles went on a full-scale offensive, crossing the Danübe River, where he met, fought, and defeated another Russian-Polish-Saxon army at Dünamünde on June 18, 1701.

As a result, he came to occupy Kurland (in western Latvia) and from there launched an invasion of Lithuania, a campaign that spanned August to December 1701. He advanced next against the Polish capital of Warsaw, occupying it on May 14, 1702, and installed on

Dowager Regent

As the dowager—the property-holding twenty-four-year-old widow—of Charles X Gustav, it fell to Queen Hedvig Eleonora of Holstein-Gottorp to serve as regent in the aftermath of her husband's death and during the minority of her son, Charles XI, and years later of her grandson, Charles XII. More precisely, she chaired a kind of board of regents, men assigned to govern in the place of the hereditary monarch while that individual was underage.

In 1697, at the age of sixty-one, she eagerly relinquished the regency of fifteen-year-old Charles XII when she determined that the remarkable teenager was quite capable of ruling in his own right. While the boy was off fighting the Great Northern War, however, Hedvig Eleonora was again called on to serve as regent at home in Sweden.

Her office as substitute head of state did not so much oppress as bore her, as she much preferred to occupy her time with parties and at least three lovers. Foreign ambassadors who came to call on her at court were invariable chagrined by the greeting she extended to them—typically dismissive laughter or bored silence.

Charles XI, father of Charles XII, was slavishly devoted to his mother, and even as an adult, long after her regency had ended, he made it a practice to speak to members of parliament and other government officials exclusively through Hedvig Eleonora. This was not a political gesture, but apparently a symptom of acute shyness. The queen would appear in parliament with her son, Charles would whisper his questions to her, and she would repeat them—in a loud voice—to the members of the parliament. This she considered her duty as a doting mother since she clearly had no interest in politics. She relied wholly on her advisers and signed whatever documents and decrees they set before her—even as the European continent roiled in the Great Northern War. Hedvig Eleonora died in 1715 at age seventy-nine.

the throne there a puppet ruler, Stanislaus Leszczynski, even as the Poles and Saxons continued to fall back before his advance. At last, at the village of Klissow, more than 100 miles (161 km) southwest of Warsaw, the defenders rallied for a stand against the Swedish army.

Combined, the Poles and Saxons mustered about 25,000 men. Outnumbered as usual, Charles attacked on July 13 with just 12,000 soldiers—but did so with a swift and crushing force that more than compensated for the disparity in numbers. It was an eighteenth-century version of the tactic that would be dubbed blitzkrieg—"lightning war"—in World War II. Charles inspired his men to defy the odds with a relentless onslaught in which the key elements were speed and sheer violence. First the Polish lines caved, and then the Saxon units followed. Charles now found his way clear to Krakow on the Vistula River. He led his army on a 45-mile (72 km) march to the ancient Polish city, took it, and then boldly doubled back in search of Augustus II, the deposed king of Poland who was in hiding.

AUGUSTUS THE STRONG YIELDS

It was at Pultusk, 32 miles (51 km) north of Warsaw, that Charles encountered Augustus II and another Saxon army, this one consisting of perhaps 10,000 men, evenly matched with his own forces. The Swedish king sighted the enemy on April 13, 1703, but bided his time until April 21 when he launched a lightning assault that almost instantly broke through the defenders' positions. The terrified Saxons offered scarcely more than token resistance before they broke and ran, leaving behind no more than 600 of their number killed and giving up perhaps 1,000 as prisoners of war. On the heels of this victory, the Polish legislature acclaimed Charles's candidate, Stanislaus Leszczynski as Stanislaus I, king of Poland. By 1705, after additional victories at Punitz and Wszawa, Charles had wholly subdued Poland.

Two years after conquering Poland, Charles invaded Lithuania and pursued the elusive Augustus II back into his native Saxony. Now fighting in his homeland, Augustus was able to fight Charles to a standstill, but unable to eject him from Saxony. He concluded with the Swedish king the Treaty of Altranstädt on October 4, 1706, by which he renounced once and for all—and after six hard years of fighting—his royal claim on the Polish throne in favor of Stanislaus I. He also pledged to end the Saxon alliance with Russia.

TARGET: RUSSIA

Returning to the Baltic, the tireless warrior king relentlessly drove the Russians out of Lithuania, pushing the army of Peter the Great as far as Pinsk during the late summer and early autumn of 1705. With the defeat of Augustus the Strong, Peter lost both his Polish and Saxon allies and therefore saw no choice but to offer Charles highly favorable terms for peace. The Swedish king, who had first engaged in war because he had been forced to, now found himself moved by visions of ever greater glory. Accordingly, he spurned the czar's terms, and to demonstrate his contempt for the czar as well as his offer, he ordered the arrest of the Russian ambassador at Dresden. Citing the fact that the ambassador had been born in Livonia, now a Swedish possession, he accused the diplomat of treason and ordered his public execution. Simultaneously, he set about raising more troops for his army and during 1707 stockpiled weapons and other supplies. On New Year's Day 1708, twenty-six-year-old Charles commenced an invasion of Russia itself.

For his part, Peter the Great was unwilling to play the role of passive victim. While Charles was fighting and chasing Augustus the Strong, Peter reorganized the Russian army and secured his nation's footing on the east coast of the Baltic in 1703 by founding what he called his "window on the West," Saint Petersburg, as well as a modern naval port at Kronstadt. Thus, when Charles marched from Saxony in September 1707 at the head of

an 80,000-man army of invasion, passing through Poland, Lithuania, and then finally into Russia, the czar was quite prepared to receive him.

BELORUSSIAN ODYSSEY

It began as all of Charles's campaigns had begun: apparently unstoppable. On January 13, 1706; 20,000 Swedes marching from Poland crossed the Neman River and pushed back Russian cavalry units, forcing them to fall back on Minsk. This retreat cut off from the outside world the 23,000 Russian troops who garrisoned Grodno on the Neman River, in modern Belarus. Charles set up a siege of the city and dispatched units to occupy the town of Nesvizh and also to lay siege to Lyakhovichi, where another Russian force was concentrated. Without food or fresh water, the Grodno garrison languished, some 8,000 Russian soldiers falling prey to privation and disease.

The Grodno blockade left Czar Peter with just 12,000 Russian soldiers in all of Belarus. Seeking reinforcements, Peter, from his headquarters in Minsk, ordered some 14,000 Ukrainian Cossacks under their remarkable hetman (leader) Mazepa to make continuous harassing attacks against the besieging forces of Charles; however, Peter refused to aid the Grodno garrison directly, because he dared not engage the Swedes in open battle so far from his main sources of supply in Russia proper. At the same time, he forbade the Grodno garrison to surrender, ordering them to hold out until the spring thaw when the Neman would be free of ice and navigable, affording an avenue of retreat to the Dnieper River.

Charles grasped Peter's strategic intentions, but he guessed wrong about the direction of the retreat of the Grodno forces, expecting that they would withdraw eastward, where he positioned his principal forces to intercept them. In May, he discovered—too late—that the Russians were moving out of Grodno and toward the southwest. In desperation, he decided to pursue them by cutting through the treacherous Polesye swamps. The season's rapid thaw made this route impassable, however, and Charles was forced to break off his pursuit.

The Swedish leader decided to advance next against the ancient Belorussian city of Minsk. He did not cross the River Berezina until July 12, 1708, after encountering a large Russian army at Golovchino, on the Vorskla River, a tributary of the great Dnieper. He

◄

Like Napoleon and Hitler long after him, Charles XII was swallowed up by Russia when he attempted to conquer it. His defeat left Czar Peter the Great, shown here, the most powerful ruler on Europe's eastern frontier.

handily defeated it and pressed on to the larger river. His vanguard entered the Dnieper village of Mogilev on July 18 and there brushed aside parties of Russian skirmishers. From here, the Swedes wheeled west and advanced on Minsk itself, which after a long and exhausting march, they entered unopposed, Peter and his army having withdrawn long before.

SWALLOWED UP

It was at this point that the Swedish invaders began to taste the fate that sooner or later befalls most invaders of Russia. Increasingly, the emperor and his men sensed the capacity of the vast land to swallow up whole armies. Minsk was a ghost town, and Czar Peter had imposed on his people a scorched earth policy, which scoured the surrounding countryside and left the invaders nothing on which to subsist. Famine swept the Swedish ranks. Deciding that it was better to starve on the march than remain holed up in Minsk, Charles ordered his exhausted troops to advance on Moscow.

On September 11, Charles defeated a small Russian force at Dobroje, where he also encountered Mazepa and his Ukrainian Cossacks. The hetman, at the time perhaps the single largest landowner in all of Europe, had become weary of Peter's policy of extending imperial control into the Ukraine and encroaching on the autonomy the Cossacks had enjoyed under the Treaty of Pereyaslav, which had been concluded a half-century earlier in 1654. In the current war, Mazepa had answered the czar's call and had faithfully led his Cossacks against the Swedes. But the Pereyaslav treaty that bound him to defend the interests of the czar in Ukraine in turn bound the czar to defend the Cossacks.

In the Treaty of Pereyaslav, the Cossacks had agreed to fight for the czar only on their own land against regional foes. Livonia and Lithuania, to which Mazepa and his men had been sent, were remote, and fighting far from home in the service of the czar left the Cossacks' families back in the Ukraine exposed to the depredations of the Tatars and Poles. Worse, although the Cossacks had a much-deserved reputation for ferocity in battle, they were poorly armed and had not been trained to the rapidly evolving modern standard of other European armies. Adding insult to injury, the Russian commanders, as well as the

▶

A detail from Jean-Marc Nattier's (1685-1766) sweeping portrayal of the Battle of Poltava, where Peter the Great defeated Charles XII on July 8, 1709.

Saxon generals who had defied Augustus the Strong and remained in the service of the czar, looked upon the Cossacks as uncivilized brutes whose lives were entirely expendable. As poorly as the Russian soldiers and officers treated the Cossacks, the Russians were even more insulting and burdensome to the civilian population of Ukraine, looting and pillaging the cities and villages in which their garrisons were quartered.

For Mazepa, the tipping point came when he heard a rumor that Czar Peter intended to remove him from command of the Cossacks and replace him with a Russian general. Moreover, Peter refused to send Russian troops to defend Ukraine against Stanislaus Leszczynski, the puppet monarch Charles had put on the Polish throne, who late in 1708 began rattling his saber against Mazepa. Deeming the failure to come to Ukraine's defense as the equivalent of tearing up the Treaty of Pereyaslav, Mazepa struck a deal with Charles on October 28, 1708 and aligned himself with the Swedes.

Outrage against Peter the Great had blinded Mazepa to the enduring loyalty his Cossacks bore to the czar. Between 2,000 and 3,000 followed the hetman into his new allegiance with Charles XII. For his part, however, Peter repaid the loyalty of the majority of Cossacks by taking indiscriminate vengeance on all Cossacks. The Russian army stormed into the Cossack capital of Baturyn, slaughtered the small garrison there along with the entire civilian population, and then put the town to torch. As if this were not message enough, the Russian troops collected the Cossack corpses, tied them to improvised wooden crosses, and set them floating down the Dnieper River to its mouth at the Black Sea. Peter intended that all who were inclined to betray him by swearing fealty to Mazepa would see this grim spectacle and think the better of it.

At first greatly heartened by the defection of Mazepa, Charles was soon dismayed by the small number of troops he brought to the alliance. Charles himself now faced a prospect he had never encountered before—mass desertion and grumblings of mutiny. It is a testament to the force of his personality that he kept his cold, sick, starving army intact during the typically terrible Russian winter of November 1708 to April 1709. Believing that only action would save his cause, he advanced on Voronezh at first thaw, pausing to lay siege against Poltava in central Ukraine on May 2.

POLTAVA

No general is eager to lay siege, and no army relishes it. Siege work is often as hard on the attackers as on their target. The success of such a campaign depends on the besieging army's being adequately supplied and sheltered. In the case of Charles's army, it suffered from an acute shortage of everything needful, from basic provisions to ammunition to powder to artillery. His supply column from Riga had been virtually destroyed. Even with the addition of Mazepa's greatly reduced cavalry, Charles commanded no more than 20,000 men, the majority weak with hunger and sickness.

Recognizing the vulnerability of his enemy, Peter was quick to pounce. He assembled an army of 60,000 Russians to lift the siege, sending all but 10,000 of these troops across the Vorskla River and entrenching them just north of the Swedish siege lines at Poltava. The entrenchments were deep and well fortified, and Peter had deployed artillery to cover them. He mounted a classic, overwhelming countersiege, which succeeded in doing just what he wanted. Unable to withstand continual artillery bombardment, Charles ordered his men out of their trenches and into the open for a showdown battle on July 8, 1709.

The king himself had suffered a crippling wound in the foot in an earlier tangle with Russian skirmishers and had to be carried into battle on a litter. Assaulting well defended, firmly dug-in forces was always a high-risk gamble. As a youth, Charles had triumphed in a situation like this at Narva, prevailing against 40,000 Russians with just 8,000 Swedes. But now his outnumbered army was disheartened and depleted. Nevertheless, the king rolled the dice.

The Swedes valiantly withstood relentless fire from the Russian redoubts, and at times, here and there, the Russian lines seemed on the verge of giving way. But they held, and the covering artillery fire took a devastating toll on the attackers. After two hours, it was clear to Peter that Charles's attack was losing momentum. His moment had come.

The czar order a counterattack, sending his men out of their entrenchments and squarely into the body of the Swedish army as well as against both its left and right flanks—a triple envelopment. Since the Swedes' backs were to the Vorskla and Dnieper rivers, it was the equivalent of a total envelopment. Despite the desperate nature of their situation, the Swedes at first showed incredible discipline as they made a fighting withdrawal. But then something simply broke. The retreat became a rout, and the Russians, thirsting for vengeance against the hated invader, pressed forward, forcing the backs of the Swedes into the angle formed by the confluence of the two rivers. Further retreat was impossible. Having bagged the invaders, the Russians killed or captured all except for Charles, Mazepa, and perhaps 1,500 officers and men, all of whom fled to the Turkish fortress of Bendery, about three days' forced march.

CODA

The Battle of Poltava did not immediately end the Great Northern War, but it did put a lasting period to Swedish military power. Never again would the far north be in a position to seriously contend for control of Europe. Even more important, the battle instantly precipitated the rise of Russia to eventual dominance in Eastern Europe: first under the czars and then after the Russian revolutions of 1917 under the dictatorship of Lenin and especially Joseph Stalin.

What remained of the Great Northern War after Poltava was a kind of coda, an anticlimax of misery. Mazepa sickened and died in Turkish Moldava on October 2, 1709. In the fortress town of Bendery, the Turks, who regarded any enemy of Russia as a friend of theirs, treated Charles as an honored guest for a very long time, from 1709 to 1714. At length, however, the Swedish exile wore out his welcome by his incessant political intriguing aimed at dragging the Ottomans into an all-out war with Russia. Sick at last of his undermining influence, the sultan ordered the arrest of Charles XII, who gave himself up only after a sharp battle between Turkish Janissaries and his own corps of bodyguards. The Turks had no real desire to hold the king, and he was allowed to slip out of Moldava quietly in the fall of 1714. He made his way to Swedish Pomerania, in Poland, reaching Stralsund on November 21. In an effort to capture or kill the monarch, the forces of Russia and its allies laid siege for a year against Stralsund and neighboring Wismar, in Germany, but Charles made good an escape to Sweden in December 1715.

In the meantime, while Charles had been away in Bendery, a great deal had come to pass. Augustus the Strong had returned to Poland, overthrew Stanislaus, and resumed the throne. Czar Peter had invaded Ingermanland on the Gulf of Finland and Lake Ladoga, in the vicinity of Saint Petersburg, as well as Livonia and Finland. His valued ally, Prussia, conquered Swedish-held Pomerania, Poland, Russia, Saxony, Hanover, and Denmark-Norway.

CHARLES TRIES AGAIN

The Swedish government was in the process of negotiating an end to the Great Northern War when Charles returned to his homeland and began putting back together the ragged pieces of what had been a great army. While he did this, the Swedish king also offered terms to Peter, agreeing to cede to Russia all of Sweden's Baltic provinces. Peter held him in at arm's length; however, as a Danish–Norwegian force invaded Swedish soil at Scania in the summer of 1716.

After driving them off, Charles prepared to retaliate by invading Norway, hoping that from there he could launch an invasion in an entirely new direction: Scotland. His purpose was to build an impregnable position from which he could force a favorable negotiated peace with the many enemies arrayed against him.

The king led a thrust into Norway and by November 30, 1718, he had penetrated as far as the fortified town of Fredrikshald (modern Halden), near Christiania (modern Oslo). While laying siege to Fredrikshald, Charles XII Gustav was struck in the head by a musket ball. He died instantly. Without their leader, the invaders simply turned around and marched home. Free now to make peace, the war-weary Swedish government leaped into the negotiations that resulted in the Treaties of Stockholm (1719–1720) and Nystad (1721), which brought a definitive end to the war in 1721. By these treaties, Hanover collected from Sweden the duchies of Bremen and Verden.

To Prussia went the Baltic port of Stettin and parts of Pomerania. Denmark gave up most of its territorial gains, except for Schleswig, in exchange for a badly needed cash indemnity. Sweden ceded Livonia, Ingermanland, a portion of Karelia (in modern Finland), and a number of Baltic islands to Russia, which in return relinquished the bulk of Finland. Even with that concession, the realm of Czar Peter the Great emerged as the dominant power in Eastern Europe whereas Sweden was ever afterward marginalized in Europe—geographically, economically, culturally, and militarily.

THE FIRST WARS ON TERROR: THE UNITED STATES VS. THE BARBARY PIRATES

1801–1815

America's very first overseas wars were fought barely a quarter-century after
the United States declared independence, but they really started about 700 years
before the American Revolution, when the Knights Hospitaller were created
in 1080 to care for sick and wounded Christian pilgrims and Crusaders in the Holy Land.
Five centuries later, in 1530, King Charles of Spain installed the Knights Hospitaller in
and around Malta, which was the frontier between Christian and Islamic lands,
to defend Rome, the seat of Christianity, against the danger of Muslim invasion.

B y the 1500s, the Knights had already compiled a long anti-piracy résumé. When they had occupied the Greek island of Rhodes beginning in the early fourteenth century, they routinely fought the so-called Barbary Pirates, Muslim "privateers" (state-sanctioned pirates) operating from the North African ports of the Barbary Coast: Tunis in Tunisia, Tripoli in Libya (at the time called Tripolitania or simply Tripoli), Algiers in Algeria, and various ports in Morocco. Their prey was the ships and sailors of Christian nations.

After they moved to Malta in 1530, the Knights—now renamed the Knights of Malta—expanded their war on the Islamic privateers, claiming as their battlefield the entire Mediterranean Sea. For the next three centuries, the Knights of Malta policed these waters, transforming their island stronghold into a Christian bastion against Islamic invasion and sustaining themselves with the booty recovered from the privateer vessels they took as prizes.

Then in 1798, Napoleon Bonaparte changed everything. Bound for Egypt and what would be his own doomed campaign in the Islamic world, he decided to scoop up Malta en route and claim it for France. Instead of presenting himself as a conqueror, however, he merely asked the Knights to grant his ships safe harbor so that they could be refitted and resupplied. He and his vessels were welcomed in the spirit of Christian charity, but no sooner had the ships entered the Maltese port then Napoleon ordered them to turn their cannon on the fortress of the Knights. Impregnable from the open sea, the Maltese stronghold was completely vulnerable to attack from the inside. The Knights abandoned Malta and the Mediterranean with it. The pirates of Islam now owned that sea.

FAITH AND TRIBUTE

In the long and still unwinding struggle between Christianity and Islam, the Christians have been historically unwilling to make any compromises. The Crusades, after all, were about conquest, not negotiation. In contrast, the Islamic rulers of the North African states, who employed the Barbary pirates, were eager to bargain with their Christian enemies. Even when the Knights of Malta still patrolled the Mediterranean, a sufficient number of pirates evaded their patrols to wreak a low but sustained level of havoc on the commerce of Europe.

During the seventeenth and early eighteenth centuries, the European states agreed to varying schemes of extortion, paying

◄

This is the *Grand Master and Chaplains of the Knights of Malta* by Antoine de Favray (1706-1791). Originating as the Knights Hospitaller in 1080, the Knights of Malta were a powerful force against the Barbary pirates until Napoleon drove them out of their island fortress.

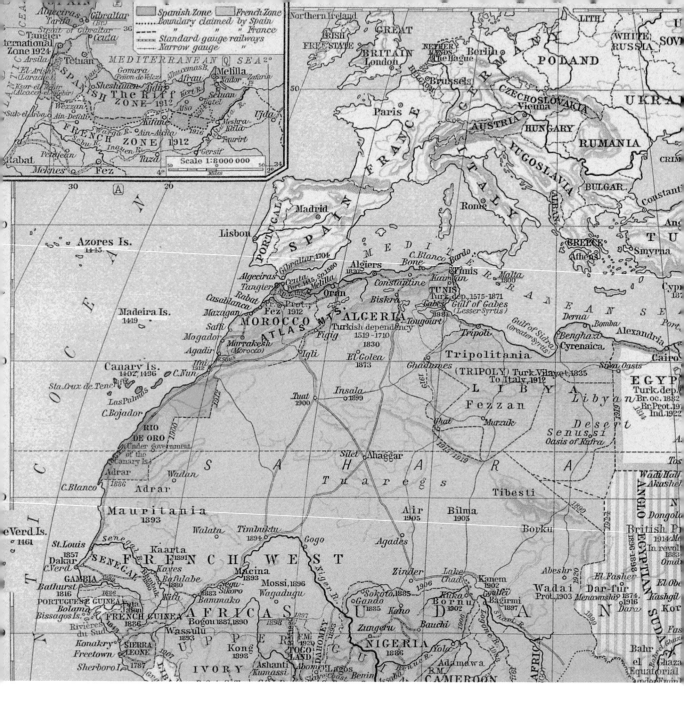

the Islamic potentates protection money—it was called "tribute"—in exchange for their pledge of safe passage through Mediterranean Sea lanes. This was cheaper than financing major naval patrols, but after the Knights of Malta were forced out, tribute provided insufficient protection from piracy, and European navies had to use force to take up where extortion left off.

Ships that plied the waters off the Northern Africa were vulnerable to attack by the pirates of the Barbary Coast—the Islamic states of that area, that included modern Libya, Tunisia, Algeria, and Morocco.

Before the American Revolution, colonial shipping was protected in the Mediterranean by a combination of British-paid tribute and Royal Navy patrols. During the revolution—at least from 1778—the U.S. alliance with France put U.S. vessels under French protection. But at the end of the war, with independence won, the United States had to take sole responsibility for the safety of its commerce.

A BAD BUSINESS

Without a navy to speak of, the U.S. Congress in 1784 appropriated funds for tribute money and commissioned John Adams and Thomas Jefferson to negotiate with the Barbary States, Tripolitania (modern Libya), Tunisia, Algeria, and Morocco. In 1786, these two men met with the Tripolitan envoy to Britain and asked him point-blank why his country would "make war upon nations who had done them no injury."

The envoy responded that the "Koran poses as a right and duty the plundering and enslavement of those who do not follow the Prophet and that any Muslim who dies in this service is assured a place in paradise." Based in part on this reply, Jefferson advised that paying tribute would only encourage more attacks. While Adams agreed, he also pointed out the need to buy time to build a credible U.S. navy. In the end, the United States paid some $1 mil-

The New Piracy

Somalia, on the Horn of Africa, thrusting between the Indian Ocean on the southeast and the Gulf of Aden to the north, is a failed state that has long been torn between competing warlords. The prevailing anarchy has contributed to the development of piracy in the region, perpetrated by young men, mostly between twenty and thirty-five years of age, formed (as of this writing) into perhaps five active pirate gangs. Recruits include local fishermen, whose knowledge of the coastal waters is extensive; ex-militiamen formerly in the employ of Somali warlords, who are accustomed to handling weapons; and young men who possess the technical sophistication to operate radar and GPS systems.

Although this region of Africa is overwhelmingly Islamic, the pirates are not motivated by religion—indeed, they have clashed with local Islamic groups—but by a gangster-like desire to make a lot of money, regardless of the risk. Captured vessels, their cargoes, and crews are typically held for ransom, which runs into the hundreds of millions of dollars annually.

Somali-based piracy began during the especially chaotic Somali Civil War of the 1990s and as of 2009 has become increasingly intense, with a high volume of incidents driving up shipping costs and interfering with humanitarian shipments of food and other supplies to the impoverished region.

lion annually in tribute and ransom to the Barbary States. By 1800, when Jefferson was elected to the presidency, the young republic was turning over to the Barbary States a staggering one-fifth of its annual revenues.

The situation was made worse for the United States by the conniving of the British, who in 1785 had actively encouraged Algiers to capture two U.S. vessels. In his capacity as U.S. minister plenipotentiary to France, Jefferson tried to recruit the aid of Portugal, Naples, Sardinia, and Russia, as well as France, in an anti-Algerian alliance. When France bowed out, however, the alliance died aborning, and the British were emboldened to encourage more Algerian piracy, which resulted in the capture of a dozen U.S. ships and the imprisonment of more than 100 U.S. sailors. The government of President Washington negotiated a treaty with the bey of Algiers in 1795, pledging tribute to secure release of the captives and to ensure freedom of navigation. This was followed by similar treaties with Tunis and Tripolitania.

UNLIKELY WARRIOR

Despite the treaties, the notion of tribute sat so uneasily with both Washington and Adams that they delayed sending the tribute money, and it had yet to be paid in 1800 when Jefferson defeated Adams in his bid for reelection. Jefferson came into office intent on reducing the scope, size, and authority of the federal government, including cutting back military spending. As governor of Virginia during the American Revolution, Jefferson had shown himself to be downright inept as a commander in chief.

The fact was that Jefferson abhorred war, but he did not believe that purchasing peace with ever-increasing tributes and ransoms was an acceptable alternative. Moreover, he was convinced that each payment further undermined the nation's claim to sovereignty. Accordingly, shortly after his inauguration in 1801, when Yussif Karamanli, pasha of Tripolitania, demanded nearly a quarter-million dollars from the incoming administration, Jefferson simply refused. The pasha responded in May by chopping down the flagstaff that adorned the U.S. consulate at Tripoli, a gesture Jefferson accepted as a declaration of war. Morocco, Algiers, and Tunis allied themselves with Tripolitania.

Jefferson dispatched the U.S. navy's newly built warships, the USS *Argus*, *Chesapeake*, *Constellation*, *Constitution*, *Enterprise*, *Philadelphia*, and *Syren* under Commodore Edward Preble to patrol the Barbary coastal waters. Only after

John Adams, Father of the U.S. Navy

Thomas Jefferson had come into office threatening to dismantle much of the U.S. Navy, which his predecessor and political rival, John Adams, had recently built. Adams had not favored the establishment of a large standing army, but he did believe that the nation needed "wooden walls"—stout frigates and other ships of war—to defend itself against threats from abroad and to secure free passage of U.S. seagoing commerce.

In 1794, during the Washington administration, Congress authorized six frigates to be built or purchased, and on April 30, 1798, at the behest of President Adams, Congress formally created the Department of the Navy, including the office of secretary of the navy. Five days later, Congress authorized the president to build or buy ten small ships for coastal defense. When an undeclared naval war broke out between the United States and France later in May, more ships were ordered, but after peace came in 1801, Congress reduced the authorized strength of the U.S. Navy from thirty-three to thirteen ships.

After he took office in March of that year, President Jefferson, worried that large oceangoing warships would inevitably involve the United States in foreign wars, called for the creation of a "gunboat navy," consisting of small vessels, mounting only one or two guns each, intended strictly to defend the coasts from invasion. His decision to defy the Tripolitan pasha's tribute demand, however, stayed Jefferson's hand, and he made full use of every frigate and schooner in the fleet.

he had dispatched the fleet did he inform Congress, which declined to declare war on any of the Barbary States, but did ratify Jefferson's action and further authorized him to enlarge the navy's mission beyond mere patrol. Jefferson now instructed his commanders to intercept and seize all vessels and cargo belonging to the Tripolitan pasha and to act as if a state of war did exist.

In the meantime, Jefferson built an international coalition among Sweden, Sicily, Malta, Portugal, and even Muslim Morocco against Tripolitania. By October 1803, Preble had established a naval blockade of the Barbary ports and carried out a series of attacks and raids against those ships that ventured out of port.

BIRTH OF A U.S. HERO

Naval blockade duty was a blend of nearly unendurable tedium—ships riding at anchor for days under the scorching Mediterranean sun—and extreme hazard. On October 31, 1803, the frigate USS *Philadelphia* ran aground on a coral reef. Helplessly exposed, it was boarded by sailors of the Tripolitan navy, who captured the crew, 307 officers and men. When a storm drove the ship off the reef days later, the pasha's men steered it into the harbor, where they anchored it and used it as a stationary gun battery to pound the blockade squad.

It became apparent to Commodore Preble that the Tripolitan navy did not have the manpower to sail the *Philadelphia*, but even anchored its thirty-six cannons made formidable weapons. Because the harbor was well fortified, Preble decided against attempting to recapture the ship. It would have been hammered to bits by shore batteries before it could make its way out of the harbor. Instead, he chose to send a small raiding party into the harbor under cover of night. Its mission would be to set fire to the ship and deprive Tripoli of the prize.

It would be, Preble explained, very likely a suicide mission, but the promise of danger served only to increase the number of volunteers. They were put under the command of the young skipper of the twelve-gun schooner *Enterprise*: Lieutenant Stephen Decatur, who had captured the Tripolitan ketch *Mastico* on December 23, 1803. Sailing in this, the raiders would have a better chance of slipping into the harbor undetected. They christened their prize vessel, appropriately, *Intrepid*.

Decatur put out from Syracuse, Sicily, on February 3, 1804, with volunteers drawn from *Enterprise* and *Constitution*. A Sicilian familiar with the Tripoli Harbor volunteered to pilot the raiders. Their first and fiercest enemy was the weather. The 350-mile (563 km)

◄

Stephen Decatur's daring operation to destroy the captured U.S. frigate *Philadelphia* in Tripoli harbor on February 16, 1804, enflamed the world's imagination. The small vessel in the foreground is a ketch the U.S. Navy captured from locals and rechristened the *Intrepid*. On it, Decatur and his men sailed into Tripoli harbor, boarded the *Philadelphia*, put it to the torch, and reboarded the *Intrepid*, on which they made good their escape.

voyage should have taken at most three or four days, but storms pounded the tiny twin-masted ketch, forcing *Intrepid* to ride out the weather at sea for almost two weeks. Packed into the vessel's tight quarters, the vessel stocked with little water and less food, the crew, many violently seasick, suffered mightily. At last on February 16, Decatur had Tripoli Harbor in sight. Eager as the men were to escape the filth and close air below deck, Decatur kept all but a few confined, hoping to pass off the ketch as a local commercial trader as it felt its way by moonlight into the harbor.

Intrepid drifted toward *Philadelphia*. The Sicilian pilot called out. Their ship had lost its anchors, he shouted. And he asked permission to tie up, right here, alongside the big black frigate.

It worked—at least at first. *Intrepid* was invited to tie up, but as she closed with *Philadelphia*, the disguise became all too apparent and a cry went up. There was nothing for it to do but to board—*now*—and the men, as if their long, miserable confinement had coiled them tight, burst onto the deck of their ketch and crossed to the captive U.S. frigate. They moved so quickly that the Tripolitan guards were overwhelmed. Most simply leaped overboard, swimming for shore while the Americans set their fires. Within little

The Dashing Decatur

Stephen Decatur was born in 1779 on Maryland's Eastern Shore, but was raised in Philadelphia, where he attended the University of Pennsylvania, leaving it to join the navy as a midshipman in April 1798. After he led the raid to burn USS *Philadelphia* in Tripoli Harbor on February 16, 1804, the navy elevated Lieutenant Decatur to the lofty rank of captain in May—at age twenty-five, the youngest man ever promoted to that naval rank before or since. A grateful Congress also presented him with a sword of honor.

In 1808, Decatur served on the court-martial board that suspended Captain James Barron for negligence in the infamous *Chesapeake–Leopard* incident of June 22, 1807, in which the USS *Chesapeake* was intercepted by the British frigate HMS *Leopard* off Norfolk, Virginia and four seamen were "impressed" (forcibly abducted) into the British service and others killed in an exchange of gunfire. The British policy of impressment on the high seas was one of the precipitating factors in the War of 1812. At the outbreak of the war, Decatur received command of the forty-four-gun frigate *United States*, with which he engaged and captured the thirty-eight-gun British frigate *Macedonian* 500 miles (805 km) south of the Azores on October 25, 1812.

Promoted to commodore, Decatur was charged with the defense of New York Harbor (1813), and during June 13–15, 1813, he attempted to run the British blockade of the harbor in the forty-four-gun USS *President*. He damaged the twenty-four-gun HMS *Endymion*, but was forced to surrender to superior British forces. Taken prisoner, he was subsequently paroled.

With the outbreak of the Algerine War in May 1815, Decatur was dispatched on the 20th to the Mediterranean once again to fight the Barbary pirates. On June 17 he captured the forty-six-gun Algerian flagship *Mashouda*, after which four vessels of his squadron ran the twenty-two-gun *Estedio* aground off Cabo de Gata, Spain. It was Decatur who dictated—"at the mouths of cannon"—highly favorable peace terms, not only secur-

ing release of all U.S. prisoners and an end to tribute payments, but also an indemnity payment from Algiers.

Decatur returned triumphantly to the United States, where he was appointed to the newly created Board of Naval Commissioners in November 1815. Five years later, James Barron resurfaced, embittered by the disgrace he had suffered in the *Chesapeake–Leopard* court-martial. He challenged Decatur to a duel, in which he fatally wounded the naval hero on March 22, 1820, at Bladensburg, Maryland.

◄

Boatswain's mate Reuben James thrust himself beneath a pirate's sword to save his captain, Stephen Decatur, in a scuffle on board the USS *Philadelphia* during the mission to burn the vessel. Though wounded, James survived and recovered. Three modern U.S. Navy ships have been named for him: a destroyer, DD-245, launched in 1919; a destroyer escort, DE-153, launched in 1943; and a guided missile fast frigate, FFG-57, launched in 1985.

more than a quarter-hour, the ship was ablaze and the raiders cast off, the flames licking at their backs.

They rowed *Intrepid* out of a harbor now brightly illuminated by the blazing vessel. Sporadic gunfire rang out after them, but all hands made it out of the harbor. One raider was wounded, but none killed. And USS *Philadelphia*, burned down to her waterline, sank in the shallows. The Royal Navy's Admiral Horatio Nelson proclaimed the raid "the most bold and daring act of the age," and in the person of Stephen Decatur, the U.S. Navy had a worthy successor to the Revolutionary War heroism of John Paul Jones.

AFTER A HERO, A MARTYR

The Decatur raid thrilled the Western world, whose shipping was chronically menaced by Barbary piracy. The United States, a young republic with an infant navy, emerged as the savior of "Christian" commerce. Yet the raid hardly constituted a decisive blow against the state that sanctioned the piracy.

On July 14, 1804, Preble attacked Tripoli directly, directing cannon fire into the heart of the city and the city's port. It was the first of a series of battles that although violent proved inconclusive. The most desperate incident occurred on August 3, when Richard Somers, native of Great Egg Harbor, New Jersey, and Philadelphia classmate of Decatur, assumed command of the *Intrepid*. Somers decided to transform the captured ketch into a fire ship, what he called a "floating volcano," which he intended to sail into Tripoli Harbor and slip in close among the pirate fleet anchored in the shadow of the city's walls. Somers and his men would set explosive charges on short fuses, abandon ship in rowboats, pull like mad to get their distance, and then watch as the *Intrepid* blew up, blasting the rest of the Barbary fleet to bits.

They set out after nightfall, but before *Intrepid* got into position, it exploded, was engulfed in flame, and vanished. Either the charges had detonated spontaneously or Tripolitan Harbor gunners managed a lucky shot. In either case, Somers and his volunteer crew were killed.

THE BATTLE OF DERNE

In September, the navy replaced Preble with Commodore Samuel Barron as commander of the U.S. Mediterranean Squadron. Barron seized upon a bold plan drawn up by a daring

U.S. Army officer and diplomat named William Eaton, who proposed a coordinated sea and land attack on the Tripolitan city of Derne (sometimes spelled Derna, and today Darnah, Libya). The plan promised the decisive victory that had eluded his predecessor.

Born in Woodstock, Connecticut, in 1764, William Eaton joined the Continental Army during the waning years of the American Revolution in 1780, served in the ranks until the end of the war in 1783, and then found his way back into civilian life, graduating from Dartmouth College in 1790. Two years later, he was commissioned a captain in the U.S. Army and in 1797 left to serve as U.S. consul at Tunis. Appointed U.S. Navy agent for the "Barbary Regencies" on May 26, 1804, he set about scheming to overthrow Pasha Yussif Karamanli. Tracking down Yussif's brother, Hamet, whom Yussif had deposed in 1795, Eaton forged an alliance with him and then recruited a mixed force of 200 Christian and 300 Muslim mercenaries to capture Derne. With a detachment of ten U.S. marines commanded by Lieutenant Presley O'Bannon, Eaton led his 500 mercenaries on a nearly 600-mile (966 km) march across the Libyan Desert. During the fifty-day trek, arguments between the Christian and Muslim troops were fre-

Birth of a Legend

The "Marine Corps Hymn," composed shortly after the Civil War, commemorates two early marine exploits—participation in the capture of Mexico City during the U.S.–Mexican War of 1846–1848 ("halls of Montezuma") and the Battle of Derne thirty-three years earlier ("shores of Tripoli").

Sung to a melody resembling a marching song from Jacques Offenbach's (1819–1880) *Geneviève de Brabant*, the lyrics were written anonymously:

> From the Halls of Montezuma
> To the Shores of Tripoli;
> We will fight our country's battles
> In the air, on land and sea;
> First to fight for right and freedom
> And to keep our honor clean;
> We are proud to claim the title
> of United States Marine.
>
> Our flag's unfurled to every breeze
> From dawn to setting sun;
> We have fought in ev'ry clime and place
> Where we could take a gun;
> In the snow of far-off Northern lands
> And in sunny tropic scenes;
> You will find us always on the job—
> The United States Marines.
> Here's health to you and to our Corps
> Which we are proud to serve
> In many a strife we've fought for life
> And never lost our nerve;
> If the Army and the Navy
> Ever look on Heaven's scenes;
> They will find the streets are guarded
> By United States Marines.

quent, at one point verging on mutiny. Eaton kept his forces both mollified and focused with the promise that supplies and pay were waiting on the coast, and when this promise proved insufficient to enforce discipline, he extorted compliance by withholding rations, threatening everyone with starvation.

In late April, the expedition reached the port city of Bomba, up the coast from Derne. Here the three ships of Barron's squadron, *Argus*, *Nautilus*, and *Hornet*, under the general command of Captain Isaac Hull, were waiting. They were loaded with the supplies and pay Eaton had promised his mercenaries.

On April 27, two days after the rendezvous at Bomba, Hull sailed into position off the coast at Derne and bombarded the city's defensive batteries for an hour. Eaton, in the meantime, deployed his forces to make two separate attacks. The Arab mercenaries were put under Hamet, who led them southwest of Derne, where they were to cut off the road to Tripoli and then attack the city from the left with the object of storming the palace of the governor. At the same time, Eaton, leading the Christian mercenaries along with the marines, would concentrate on the harbor fortress.

EATON KEPT HIS FORCES BOTH MOLLIFIED AND FOCUSED WITH THE PROMISE THAT SUPPLIES AND PAY WERE WAITING ON THE COAST, AND WHEN THIS PROMISE PROVED INSUFFICIENT TO ENFORCE DISCIPLINE, HE EXTORTED COMPLIANCE BY WITHHOLDING RATIONS, THREATENING EVERYONE WITH STARVATION.

The attack stepped off at 2:45 in the afternoon, with O'Bannon and his marines in the vanguard. Resistance from the harbor defenses was heavier than expected because they were reinforced; however, the reinforcements had been taken from the western approaches to the city, which therefore meant that the Arab mercenaries' mission to cut

◄

Artist C. H. Waterhouse, who was active around 1812, painted a watercolor of U.S. Marines capturing the Barbary pirate fortress at Derne, Tripoli, on April 27, 1805. The event is alluded to in the lyrics of "The Marine Corps Hymn" as "the shores of Tripoli."

the road to Tripoli was unopposed, as was their advance into Derne. While the Arabs rushed in the back door, as it were, Eaton rallied his contingent at the fortress by lofting his rifle in the air, shouting *"Charge!,"* and leading them up and over the fortress walls, taking a musket ball to the wrist as he did so.

It did not matter. The marines and the Christian mercenary contingent poured over the walls in such a torrent that the garrison abandoned its loaded cannon, unfired, and fled. O'Bannon withdrew a folded U.S. flag from his uniform jacket and raised it over the fortress—the first time the Stars and Stripes were flown over a conquered land.

By now, Hamet's Arabs held the Governor's Palace as well as the entire west end of Derne. The retreating garrison fortress fled directly into the unwelcome embrace of the Arab mercenaries. By 4 p.m., Derne was a captive city. Ten U.S. Marines and 500 mercenaries had defeated at least 4,000 of the pasha's soldiers.

DERNE AFTERMATH

Learning of the attack on Derne, Pasha Yussif dispatched reinforcements, which arrived only after the city had fallen. The new arrivals dug in south of Derne, preparing to invest the city and retake it. Eaton responded by fortifying the captured fortress, and Hamet, using the Governor's Palace as his headquarters, sent Arab patrols to the outskirts of town.

On May 13, Yussif's reinforcements attacked, driving the Arab mercenaries back upon the Governor's Palace, which was on the verge of falling to the pasha's men when the USS *Argus* and the batteries of the captured fortress pounded the attackers into a panicked retreat. By sunset, the reinforcements had withdrawn, and the Arab mercenaries returned to the positions from which they had been driven. The next several weeks saw scattered skirmishing, but no serious attempt to retake the city. From Derne, Eaton prepared for another cross-desert march, this time to make an overland attack on Tripoli. Shortly after he set off, however, word caught up with him that Tobias Lear, Thomas Jefferson's envoy to the Barbary States, had concluded a favorable treaty with Yussif Karamanli.

The June 4, 1805, document ransomed all U.S. sailors for a one-time payment of $60,000, and while it did not explicitly mention the subject of tribute, it nevertheless put a de facto end to the practice by establishing free and unhindered commerce between the United States and Tripoli.

ACT II: THE ALGERINE WAR

While Tripoli-based piracy was largely suppressed by the 1805 treaty, it still required continual U.S. navy patrols to discourage other Mediterranean pirates, and when the War of 1812 (1812–1815) broke out between the United States and Britain, the U.S. ships of the Mediterranean Squadron had to be recalled for duty closer to home. This encouraged the dey of Algiers to resume preying on U.S. commerce in the region.

After expelling the U.S. consul and imprisoning and even enslaving U.S. nationals living in his country, he declared war on the United States for having violated the 1795 tribute treaty. The dey's timing was not ideal, however, since the War of 1812 was coming to an end, and when it did, Commodore Stephen Decatur was dispatched with a ten-ship squadron back to the Mediterranean. Operating in these waters between March 3 and June 30, 1815, Decatur captured two Algerian warships and then sailed directly into the harbor of Algiers.

He trained the massed firepower of his squadron on the city and demanded cancellation of all tribute and the release of all U.S. prisoners without ransom. Concluded on June 30, 1815, the Treaty of Peace with Algiers included the dey's pledge to permanently end all state-sanctioned piracy.

From Algiers, Decatur sailed to Tunis and Tripoli, using the same forceful tactics to extract similar treaties. He also negotiated compensation for U.S. vessels that had been seized at the behest of the British during the War of 1812.

ENDURING CONFLICT

Despite the treaty of 1815 and another concluded the following year, Algerian piracy remained a chronic, albeit diminished threat to the shipping of the United States and other non-Muslim nations until 1830, when French forces captured Algiers in 1830. Nevertheless, the two Barbary Wars were a triumph of sovereignty for the young republic and enhanced the nation's international standing.

The two wars, international in scope but small in scale, were episodes in a vaster, far more enduring conflict between two cultures, each steeped in its own religion. Their actions although at times coinciding with and supported by governments and heads of state were also at times beyond the control of any national authority. If piracy is terror, then these wars at the start of the nineteenth century were the United States' first wars on terrorism, born of a conflict as old as the Muslim conquest of Spain in the eighth century and the Christian invasion of Muslim lands known as the Crusades during the eleventh through thirteenth centuries. Treaties among governments notwithstanding, it would be a war destined to reignite throughout the twentieth century—in, for example, the Armenian genocides at Turkish hands during 1915–1917 or the war of "ethnic cleansing" in the Balkans during 1992–1995. For Americans, the struggle would explode in the terror attacks by Islamic extremists on September 11, 2001. So far, the twenty-first century promises no enduring resolution of the conflict.

EASTERN SUNSET:
THE FIRST AND SECOND OPIUM WARS

1839–1842 and *1856–1860*

Defending its massive trade in opium, the British waged two wars against China, forcing the country into economic subjugation to the West and hastening the demise of the Qing dynasty. These events ushered in a period of twentieth-century revolution that ended in the founding of the world's biggest Communist state and one of the most formidable economic powers on the planet.

At first glance, the room appeared to be a prison dormitory, filthy, with squalid plank bunks stacked three high like racks against the walls. But no prison was ever lit like this, by the guttering orange glow of oil lamps on each bunk, and no prisoners ever lounged on those bunks as these did. The men were young Chinese in loose-fitting, threadbare garments, their hair shaved off above the temples at the front of the head, the rest braided into a long queue in token of their complete submission to the Qing emperor. Here they reclined as if they themselves were potentates, propping head on arm or sweat-stained pillow as they drew deeply on long opium pipes heated over the oil lamps.

Each pipe was loaded with the drug, the heated vapor of which brought euphoria, a feeling of utter detachment from the world, an absence of pain, and sometimes visions of a most delightful nature. There had been a time when only the wealthy could purchase such bliss, but by the 1830s, opium was so plentiful in China that even the commonest of common laborers could afford it.

Not that the true price of opium could be counted in the few copper coins that were the cost of a pipeful.

REIGN OF THE POPPY

By the 1830s, 90 percent of all men under the age of forty in China's coastal cities were addicts. A British physician practicing in Canton (today called Guangdong) estimated the number at twelve million. As a result, commerce and government alike were consumed in a somnolent smoke, and the Chinese national economy drifted into a torpid slumber. In 1839, the Chinese government spent forty million taels to run the country. That same year, the country's opium smokers paid an estimated 100 million taels for their drug. The imperial commissioner at Canton, Lin Zexu, the man who compiled the shocking statistics on opium use, reported to the Daoguang Emperor that if the opium trade were allowed to continued, "in a few dozen years we will find ourselves not only with no soldiers to resist the enemy, but also with no money to equip the army."

Chinese law had prohibited opium consumption except for medicinal use since 1796, but drug dealers, ever heedless of the harm they inflict, have never obeyed laws banning the drugs they deal, not when fortunes are to be made. And by the

This hand-tinted photograph shows opium smokers in Hong Kong about 1900. The setting is more genteel than the typical working-class opium den of the era, but the men have still cut their hair in the traditional braided queue, in token of their abject subjugation to the Qing emperor.

Narcotic Empire

Opium is derived from the latex—the sap—that oozes from immature opium poppy seed pods when they are scored (cut with a knife). The principal narcotic ingredients in this resin are morphine and codeine, which can be processed into powerful illicit drugs (such as heroin) as well as medicinal drugs (such as medical-grade morphine), but as far back as the Stone Age, some 10,000 years ago, opium poppies were used medicinally and recreationally, as well as for ritual purposes. All of the ancient civilizations of which we have knowledge used opium, often as a pain reliever or even a surgical anesthetic. Only in the mid-nineteenth century did morphine begin to displace raw opium for medical applications.

The Chinese used opium recreationally at least as early as the 1400s, but the drug remained an expensive luxury until the seventeenth century, when costs were reduced somewhat by mixing it with tobacco for smoking. As use increased, Chinese authorities began to recognize that the drug was addictive, and throughout the eighteenth century passed laws first to restrict opium use and then to ban it completely. Despite the legislation, opium use continued to increase dramatically. By the nineteenth century, British merchants were flooding China with opium from India.

After the two Opium Wars failed to suppress the trade, the rate of use and addiction among Chinese men continued to rise. Beginning in the 1880s, the Chinese government gave up on trying to restrict opium use and allowed—albeit unofficially—opium to be grown domestically. The result was a rapid decline in opium imports, but an increase in opium use, so that by the beginning of the twentieth century, an estimated one-fourth of the nation's entire male population was addicted.

A combination of Chinese nationalism, revulsion against all things associated with the corrupt Qing Dynasty, and the displacement of opium by more sophisticated opiate drugs (such as morphine and heroin) reduced the demand for opium in China. Anti-drug laws under the Communist regime of Mao Zedong were stringent, but so were restrictions on information about drug use and all other aspects of Chinese society. It is therefore difficult to assess the decline in the nation's opium consumption and the rise, if any, in the use of other drugs.

1830s, those fortunes were mostly in the hands of Englishmen. The merchants of Queen Victoria's Britain had created the greatest drug-trafficking criminal enterprise in the world. When the Qing government finally moved against it, the pushers, prosperous English gentleman all, demonstrated that their government backed them—all the way.

About 30,000 chests of opium were smuggled into China annually, mostly through Canton, the chief port open to foreign trade. On March 30, 1839, Lin Zexu took action. After making some 1,600 arrests, he confiscated and destroyed about 11,000 pounds (5 metric tons) of opium in British warehouses and on board ships. He then appealed to the British merchants for help in rounding up their Chinese customers. They refused, citing "humanitarian" reasons: the Qing government routinely subjected prisoners to torture.

At this point, Charles Elliot, chief superintendent of trade and British minister to China, sent word from his office in Macau that he wanted to negotiate. Apparently interpreting this as the prelude to a bribe, Lin Zexu—that rarest of Qing officials, an incorruptible, unbending man—responded in June by arresting and holding hostage all British traders in Canton. He told the merchants that he would release them after they had turned over all opium stocks still in foreign-controlled portside processing factories and warehouses. Elliot persuaded them to comply, promising that Her Majesty's government would compensate them for their losses. Accordingly, the traders surrendered an additional 20,000 120-pound (54 kg) crates of opium, stores worth $9 million 1839 dollars. This mountain of drugs Lin Zexu ordered publicly destroyed.

Lin Zexu's next act was to close Canton to all foreign merchants and write a respectful but unsparing letter (officially called a "memorial") to Queen Victoria, requesting that Her Majesty order an end to the British trade in opium. Lin Zexu explained that he based his request on the fact that British law recognized the harmful effects of opium by banning its sale and consumption in Great Britain; therefore, Great Britain should not export harm to other nations.

INCIDENT AT KOWLOON

Pursuant to the closure of Canton, the Chinese coast guard at the end of June arrested the comprador (the Chinese agent employed by the British as an interpreter and commercial negotiator) serving aboard the British clipper *Carnatic*.

Tensions were thus running high when, in July 1839, a gang of U.S. and British sailors (including the *Carnatic* crew) on Sunday shore leave roamed the byways of Kowloon (now part of Hong Kong), at the time a supply depot for foreign ships. The sailors got into a stash of *samshu*, rice liquor. They drank it down and stormed into the local village of Chien-sha-tsui, where they vandalized a Taoist temple, killed a villager named Lin Weixi, and touched off a riot.

No one, not even the British authorities, denied that the sailors were guilty of grave wrongdoing, but citing the absence of trial by jury under Chinese law (indeed, Chinese judges served as prosecutors as well as executioners), Elliot demanded that the sailors be tried as British subjects by a British court. The Qing officials indignantly refused and demanded that they be turned over to local magistrates for immediate prosecution. Elliot had been an officer in the British Royal Navy since 1816. He had taken part in the bombardment of Algiers and had served as a colonial administrator in India, Africa, and the West Indies. He believed he knew very well how to deal with the "lesser races": stand firm—stand firm in everything.

He now stood firm. He not only refused to surrender the six sailors involved in Lin Weixi's death, but he convened and personally presided over their immediate trial in Canton. Found guilty, they were shipped off to England—where (to Elliot's consternation) they were set free on the patently spurious grounds that Elliot had no right to try anyone.

Lin Zexu announced that Canton would remain closed to British traders until all European merchants signed a bond, guaranteed by their very lives, pledging to smuggle no more opium and agreeing to submit to Chinese law. Elliot forbade any British subject from signing such a bond, and he ordered all Britishers to evacuate from Canton. He then prohibited all trade with the Chinese, confident that this embargo would bring such financial hardship upon the Qing government that it would have no choice but to force Lin Zexu to reopen Canton and grant British nationals "extraterritorial" legal status, giving them immunity from Chinese law and law courts.

A Righteous Man

Lin Zexu was born in 1785 in Fuzhou, Fujian province, and was trained for Chinese government service, earning the highest marks in the imperial examinations. As governor-general of Hunan and Hubei in 1837, he initiated a campaign to suppress opium use. This so impressed the Daoguang Emperor that Lin was transferred to Guangdong as an imperial commissioner, tasked with halting the smuggling of opium by the British.

His vigorous campaign of enforcement resulted in confiscation of some 2.6 million pounds (1200 metric tons) of opium during 1839. His famous "memorial" to Queen Victoria argued that it was immoral for Great Britain to export a drug that the British government itself had outlawed as harmful. Deeming the memorial impertinent, Victoria's counselors declined to deliver the document into her hands, but it was published in *The Times* of London, where it roused many Whig (liberal) politicians to join Lin Zexu in calling for an end to the opium trade.

The First Opium War (1839–1842) dealt the Chinese a humiliating defeat, for which the Qing government scapegoated Lin Zexu. In 1840, he was demoted and sent to a remote outpost in Xinjiang. The stoic Lin used his exile to study the local Muslim culture in the region and collected local folklore that scholars today consider of great value.

After a time, realizing its desperate need of him, the Qing government reinstated Lin Zexu. He died in 1850 en route to Guangxi, to which his government had dispatched him to aid in the suppression of the Taiping Rebellion. Today, Lin Zexu is revered in China and Chinese communities worldwide as a heroic example of selfless service to the people. In New York City's Chinatown, he is even memorialized by a statue on Chatham Square.

▲ Lin Zexu, an upright man in a corrupt age, campaigned against the British opium trade in China.

◄ British warships bomb Canton (today Guangzhou) during the First Opium War.

FIRST MOVES, FIRST OPIUM WAR

Elliot's economic strategy might have worked had it not been for a number of merchants—those who did not deal in opium—who defied his order, willingly signed the required bonds, and continued trading. Now there seemed no choice but war. On August 23, 1839, British troops seized Hong Kong, at the time a semi-rural trading outpost, and garrisoned it as a base of operations. Both sides now awaited some incident to precipitate actual combat. They did not have to wait long.

The British merchant ship *Thomas Coutts* sailed into Canton harbor late in October 1839. Owned by Quakers, who refused on moral and religious grounds to transport opium, the *Coutts* put into port. Its skipper, convinced that Elliot had no authority to close down trade, personally negotiated with the Cantonese governor for permission to unload his ship at Chuenpeh Island, near Humen, and to permit all other British ships to do the same. Learning of this, Elliot ordered an armed naval blockade of the Pearl River, the waterway between Hong Kong and Canton, to intercept and turn back any ships approaching Chuenpeh.

On November 3, a British merchantman, the *Royal Saxon*, defied the blockade by approaching the island. The HMS *Volage* and *Hyacinth* each fired warning shots across the *Royal Saxon*'s bow. This action gave the Qing navy the unusual opportunity to claim that it acted to defend the British merchantman against a British attack. As Elliot saw the situation, any British vessels in the area were subject to Chinese attack, both from the junks of the Qing navy and from a pair of land-based artillery batteries defending the approach to Chuenpeh. Accordingly, he sternly ordered all British ships out of the waters around Chuenpeh. Chastened by the Royal Navy action against the *Royal Saxon*, every British vessel weighed anchor and made for the port of Tung Lo Wan, a short distance from the Portuguese colony of Macau. Once the merchant ships had cleared out, Elliot engaged the junk fleet, sinking several Chinese vessels.

Seeking an alternative to Canton, Elliott asked the governor of Macau to permit British ships to load and unload there in return for the payment of rent and any reasonable duties. It was a tantalizingly profitable offer, but the governor refused, fearful that the Qing government would cut Macau off, denying it the regular shipments of food and other provisions on which its people depended. Noting this fissure in European solidarity, the Qing emperor, on January 14, 1840, requested that all foreigners who resided in China refrain from aiding any British subject in the country.

CAUSE FOR WAR

It was at this point that Britain's prime minister, Lord Palmerston, authorized a full-scale war. The causes he argued before Parliament were the attacks on British merchants and the brief battle off Chuenpeh, but his more pressing motive was to extort an indemnity from the Qing government to reimburse the merchants for the opium Elliot had persuaded them to yield. To many members of Parliament, no aspect of Palmerston's rationale for war seemed legitimate, and a young William Gladstone—future prime minister—led the opposition's denunciation of an unjust war waged to protect the commerce of drug dealers.

The objections notwithstanding, in June 1840, Palmerston authorized a British expeditionary force consisting of fifteen troop transports (called at the time "barracks ships"), four steam-powered gunboats, and twenty-five smaller vessels. The expedition included an amphibious contingent of 4,000 marines under an officer named James Bremer.

Backed by his ships and marines, Bremer presented Qing representatives with a demand for payment of an indemnity to compensate British merchants not only for losses actually suffered, but for business lost on account of interrupted trade. While Bremer presented his demands, the expedition's vessels augmented the original Pearl River blockade. When the Qing government spurned Bremer's demands, a portion of the expeditionary force marched north to take Zhousan (Chusan), at the mouth of Hangzhou Bay, which provided access to Shanghai, another principal port used by Westerners.

The war continued at a low level until January 1841, when the British force assaulted and seized the Bogue forts guarding the mouth of the Pearl River. In short order, the British fully blockaded and completely cut off Hangzhou (Hangchow), Hong Kong, and Canton. An amphibious detachment from the expeditionary force sailed up the Pearl to attack the fortifications surrounding Canton. The city itself fell in May 1841, followed soon by Xiamen (Amoy) and Ningbo (Ning-po).

CHINA BOWS WESTWARD

After these victories, dysentery and other diseases ravaged the expeditionary force, retarding its advance. It was early 1842 before the marines had sufficiently recovered to continue their campaign, brushing aside all Chinese resistance at the mouth of another key river, the Yangtze. This accomplished, the British occupied Shanghai.

Militarily, Western weaponry and tactics overmatched Qing land and naval forces. In August 1842, the emperor agreed to the Treaty of Nanjing, by which China obligated itself to pay a $20 million indemnity and to open to British trade and residency the ports of Canton, Xiamen, Fuzhou (Foochow), Ningbo, and Shanghai. The Qing government also yielded on the issue of "extraterritoriality," exempting British residents from Chinese legal jurisdiction and entrusting them to the jurisdiction of British consular courts. These were all heavy concessions, but the heaviest of all was Hong Kong, ceded to the British crown—and thus denominated a "crown colony"—in perpetuity. Inevitably, Chinese authorities extended to other Western nations the trading rights acquired by the British.

THE *ARROW* FLIES

The First Opium War satisfied no one fully. Many Chinese, in government and out, were outraged by the opening of China to the "foreign devils" and the relinquishment of sovereignty to foreign powers. The French and U.S. treaties with China, negotiated in the wake of Britain's Treaty of Nanjing, contained clauses specifying the right of renegotiation after a dozen years. Fearing that renegotiation would give France and the United States a trading edge, the British government now demanded that the Qing renegotiate the Nanjing agreement—one-sided though that already was.

The new British demands were breathtaking. It began with Chinese legalization of opium (still illegal in Great Britain and most other Western nations) and included the opening of all of China to British trade, the lifting of most duties, the regulation of the "coolie" (unskilled labor) trade, and installation of the British ambassador in Beijing, hitherto absolutely closed to foreigners and to many Chinese as well.

Not surprisingly, the Qing government rejected these demands, as it also spurned the demands for renegotiation made by France and the United States. Once again, the powder was packed in the keg. All that was needed was a single spark to set off the explosion.

That came on October 8, 1856, when Qing customs officers boarded the *Arrow*, an indigenous Chinese sailing craft called a lorcha, suspected of smuggling as well as piracy. According to its papers, the ship was registered in Hong Kong, but when the officers arrested twelve sailors, all Chinese subjects, the British consulate in Guangzhou demanded their release. They claimed that the *Arrow* was actually a vessel of British registry and was therefore protected by the extraterritoriality provision of the Treaty of Nanjing. The Qing government quickly knocked down this flimsy argument, whereupon the British officials insisted that the *Arrow* had been sailing under a British flag; therefore, its seizure and the arrest of its crew had been an insult to the "national ensign." The

Chinese responded that the lorcha had flown no flag of any kind. With that, negotiations were deadlocked—though the sailors were, in fact, released to the British, each bearing a letter from local officials who promised not to improperly board "British vessels" in the future.

RELATIONS BECOME POISONOUS

However slim it might have been, the "Arrow incident" was just the excuse Britain needed for a new war against China. Undoubtedly, the war would have begun instantly had the bulk of the British army in Asia not been preoccupied with another imperialist campaign, the suppression of the Indian Rebellion of 1857. But before long, it became clear to British high command that it would need only a small fraction of its military assets for this Second Opium War. At the moment, the Qing government was in no position to offer effective resistance to attack. Weakened by opium and general corruption and humiliated by the Treaty of Nanjing, the government was desperately fighting for its own continued existence by fending off the Taiping Rebellion, a major civil war fought over twenty years and that resulted in as many as thirty million killed. Accordingly, British troops were transported down the Pearl River, from which they attacked Guangzhou. The local governor ordered the garrisons of all the river forts to offer no resistance, and so Guangzhou fell.

The new war was under way, but what won over the popular support of the British public was the discovery that Chinese bakers in Hong Kong had conspired to poison all the Europeans there by baking arsenic into the bread they sold to the European community. It was not a bad plan, as mass murder conspiracies go, but in their zeal to kill the foreigners quickly, the bakers had laced their dough with so much arsenic that it was very easily detected. Instantly, runners were sent throughout the European quarters of Hong Kong to alert the residents to the danger.

The poisoning plot had unfolded in January 1857, but it took some time for word of it to reach Parliament. When it did, the news was sufficient to quiet Whig protests against yet another "unjust war" against China. Seizing his moment, Lord Palmerston dissolved Parliament and called for a new general election, which returned a Tory majority that was quick to vote a resolution demanding Chinese redress for having violated the Treaty of Nanjing by boarding the Arrow. In addition, the British government now sought an alliance with France, Russia, and the United States.

WEST MEETS EAST

Amid popular outrage over the recent execution of Father August Chapdelaine, a French missionary in Guangxi province, France eagerly joined the alliance. Both the United States and Russia showed their support by sending diplomats to confer with British authorities in Hong Kong, but no military alliance was concluded.

In reality, the Anglo-French force needed no help. Put under the unified command of Admiral Sir Michael Seymour, the combined British and French forces attacked and then occupied Guangzhou before the end of 1857. They took prisoner Ye Mingchen, the provincial governor of Guangxi, and Bo-gui, the governor of Guangdong. Bo-gui agreed to maintain order under Anglo-French occupation, whereas Ye Mingchen was deported to British Calcutta, where he embarked on a fatal hunger strike. The foreign occupation of Guangzhou would last nearly four years.

WHEN PEACE TREATIES BROUGHT WAR

In May 1858, coalition forces sailed north, easily capturing the Dagu Fort near Tianjin. After their loss, the Qing government agreed to renegotiate treaties with Britain, France, Russia, and the United States. The new treaties proved significant because they not only opened eleven more ports but also opened much of the interior. Britain, France, Russia, and the United States received permission to establish legations in Beijing, China agreed to pay even heavier indemnities to Britain and France, and the Kowloon Peninsula, a portion of the Chinese mainland, was added to Britain's Hong Kong colony. Additionally, a large tract beyond Kowloon, together with the islands surrounding it, was leased to Great Britain for ninety-nine years as the "New Territories."

It was all too much for many of the emperor's ministers to swallow. They rebelled by refusing to ratify the new treaties. The treaties provoked a popular uprising as well. The people of Beijing barred foreign diplomats from the city, and a mob outside of Tianjin, where the new treaties were signed, overwhelmed a British army unit there, slaughtering it to a man.

On June 2, 1858, with the people up in arms and his own ministers turning against him, the Xianfeng Emperor ordered a Mongolian general named Sengge Rinchen to lead a force to hold down, at all costs, the Taku Fort guarding Tianjin. The Mongolian installed additional artillery and brought with him 4,000 fiercely elite Mongolian cavalrymen.

The anticipated Western retaliation for the Tianjin uprising did not materialize until June 1859, when a Royal Navy flotilla of twenty-one ships carrying 2,200 troops—as well as the intrepid British and French diplomats who were to be stationed in Beijing—sailed from Shanghai north to Tianjin. At the mouth of the Hai River, below the Taku Fort, the flotilla halted as its commander, Admiral Sir James Hope, demanded safe passage inland to Beijing. Sengge Rinchen replied that the diplomats could be landed up the coast, from which they might then proceed overland to Beijing—but no troop escort would be allowed. Admiral Hope announced that this was unacceptable and withdrew.

His retreat was temporary. Under cover of darkness on June 24, 1859, a British engineer detachment blew up the iron obstacles the Chinese had positioned to block the Baihe River. On the 25th, Hope sailed up the Baihe and began bombardment of Taku Fort. Sengge Rinchen replied with his augmented artillery, sinking four British gunboats and damaging two others. In blatant violation of declared U.S. neutrality, Commodore Josiah Tattnall, U.S. Navy, who had been observing the action, led his U.S. naval squadron into position to provide covering fire for Hope's withdrawal.

The Russians Score

Beginning in the reign of Czar Peter the Great (who ruled from 1682 to 1725), Russia sought to end its isolation and become a world power. To build a naval presence in the Pacific, Czar Peter authorized naval bases to be built in Chinese territory near the Amur River, which became the nuclei around which small Russian communities developed.

Subsequent czars quietly built up military strength on both sides of the Chinese–Russian border in the region. Because the Qing government proved unable either to govern or police the area, the communities grew unchecked. At the time of the Second Opium War, the government of Czar Alexander II decided simply to annex the Amur territories. Qing military commanders wildly overestimated the Russian military presence in the region, and when Russia's ambassador to the Qing court threatened war, the Chinese folded, immediately agreeing to negotiate.

On May 28, 1858, Russian and Chinese officials concluded the Treaty of Aigun, which redrew the Russian–Chinese border. The czar's representatives grabbed the left bank of the Amur River and pushed the international border back from the Argun River. Even more important to the future of Russia, the czar acquired control over a portion of the Pacific coast that never froze and therefore provided a year-round port. Here the new city of Vladivostok was established in 1860.

THE ANGLO-FRENCH FORCES RETALIATE IN STRENGTH

Having previously experienced only the weakness of the Qing, Admiral Hope had badly underestimated the government's renewed will to resist. It was an error that would not be repeated.

In the summer of 1860, British general James Hope Grant, leading 11,000 men, and French general Charles Cousin-Montauban, with 6,700, sailed together in a fleet of 173 ships from Hong Kong. They quickly took the port cities of Yantai and Dalian, thereby seizing control of the Bohai Gulf. Then, at Bei Tang, just below the Taku Fort, the fleet landed a large contingent of troops, which laid siege to the fort beginning on August 3. It fell three weeks later, on August 21.

In the meantime, another portion of the Anglo-French force captured Tienstin on August 3 and then advanced inland toward Beijing. In a panic, the Xianfeng Emperor sent his ministers to negotiate peace, but a renegade Chinese general arrested the British envoy, Harry Parkes, on September 18 in the midst of negotiations. He and his attaches were locked up and tortured—some to death. Fortunately for Parkes, he was released just before imperial orders arrived authorizing his execution.

On the very day that Parkes had been arrested, Anglo-French forces engaged Sengge Rinchen's Mongolian cavalry, defeating them at Zhangjiawan. Following this victory, the Europeans advanced to the environs of Beijing.

On September 21, Sengge Rinchen massed everything that remained to him, 10,000 troops, including the surviving members of his Mongolian cavalry. He intended to force a decisive battle at Palikao.

And decisive it proved to be—but not in the way he wanted. Armed with obsolete weapons, Sengge Rinchen's forces were overwhelmingly outgunned. The Mongolian gen-

▲

British forces clash with Sengge Rinchen's Mongolians near Beijing in the Second Opium War.

eral ordered one head-on charge after another, sending his men directly into the modern artillery, rifles, and rapid-loading carbines of the European troops, who slaughtered them. Now unopposed, the Anglo-French army entered Beijing on October 6.

PRELUDE TO AN END

His army having melted away, the Xianfeng Emperor fled Beijing, turning over negotiations to his brother, Prince Gong. In the meantime, Britain's Lord Elgin, who was now in overall command of the war, turned the Anglo-French troops loose on the Summer Palace and the Old Summer Palace. They looted these magnificent seats of imperial Chinese power, stripping them bare of priceless artworks. It was an act of revenge for the murders of the diplomats and other Westerners. And after Parkes and the surviving members of his diplomatic party safely returned, Elgin ordered the looted palaces razed.

On October 18, 1860, the same day that the destruction of the Summer Palaces began, Prince Gong signed the Convention of Peking, which included ratification of the earlier Treaty of Tianjin. This bought an end to the Second Opium War, but only the beginning of the dissolution of imperial China. Even larger indemnities were levied, intended to drain the Qing treasury. The country was thrown wide open to a commercial, political, cultural, and spiritual invasion by the West. The convention granted "Christians" all civil rights and gave missionaries authority to make converts. At the same time, the document legalized the trade in opium.

The victory of the Western allies plunged China into a century of abuse, degradation, and humiliation at the hands of foreign powers, hastening the decay and downfall of the Qing dynasty, an event that was followed in the first half of the twentieth century by revolution, civil war, and the ascendancy of Communism. The Communist regime transformed China into a military force to be reckoned with. Next, in a historic irony of epic proportion, this same government transformed itself ideologically and economically, making of China the greatest nondemocratic capitalist power the world has ever known.

RISING SUN:
THE MEIJI RESTORATION

1860—1868

The war by which Emperor Meiji reestablished imperial supremacy over Japan

produced consequences far out of proportion to its brevity and scope,

rapidly converting Japan from a collection of feudal domains into a modern nation,

a formidable industrial power, and a military juggernaut destined to have an impact

on the world that was at first devastating and then transformative

They were the USS *Mississippi, Plymouth, Saratoga,* and *Susquehanna,* ordinary vessels of the U.S. Navy, but to the Japanese who saw them sail into Uraga Harbor, near Edo (modern-day Tokyo), on July 8, 1853, they were *kurofune,* the "black ships," iron hulls painted a dull black and belching from their single stacks a thick black smoke that surely boded nothing good. The woodblock portraits that popular *ukiyo-e* artists made of the flotilla's commander, Commodore Matthew Calbraith Perry, accentuated drooping eyes under heavy eyebrows and portrayed a hard, unsmiling mouth beneath a long nose. One could conclude that the Japanese engravers purposely made him look like a monster were it not for the daguerreotypes by Western photographers that show Perry looking much the same way.

Perry met with officials of the shogun—the man who led the government with the blessing of what was then a figurehead emperor—who instructed him to sail on to Nagasaki, about 1000 miles (1609 km) from Edo, the seat of the shogunate government. Nagasaki, far from the center of power, was the only place Europeans were permitted in any number, and only the Dutch were allowed to trade with Japan. That, Perry was told, was the law.

But the commodore stood squarely in the shadow of his own law, the black cannon of his black ships, and standing thus, he told the officials no; he would not leave Uraga Harbor until he had been given leave to present a letter he carried from President Millard Fillmore.

Under the shoguns of the Tokugawa era (also called the Edo Period, 1603–1858), Japan had enjoyed some 250 years of peace occasionally punctuated by minor peasant revolts, which were quickly crushed. The shogunate possessed a small army consisting of samurai without modern rifle muskets or major land artillery; the vessels of its wood-and-sail navy had only small guns. Mindful of the black ships, the officials backed down, giving Perry the permission he demanded. They told him to sail to nearby Kurihama (part of modern Yokosuka), where he could present his president's letter to a senior delegation.

This he did on July 14, 1853, and neither Japan nor the rest of the world was ever the same.

◄

This is Commodore Matthew Calbraith Perry, United States Navy, as the Japanese saw him. This woodblock print from about 1854 is titled *Kita Amerika jinbutsu: Peruri z (A North American: Portrait of Perry).*

AMITY AND COMMERCE

Perry left Kurihama for China, promising that he would return in several months to receive the shogunate's response to President

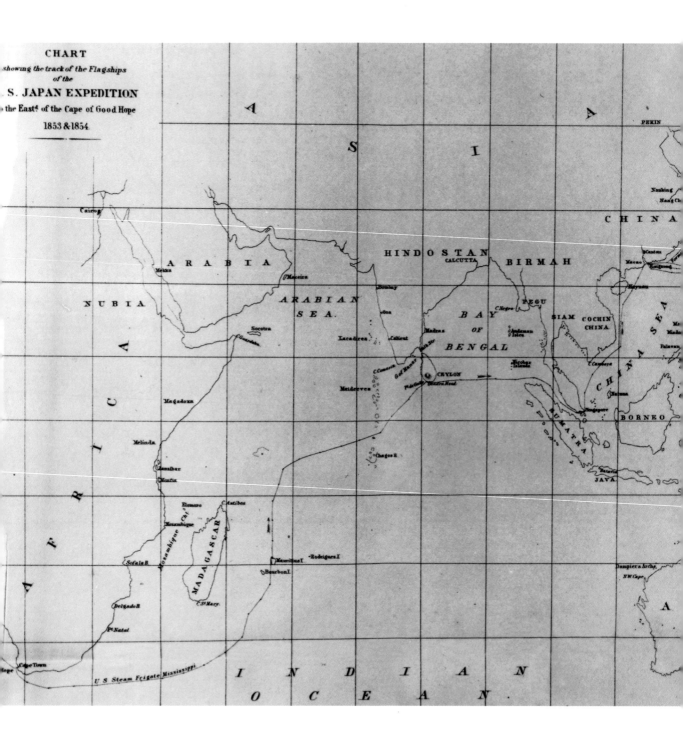

CHART
showing the track of the Flagships
of the
U.S. JAPAN EXPEDITION
to the East. of the Cape of Good Hope
1853 & 1854

From Commodore Perry's own 1856 account of his mission to China, the map shows the route of his "black ships."

Fillmore's letter. With three more ships added to his flotilla, he returned in February 1854, delighted to discover that the shogun's ministers had already drafted a treaty that met all of the U.S. president's demands. The Convention of Kanagawa, as it was called, was signed on March 31; it opened two major Japanese ports to United States trade, granted refuge to shipwrecked U.S. sailors, and established a U.S. consulate. The convention led to a full Treaty of Amity and Commerce, signed on July 29, 1858, which opened even more ports to the West, set low import–export duties (subject to international, not Japanese, control), and put all Westerners living in Japan under the legal jurisdiction of consular courts instead of Japanese law. Almost immediately, Holland, Russia, France, and Britain followed suit with treaties of their own.

Japan had been closed to the West ever since there was a Japan, and for the two and half centuries before Perry and his black ships, the *bakufu*, or "tent" as the Tokugawa shogun's government was called, had exercised feudal rule over the Japanese, who numbered some 30 million by the mid-nineteenth century. By Western standards, the country seemed backward; nevertheless, it was both peaceful and prosperous. Never in its history had Japan suffered successful invasion by a foreign power, and now under the cannons' mouths, but without a shot having been fired, the shogun surrendered to the will of Perry, Fillmore, and the merchants of the United States and Europe. What compelled him?

Perhaps the best answer is that, at 250 years old, the Tokugawa shogunate was showing its age. More remote, even provincial, regions of Japan were beginning to overtake the central domains in wealth and political dynamism. In contrast to these vibrant realms, the Tokugawa bureaucracy had become so stultified that one young

Japan's Emperors: Divine Prisoners

A document from 712, the *Kojiki* ("Record of Ancient Matters") and the *Nihongi* ("Chronicle of Japan"), from 720, relate how two gods, Izanagi (male) and Izanami (female), descended from heaven to create the islands of Japan. Izanagi and Izanami brought to existence on earth *kami* (deities) that exert an influence on the sea, rivers, wind, woods, mountains, and other natural features and phenomena. Two of these kami, the Sun Goddess, Amaterasu Omikami, and her brother, the Storm God, Susano-o, fought one another, Amaterasu emerging victorious. It was she who sent her grandson, Ninigi, to reign over the sacred islands.

Ninigi brought to the task three items, a curved jewel (*magatama*), a mirror, and a sword hammered out from gathered clouds. With these, he ruled over the island of Kyushu. His great-grandson, the semi-legendary, semi-historical Jimmu, is regarded as Japan's first human emperor. According to tradition, his imperial reign began in 660 BCE, when he conquered the other Japanese islands, including the principal island of Honshu, on which he founded the unbroken line of imperial descent from Amaterasu reigning over the Land of the Rising Sun.

In 663 BCE—again, according to tradition—Jimmu founded the throne of the mikados, who were the spiritual rulers of Japan, reigning in parallel with the shoguns (sometimes translated as "tycoons"), who held sway over temporal matters. From the inception of the mikado's throne to the end of the twelfth century,

the mikado was the dominant sovereign: the emperor. Yet Japan was hardly a nation-state in the modern sense. It was a feudal realm in which feudal lords and princes contended for power with one another and with the mikado. To deal with this, a class of military rulers emerged, assuming greater and greater power in proportion to which the authority of the mikado was reduced until in 1585 Toyotomi Hideyoshi created the shogunate. From this point forward, rule in Japan was ever more sharply divided between the spiritual head, the mikado, and the secular shoguns.

It would be a mistake to regard the mikados as mere figureheads. In fact, as they withdrew from temporal matters, their divine character became increasingly exalted. They were worshiped as earthly manifestations of the gods, the very embodiment of the Japanese national religion, Shinto, and as such, they were a source of inspiration for the temporal rulers. In theory, this elevated the mikados, the emperors, to a kind of absolute power. In practice, however, they were effectively held hostage by the shoguns, who used the emperor's divinity as a means of legitimating their own claims to authority. Thus, for some eight centuries prior to the Meiji restoration, the emperors of Japan, imbued with godhood, were nevertheless the political—and often physical—captives of the shoguns and their military regimes. Among rival shoguns, whoever retained control of the emperor had the greatest claim on legitimate power.

official described his colleagues as so many "wooden monkeys." Trade with the West, which offered profit as well as the kind of modern technology embodied in those black ships with their big guns, seemed to promise an injection of new life for the tired old shogunate.

FROM THE MEN OF SPIRIT TO THE YEAR OF THE DRAGON

The treaties with the West incited members of the lowest class of samurai, called shishi ("Men of Spirit"), to rise against the influx of foreigners. On the one hand, the Men of

Spirit occupied a position so far out on the periphery of political power that they posed no grave threat to the Tokugawa shogun and his government; but on the other hand, they were numerous, they were angry, and they were armed. They terrorized Edo and other political centers with acts of violence, including random assaults, destruction of property, and even murders, which brought much of Japan to a low level of continual civil war.

The shishi reign of terror was ended by an unlikely alliance between shogunate forces and those of its traditional political rivals, the daimyo, the feudal lords of western Japan. In the beginning, the daimyo, like the Men of Spirit, were opposed to the influx of foreigners, but they soon came to see the same advantages to trade that were apparent to the shogun. But the daimyo also believed that one of the chief advantages of opening the country to Western trade would be the eventual dissolution of the shogunate itself; therefore, once the shishi had been suppressed, the daimyo approached the foreign traders and endeavored to talk them into bypassing the shogun's agents to deal directly with the representatives of the emperor.

This maneuver suddenly put the shogun at odds with the traders, but when a combined fleet of Dutch, British, and French commercial vessels steamed into port escorted by a full contingent of modern warships in November 1865, Shogun Tokugawa Iemochi himself came forward with an offer to intercede with the emperor in order to conclude an even more comprehensive trade treaty.

▲

A samurai poses with the banner of his clan. His late-period armor, consisting of many metal plates bound together by leather bands, was ingeniously constructed to provide protection without compromising mobility. The samurai carries two swords, the long katana and the short wakizashi. Also note his ornate helmet on the stand to the right.

The Sun Sets on the Samurai

During the Tokugawa shogunate, the samurai enjoyed high noble status, but unlike other nobles, they were obliged to work. The shoguns, the daimyo, and members of the lesser nobility supported them with retainer stipends. Although noble, each samurai thus served a master. As the Tokugawa period developed, the role of the samurai increasingly changed from warrior to government administrator. Many samurai undertook advanced studies, especially in mathematics, although they also continued to practice the martial arts.

At the height of their status, during the Tokugawa period, the samurai were divided into three social ranks: the upper, middle, and lesser samurai (among which the shishi were most numerous). Of the three, only the upper samurai enjoyed sufficient wealth to own land. The others were obliged to live off the income provided by their masters. As the Tokugawa period approached its end in the nineteenth century, the samurai were still revered, but fewer masters employed them and as a consequence most samurai suffered financially.

They turned to the rising merchant class—the class that would rise even higher after trade was opened with the West—that became bankers and money-lenders. The samurai were obliged to show deference to these powerful men of the new middle class, even bowing to them when requesting loans. During the era of the Meiji restoration, many samurai of the lower two classes came to resent their socioeconomic subordination to the merchants and money-lenders. Worse, whereas samurai accepted obedience to a noble master, they now often found themselves serving the commoners of the middle class to whom they were indebted. Thus, by the time of the Meiji restoration, the samurai were already at the margins of society—though their warrior traditions continued to exert a strong influence on the military and the increasingly militaristic government.

Iemochi congratulated himself on thus having avoided both a foreign naval assault and exclusion from profitable trade. But his relief did not last long. In 1866, Choshu, a western province under the leadership of Kido Takayoshi, rose up against the shogun.

Over two and a half centuries, the Tokugawa shoguns had suavely continued the centuries-old delicate dance with the emperors, allowing them to enjoy their position as divinely descended sovereigns even as they, the shoguns, wielded all the practical, temporal power. Now Tokugawa Iemochi approached Emperor Komei with a request that Komei mount a military campaign against rebellious Choshu. By asking the emperor for military aid, the military leader Iemochi betrayed his weakness. Komei did invade Choshu in a brief campaign dubbed the "Summer War," but broke off combat in September 1866 as soon as Tokugawa Iemochi had died.

Now the emperor entered into an entirely new political alignment. In the course of his rebellion, Kido Takayoshi of Choshu made an alliance with Saigo Takamori, who led the Satsuma domain. With Shogun Tokugawa Iemochi's death, Takayoshi and Takamori announced their support of Komei and proposed restoring the emperor to sole and absolute power by overthrowing the shogunate. They were driven to this by the increase in trade and modernization that had begun with Commodore Perry's 1853–1854 visit. They reasoned that one nation under imperial rule could take full advantage of the new commercial opportunities by converting from the fragmented feudalism of the shogunate to the unitary order of an empire. Japan would follow the example of the empires of Europe with whom it now traded, shedding its feudal government and economy like a dead shell and becoming instead a capitalist power.

Before this new challenge to the shogunate came to fruition, however, Komei died in 1867. He was succeeded by his son, Mutsuhito, who took the throne name of Meiji. On November 9, 1867, Takayoshi and Takamori wrote a secret military order in the name of the new emperor, denouncing Shogun Tokugawa Iemochi's successor, Tokugawa Yoshinobu, as a traitor and commanding his death. But on this very day, Yoshinobu, realizing that he could not fight the combined force of Takayoshi, Takamori, the new emperor, and all that the nations of Europe and North America offered, voluntarily ceded to Emperor Meiji all of his "prerogatives," a deliberately ambiguous word by which Yoshinobu renounced his hereditary privileges without giving up most of his current power. This was a prelude to his formal resignation as the fifteenth and final Tokugawa shogun ten days later—again, a renunciation of hereditary authority without an immediate abrogation of power.

Historically, this event constituted the Meiji restoration; however, like most things in traditional Japanese government, the results of the event were far from absolute. Although Yoshinobu had resigned as shogun, a hereditary ruler whose authority would be passed to a son, he was still a very powerful man who commanded the loyalty of an army. On January 3, 1868, Meiji issued a proclamation addressed "to the sovereigns of all foreign countries and to their subjects" that the "Emperor of Japan . . . has . . . granted permission to the Shogun Tokugawa Yoshinobu to return the governing power in accordance with his own request." It was brilliantly phrased. The emperor did not concede to Yoshinobu even the power to renounce power, but retained that for himself by giving imperial permission for Yoshinobu to step down. Unwilling to relinquish the last of his real power, however, the ex-shogun took the emperor's action as nothing less than a coup d'etat, and a new civil war erupted. It would be known as the Boshin War—the War of the Year of the Dragon.

A MODEST BATTLE AT TOBA AND FUSHIMI PRODUCES MOMENTOUS RESULTS

At about four o'clock in the afternoon of January 27, 1868, the advance guard of the ex-shogun's army drew up to Toba, the fortified southern entrance to Kyoto, and demanded peaceful passage into the city. Those guarding the entrance, samurai from Saigo Takamori's Satsuma province, supporters of the emperor, responded to the demand by launching an artillery attack against the flank of the ex-shogun's forces. One shell exploded near the commander, Takigawa Tomotaka. It spooked his horse, which threw Tomotaka to the ground then stampeded wildly, an ill omen that prompted the advance guard to break ranks and run.

Observing from a distance the dissolution of his advance guard, Sasaki Tadasaburo, overall commander of the ex-shogun's forces, impulsively ordered a charge against the Satsuma gunners. What happened next was an iconic episode in the transformation of Japanese culture and technology as well as a lesson in modern warfare. The ex-shogun's men were armed as traditional samurai, with spears and swords. The Satsuma men, although they were also samurai, wielded Western weapons, the same kind of rifle muskets and artillery that the Union and Confederate armies had used in the recently ended U.S. Civil War. With these, they inflicted a slaughter.

On the next day, one of the emperor's courtiers, Iwakura Tomomi, presented Saigo Takamori and his subordinate, Okubo Toshimichi, with orders from Meiji denouncing Yoshinobu and all who followed him as "enemies of the court" and authorizing military action against them. What Tomomi did not mention was that he had written the orders himself and had forged the imperial signature on them. Moreover, Tomomi had pulled twelve-year-old Imperial Prince Yoshiaki from the Buddhist temple of Ninna-ji, where he lived as a monk, and named him commander in chief of the army. It was a symbolic gesture that instantly transformed the provincial forces of Satsuma and Choshu into an imperial army.

The forged orders and symbolic imperial commander proved a brilliant stroke. Aware that to fire on the emperor's army would be high treason, the men of the ex-shogun's army were confused and badly shaken. Nevertheless, on the next day, both sides

▶

This contemporary Japanese print of the Satsuma Rebellion shows the Satsuma men in quasi-Western military dress. Although they were samurai like the forces they opposed, the Satsuma warriors adopted some Western military methods and equipment.

新政府大総督陸軍大将西郷隆盛

惺々斎 小金丸某

警部補 西原猪太郎

Japan Modernizes—and Militarizes

The Battle Toba-Fushimi was the last in which traditional samurai fought. The differences between the samurai of the Satsuma and Choshu domains and those of the ex-shogun were extraordinary. In the battle's initial engagement, the Satsuma–Choshu force had already adopted Western arms, whereas the ex-shogun's men fought exclusively with traditional samurai weapons—and paid for this with their lives.

The battle raised the curtain on a massive and accelerated effort to modernize Japan. Nowhere was the modernization more intense than in the military. The Meiji's official restoration to full sovereign power evoked passionate study and emulation of the militaries of the west, with the main focus on Prussian models for the army and British and U.S. practices for the modernization of the navy. Equal in importance to the technological advances was the reorientation of the armed forces, which exchanged the traditional samurai's allegiance to their feudal lords for complete loyalty to the emperor. Yet, even as the army vastly expanded by conscripting common Japanese, it remained infused with the samurai spirit.

Modernization of the armed forces led the way for modernization of Japanese industry and society. This was not merely an instance of civilian Japan following the example of the military. Among the innovations the military borrowed from Prussia was the creation of a general staff that not only commanded the armed forces but also exerted extensive influence over the government as a whole. Within ten years of the emperor's proclamation of the shogun's resignation, Japan's government was well on the way to extensive militarization. This transformation was promoted from the top down as well as from the bottom up, as conscripted soldiers, having completed their four years of compulsory service, brought back to civilian life the ideals that had been instilled in them during their military experience. By the time of the Russo-Japanese War of 1904–1905, Japan was both extensively industrialized and militarized. By the era of World War II, the government of Japan was a frank military dictatorship.

hammered one another with artillery, and the ex-shogun's men, having apparently recovered their morale, held their own.

That is when the commanders from Satsuma and Choshu exhibited another forged artifact, a facsimile of the imperial banner. The trouble with this gesture was that the Japanese emperor had been a figurehead so long that few soldiers on either side had ever seen the imperial banner. Indeed, the emblem was meaningless until Okubo Toshimichi sent through his own lines, as well as forward to the commanders of the enemy force, messengers bearing an explanation of the banner's significance.

Once again reminded that they were fighting against the emperor's army, the ex-shogun's men began to break ranks. Seeing this, the Satsuma and Choshu samurai charged the wavering enemy line. This time, they set aside their modern arms and instead used the traditional samurai weapon: the sword. The ex-shogun's officers desperately attempted to rally their men, but both effort and discipline quickly dissolved, and the army was routed.

The Battle of Toba-Fushimi produced relatively few casualties, but it was a spectacular psychological triumph for the imperial cause. Those daimyo who had hesitated to side with either the ex-shogun or the emperor instantly renounced their neutrality and rallied to Meiji. Although Yoshinobu himself now yielded unconditionally to Meiji, some of his forces refused to give up and instead made their way to Hokkaido, where they proclaimed the independent Republic of Ezo. This act of defiance was crushed by imperial forces on July 4, 1868, and the diehards, some 3,000 of them, were killed.

JAPAN ASCENDANT

After two and a half centuries under the shogunate, the Japanese Empire had been, to all appearances, restored to the emperor. But this perception was compounded both of fact and fiction. While it is true that Emperor Meiji reigned supreme, the actual administration of the government was merely transferred from the hands of the Tokugawa shogun to a cartel of leaders drawn from the provinces of Satsuma and Choshu. These men assumed the role of oligarchs, wholly empowered to govern in the emperor's name.

▲

Mutushito, who took the throne name Meiji when he became emperor in January 1867, initiated a period of sweeping and profound reform in Japan. His Western military appearance in this portrait extends even to his hair style and beard, the latter cut in the "Imperial" fashion made popular by France's Napoleon III and widely adopted during this era by army officers throughout much of the world.

The oligarchs were samurai, but above all they were driven by the influences of the West that had first arrived with Perry's ships. The oligarchs were now modern military commanders, whose government took on a distinctly militaristic tone. Increasingly, the motive of capitalism, which vastly accelerated the industrialization of the country, entwined with the motives of militarism and the consolidation of government in the name of the emperor. This centralization of authority spelled the end of feudalism.

But before that end could be made final, the emperor had to formally acquire all the lands that had been subject to the Tokugawa shogun, which he did—peacefully—from 1868 to 1872. With this accomplished, the next two steps were the abolition of the samurai and the reformation of the military.

Nearly two million samurai lived in Japan in the early 1870s, each originally financed by the master who employed them, but now paid a stipend out of the imperial treasury. To eliminate this ruinous government expense and also to remove from Japanese society a class of armed men who were not under the emperor's exclusive control, the Meiji government in 1873 levied taxes on the stipends and eventually compelled the samurai to convert their stipends into government bonds. Also in 1873, the government instituted compulsory military service for every adult male, requiring four years' service in the regular army, followed by three years in the reserves.

Conscription not only accelerated the militarization of Japan—whose government was, after all, run by warriors—it also further diminished the samurai by introducing another, much larger class of armed men into Japanese society. These new warriors were entirely answerable to the state, not to their class or the traditions of their class, and to further reduce the social standing of the samurai, the emperor decreed that they could no longer wear their swords or any other weapons in public. The government quickly put down a brief samurai uprising in response to the new social order.

FOUR HUNDRED YEARS IN FORTY

Emperor Meiji reigned for forty-five years. It was widely reported that a man who had left Japan near the beginning of his reign and returned forty years later, near its end, marveled at the changes in his country. He said that he felt as if he had lived four hundred years.

Before the arrival of Perry, Japan was a feudal state: an island geographically, economically, technologically, and culturally. By 1912, when Meiji's son Taisho assumed the throne, Japan had already shocked the Western world by defeating the thoroughly modern army and navy of Czar Nicholas II in the Russo–Japanese War of 1904–1905. Six years after this, Japan was an even more formidable industrial and military power—with the emphasis on military.

For as much and as profoundly as Japan had changed, its imperial nucleus was made up of the same kind of men who had ruled Japan for hundreds of years. They were warriors—warriors whose weapons were modern, whose allegiance was to the state, but whose spirit lingered in the world of the samurai. The mix of tradition and modernity was a volatile combination almost inevitably bound to ignite, which it did in the mid twentieth century, exploding into a world war that devastated no place more terribly than Japan itself. And yet, rising from the ashes of Hiroshima, Nagasaki, and other ruined cities, Japan recreated itself yet again in the years following World War II, becoming an innovator of culture and technology where before it had been content merely to emulate and adopt the culture and technology of other nations.

CHAPTER
14

GERMANY IN THE SADDLE:
THE FRANCO-PRUSSIAN WAR

1870—1871

On July 19, 1870, when the war began, Germany did not exist.

On January 18, 1871, when the fighting was all but over, the German Empire came into being

at the very heart of Europe. Its creation had required a man who wanted war,

another willing to give it to him, and a third possessed of the military genius to win it.

I n the short term following the Franco-Prussian War, one emperor fell and another rose. In the long term, the war and its consequences were supposed to bring lasting peace to Europe, peace on strictly German terms, but peace nevertheless. Instead, the brief but bloody conflict set into motion the machinery that would grind out the two most destructive wars the world has yet endured.

BISMARCK RISING

Otto Eduard Leopold, Prince of Bismarck, Duke of Lauenburg, Count of Bismarck-Schönhausen, was born in 1815 on a Prussian estate outside of Berlin, the son of a landed retired army officer who had married a woman of even great wealth and the loftier ambition to rise through the ranks of the lesser nobility. Bismarck was born just as Britain, having led the coalition that defeated Napoleon I, was maneuvering its mighty navy to impose a "Pax Britannica" over all the other great powers of Europe. To a remarkable degree, the British effort succeeded. With no country in a position to challenge its dominance of the seas, the period between the Napoleonic Wars and the mid-nineteenth century was marked by an unmistakable reduction in armed conflict, and the British Empire became the world's champion of free trade, also taking the lead in such progressive campaigns as abolishing slavery. In a climate of relative peace, the Continent opened to dramatically increased industrial development, which in turn sparked movements toward national unification, beginning with Italy.

As Bismarck came of age and entered politics, Germany did not exist except as a loose alliance among disparate states and principalities dubbed the German Confederation. In 1851, King Friedrich Wilhelm IV appointed Bismarck as Prussia's representative to the Confederation, just then convening in Frankfurt. He served in the Confederation for seven years, in the process finding himself increasingly inspired by the early successes of Italy's remarkable chief minister, Count Camillo di Cavour, in creating a new, unified Italian state under his Piedmontese king.

In the meantime, in 1857, Friedrich Wilhelm was disabled by a stroke. His brother Wilhelm became regent and appointed Bismarck in 1859 ambassador to Russia. The assignment broadened the diplomat's horizons to a sweeping international scope. While Bismarck served in Russia, his king made two other momentous

◄

On September 2, 1870, Napoleon III met Otto von Bismarck at Donchery, in the French Ardennes, to offer surrender terms after France's final humiliating defeat, at nearby Sedan, in the Franco–Prussian War. Whereas Bismarck sits ramrod straight, Napoleon III has the bearing of a beaten man.

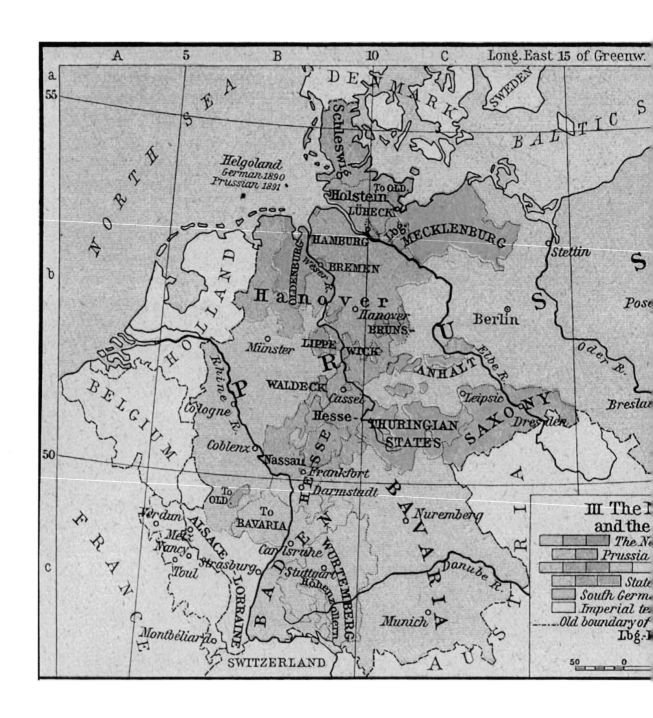

The map shows Germany with labeled regions including:

A 5 B 10 C Long. East 15 of Greenw.

a
55

DENMARK

SWEDEN

NORTH SEA

BALTIC S

Schleswig

Helgoland
German 1890
Prussian 1891

To OLD.

Holstein

LÜBECK

MECKLENBURG

Stettin

HAMBURG

b

BREMEN

HOLLAND

OLDENBURG

Weser R.

Hanover

Hanover

Berlin

S

Pose

BRUNS-

WICK

LIPPE

Oder R.

Münster

P

R

WALDECK

ANHALT

Elbe R.

Breslau

BELGIUM

Rhine R.

Cassel

Leipsic

SAXONY

Cologne

Hesse-

THURINGIAN

Dresden

Coblenz

STATES

A

50

Nassau

Frankfort

B

Darmstadt

To
OLD

HESSE

Nuremberg

FRANCE

Verdun

ALSACE

To
BAVARIA

N.

BAVARIA

Metz

Nancy

Carlsruhe

WÜRTEMBERG

Danube R.

Toul

Strasburg

Stuttgart

Höhenzollern

BADEN

LORRAINE

c

Munich

A

U

S

T

R

I

A

Montbéliard

SWITZERLAND

III The I
and the

The Ne
Prussia

State
South Germ.
Imperial te.
Old boundary of
Lbg-I

50   0

The shading and key for this map show the transformation of Germany from a collection of loosely federated states before the Franco-Prussian War to *the* German Empire following it.

20　　　E

55

oKönigsberg

ic

Vistula R.

R U S S I A

50

German Federation
n Empire, 1866-1871.
rnan Federation, 1866-71
her members of the Federation
rman Empire, 1871
North German Federal Union
bers of the Federal Union
f Alsace-Lorraine
iard. German Lorraine and Alsace
g. OLD.- OLDENBURG
1:12 000 000
100   150   200 Miles

appointments. He named Helmuth von Moltke chief of staff of the Prussian army and Albrecht von Roon minister of war. Moltke was a military genius who combined brilliance in battlefield tactics with a strategic vision that put two burgeoning nineteenth-century technologies—the telegraph and the railroad—front and center in military logistics. Roon was a thoroughgoing militarist who was determined to create the Prussian military as an unparalleled instrument of armed diplomacy.

When Wilhelm I assumed the throne after the death of his ailing brother in 1861, he pondered recalling Bismarck from St. Petersburg to become minister-president—effectively prime minister—of Prussia. He was confident that Bismarck would bring the reluctant Prussian House of Deputies (parliament) into line behind the program of militarization that Roon had designed, but the new king was taken aback by Bismarck's demand that he would accept nothing less than a dual appointment as both minister-president and foreign minister.

Otto von Bismarck was an ambitious man who was less interested in possessing power for the sake of power than in pulling the strings that controlled the powerful. He had been born into an enviable yet ambiguous social niche. He possessed money and a fine family name, but he was a long way from royalty and the inner circle of power. Nevertheless, he identified wholeheartedly with the aristocracy, even as he understood that he was not by birth invested in it and would never be admitted fully into its embrace. The most he believed he could hope for as a young man was to parlay a good education and his family name into a comfortable posting in the Prussian diplomatic corps.

As it turned out, however, the best he could manage was a series of jobs in government back offices in the western border city of Aachen and the Berlin suburb of

Potsdam. This disappointment notwithstanding, he followed in his father's footsteps by making an advantageous marriage. In 1847 he wed Johanna von Puttkamer, a noblewoman whose station was substantially higher than his own. This same year saw his first political breakthrough when he was elected to the Landtag, the newly established Prussian legislature. He used this position as a stepping stone to higher office. At first, he opposed what seemed to him a radical movement to unite Germany, believing that Prussia would be diminished in such an empire; however, as he began to realize that Prussia isolated was Prussia doomed—which meant an end to his own climb to the place where the strings were pulled—Bismarck not only decided to maneuver Prussia into a united Germany, but to put it at the union's very center.

Thus the demand Bismarck made of his king was not the product of blind ambition, but of his far-seeing ambition, a dual plan for the ascendancy Prussia and himself. In Russia, he had learned that an effective political leader had to exercise control over more than the nation's interior. He needed to determine foreign policy as well. What shook the king out of his hesitation was the stunning rejection of his proposed military budget by the House of Deputies in September 1862. Within days of this action, Wilhelm I appointed Bismarck to both of the posts he demanded.

Now Bismarck turned in earnest to the example of Italy. His intention was to unify Prussia from within while simultaneously refashioning it into the nucleus of a German empire. In 1866, over the express objections of Wilhelm I, he fomented the so-called Seven Weeks' War with the aim of ending Austria's bid for dominance over the German states. As a result of the war, the old German Confederation was replaced by the North German Confederation, which excluded Austria and thereby put Prussia in control of most of the other German states. The next step was to seduce the other south German states into joining the new confederation, which could then become an empire. Addressing the North German Reichstag (parliament) in 1867, Bismarck urged: "Let us put Germany in the saddle, so to speak—it already knows how to ride."

WIELDING THE HAMMER

The truth was that Otto von Bismarck loved war no more than a carpenter loves a hammer, but what the hammer is to a carpenter, war was to the minister-president of the kingdom of Prussia in 1870: an indispensable tool. He needed war to elbow and shove Prussia ahead of the rest of Europe so that the other German states, taking notice,

Fragmentary Origins

The Holy Roman Empire came into being in 962 under Otto the Great. It was never truly an empire, however, but a loose union of Central European territories. By the sixteenth century, it became known officially as the Holy Roman Empire of the German Nation. But there really was no such nation. Germany was a collection of disparate states united only by a common language. In 1806, at the height of the Napoleonic Wars, the Holy Roman Empire was dissolved, and nine years later the Congress of Vienna created the German Confederation as its successor.

Its thirty-nine German states were dominated by the two largest, Prussia and Austria, which were rivals for total domination. The confederation had a so-called "Federal Assembly" in Frankfurt, a forum in which ministers answerable not to the people, but to the sovereign of each state, gathered. Yet so vague was the scope and nature of the confederation that parts of Prussia and Austria did not belong to it. Most important, these major powers withheld from the confederation's federal army most of their troops. Thus both Prussia and Austria each had a toe in the German Confederation, but the other foot was firmly planted in independence.

In 1848, a series of revolutions—most of them abortive—washed across Europe, affecting the Italian states, France, the duchy of Schleswig, Austria (and other parts of the Hapsburg Empire), Hungary, Switzerland, and Poland as well as many of the German states. During this ferment, German nationalists united with German liberals in an attempt to create a genuinely unified German state, an entity that would make the German people a force to be reckoned with in Europe. Not only did the talks fail, but the German Confederation itself dissolved, only to be somewhat grudgingly reconstituted in 1850.

But the relentless rivalry between Austria and Prussia doomed the confederation. Hostility boiled over into the Austro-Prussian (Seven Weeks') War of 1866, which brought about the collapse of the confederation and the creation of the North German Confederation, dominated by Prussia, and a number of south German states, which gravitated toward Austria. With Austria out of the organization, Bismarck, once he found a catalyst in the Franco-Prussian War, was able to create a German Empire in 1871.

would rush to ally themselves with the kingdom, thereby transforming it into a German empire.

Given the choice between buying a hammer at great cost and accepting one free, as a present, the wise carpenter takes the gift. What Bismarck needed was a preemptive war with the one country that had the most to lose in a Europe suddenly dominated by a German Empire. But simply to declare war on France would alienate much of the rest of the continent. Fortunately for Bismarck, he had taken the measure of the French emperor. He knew that Napoleon III, despite the illustrious name he had taken, had a personality compounded of intense nationalist fervor and thorough mediocrity of intellect. Play on the fervor, and his will would follow—eagerly, helplessly. Play on the fervor, and you could make the Frenchman do whatever you wanted him to.

Moltke the Magnificent

Count Helmuth Karl Bernhard von Moltke was born in 1800 to an aristocratic family in the German duchy of Mecklenburg. The family's precarious finances limited their son's prospects, and so he was sent to the Royal Cadet Corps in Copenhagen for a military education. On graduation, he joined a Danish infantry regiment, but was determined to become an officer in Europe's most elite military force, the Prussian army. Despite chronic ill health, he was commissioned a lieutenant in the Leibgrenadier Regiment in 1821.

Proving to be a young officer of prodigious talent, he was enrolled in the prestigious *Kriegsakademie* (War College) and groomed for higher command, becoming chief of staff of the Prussian army in 1857, promoting his vision of the role of the railway and telegraph in military operations, expanding the army, and creating a supremely efficient system of command capable of controlling large forces deployed over vast areas. More than any other figure in the second half of the nineteenth century, he brought warfare into a new age.

▲

Helmuth von Moltke created Prussia's formidable military machine and led it to rapid victory against the French. With his emphasis on the military application of such technologies as telegraph communications and rail transport, he brought warfare into the modern age.

INCIDENT AT BAD EMS

In 1868 a revolution vacated the Spanish throne. Two years later, the new Spanish government, seeking a monarch from outside the country, offered the throne to Leopold of Hohenzollern-Sigmaringen, a German prince. Predictably, the French government not only moved to block Leopold's ascension, it demanded that the North German Confederation guarantee that no Hohenzollern would ever become king of Spain. When the Confederation withheld its response, Napoleon III and his people did what Bismarck knew they would do. They contemplated war against their traditional German enemy.

On July 7, the French ambassador approached the Prussian king, Wilhelm I, who was enjoying the curative waters at fashionable Bad Ems, a German spa. Adopting a manner one does not use with a king, especially when the king is trying to relax, the diplomat imperiously demanded that Wilhelm promise—then and there—to withdraw the candidacy of Leopold. Taken aback, the monarch glared at the ambassador. He could make no such promise, he said, because he was not responsible for Leopold's candidacy in the first place. With that, the ambassador withdrew, only to stalk back to the spa four days later to press his demand again.

In fact, there was no need for him to have returned. Leopold, as it turned out, had no stomach for a crisis and voluntarily withdrew himself from consideration—without anyone having asked him to. This would have settled the matter and defused the crisis had the French foreign minister refrained from intervening by ordering his ambassador to demand from Wilhelm I a full formal endorsement of Leopold's demurral in addition to a solemn pledge that the Confederation would never support a Hohenzollern as Spanish king.

It was a demand even more impertinent than the original one, and Bismarck was determined to make the most of it. On July 14, the great French Bastille Day holiday, he released to the European press a telegram the king had sent from Bad Ems to the Prussian foreign office reporting his confrontation with the French ambassador. Without bothering to consult the king, however, Bismarck had edited the dispatch, transforming Wilhelm's bland report of his refusal to assent to the formal agreement the French demanded into a statement roughly tantamount to a severance of diplomatic relations, which is almost inevitably a prelude to war.

In Bismarck's hands, the "Ems Telegram" became what he called "a red rag to the Gallic bull"—by which he meant the French people as stirred by their reliably nationalistic emperor. On July 19, 1870, a mere five days after the telegram appeared in print, France declared war on Prussia. Bismarck had his hammer.

OPENING MOVES

As Bismarck knew that the Ems Telegram would provoke France to war, so he also knew that war with Germany's perennial adversary would rally the German folk behind Wilhelm I, who thanks to Moltke and Roon now presided over the most powerful army in Europe.

As for Napoleon III, only after he had declared war did war begin to seem like a very bad idea. His armies were not only outnumbered, they were out-generaled. Whereas Moltke had been planning his "French strategy" for years, the French high command bumbled into hasty mobilization.

On the Rhine River frontier, Moltke deployed three armies totaling 380,000 men, equipped with state-of-the-art arms. Sixty thousand, under General Karl von Steinmetz, were concentrated between Trier and Saarbrücken; another 175,000 troops, commanded by Prince Friedrich Karl, were distributed between Bingen and Mannheim; and the third army, under Crown Prince Friedrich Wilhelm, consisting of 145,000 men, was deployed between Landau and Germerscheim. The three commanders of these field forces were not only highly capable officers; Moltke had also created another level of command, the general staff, whose job it was to extend and amplify his own extraordinary strategic thinking and also to see to its precise and efficient execution. This was a true innovation in the military art, providing a virtually seamless connection between highest headquarters and the officers in the field. Moltke's plan was to destroy the French armies in the field and then take Paris.

Opposing Moltke's armies were the 224,000 officers and men of the French army. This force was divided into eight corps, which were thinly stretched behind the Franco-German frontier, backed by fortresses at Metz, Nancy, and Belfort. Whereas logistics, including full exploitation of existing rail networks, was always uppermost in Moltke's planning, transport seems to have been something of an afterthought for the French, and troop movement would have to be improvised.

Improvised as well was the deployment of forces. In contrast to the Prussians, the French had virtually no military intelligence operation and therefore knew almost nothing about the enemy's movements. French war minister Marshal Edmond Leboeuf moved his armies over the field without any coherent plan of battle other than what was encapsulated in the cheer raised by the French men, women, and children who lined the routes of march: "On to Berlin!" As for Napoleon III, he issued only one strategic order: "Advance!"

FIRST BLOOD

In theory, the clash of great European armies was commanded by the monarchs of each belligerent nation. Wilhelm I had the good sense to entrust actual command to Moltke. The egocentric Napoleon III, however, put himself at the head of his forces, and it was not until the first skirmish between the French and Germans, at Saarbrücken on August 2, 1870, that the emperor made an effort to group his amorphous collection of independent corps into two functional armies. The three southernmost corps were dubbed the Army of Alsace and put under the command of Marshal Patrice MacMahon. The remaining five corps became the Army of Lorraine, under Marshal Achille F. Bazaine. This ad hoc reorganization rendered the French forces more manageable, but the two marshals lacked the kind of staff–officer organization that was a key element of Moltke's armies. Orders from the top therefore trickled down to field commanders slowly, making coordinated movement almost impossible.

Napoleon III's forces suffered three defeats in as many days along the northeast borders of France, whereupon Marshal Bazaine fell back on the Metz fortress with his Army of Lorraine. Three Prussian armies gave chase, and on August 14, at Colombey, 4 miles (6 km) east of Metz, General Karl von Steinmetz's First Army overtook the French. Both sides suffered several thousand casualties, but the French took the brunt of the losses. Bazaine, a demoralized commander leading a demoralized army, fell back across the Moselle River.

On August 16, at Mars-la-Tour, between Metz and Verdun, Prince Frederick Charles's Second Army attempted to cut off the French retreat. At first, the battle seemed to shift

The Angel of the Battlefield

Clara Barton, barely five feet tall and with a round face that made a striking contrast to her slender frame, was an American from Massachusetts who against all advice from military commanders and politicians had run a one-woman relief operation during the U.S. Civil War, bringing fresh food to the Union soldiers in the field and helping to care for their wounds.

This "Angel of the Battlefield," as she was called, worked herself to near exhaustion but did not seek rest until four years after the end of the Civil War, when in 1869 she embarked on what she hoped would be a restorative leisurely tour of Europe.

Instead, she found herself a witness to the Franco-Prussian War of 1870, and without hesitation began distributing relief supplies to the victims of combat. She was introduced to the International Red Cross, which had been founded in 1863 by Swiss humanitarians. She was shaken by the carnage of the brief Franco-Prussian War—advances in weapons technology produced casualties of a nature she had not seen even in the U.S. Civil War. Barton, on her return to the United States,

campaigned to secure the government's endorsement of the Geneva Convention, which the Red Cross had formulated to promote the humane treatment of soldiers wounded or captured in war. In 1881, she organized the American Association of the Red Cross, which became the American Red Cross.

Under her leadership—which lasted until 1904, when she was eighty-three—she wrote and engineered passage of the "American amendment" to the constitution of the International Red Cross, which expanded the brief of the institution from relief in war to include other times of major emergency, including floods, earthquakes, hurricanes, tornadoes, epidemic, and famine.

▲

Clara Barton, the genteel Massachusetts lady who brought compassion to the battlefields of the American Civil War, was vacationing in Europe when the Franco–Prussian War broke out. She immediately volunteered to distribute relief supplies to the victims of the combat.

in favor of the French, but Bazaine, operating in a state approaching stupor, allowed the Prussian Second Army to build up and block his route westward. Before it was over, the Battle of Mars-la-Tour cost more than 15,000 casualties on each side.

Instead of retreating, Bazaine turned back toward Metz and on August 18 took a stand at Gravelotte, west of the fortress. Outnumbered, Bazaine nevertheless somehow managed to rally his forces and throw back the assault of the First Army, which withdrew from Gravelotte in great disorder. At Saint-Privat, to the north, the French also took a heavy toll on the Prussian Second Army until it was reinforced by troops from Saxony. The repulse at Gravelotte and the taking of Saint-Privat had cost the Prussians 20,000 casualties against French losses of about 13,000 (plus 5,000 captured at Saint-Privat). Had Bazaine counterattacked, he might have inflicted a decisive defeat against the Prussians. Instead, he withdrew to Metz, where the Prussians held his entire army of 170,000 under siege.

With his hopes for repelling the Prussians at the frontier dashed, Napoleon III saw no alternative but to attempt to break the siege of Metz and rescue the Army of Lorraine. He took personal command of the Army of Alsace, the only French force still capable of movement, and advanced northeast leaving Paris undefended.

▶

French cavalrymen charge at Sedan. The French defeat here cost Napoleon III his throne, transformed France from a monarchy into a republic, and elevated Prussia to preeminence in the new German Empire, which became the most powerful force in continental Europe.

Anticipating this move, Moltke had blockaded Metz and under the Crown Prince of Saxony created an entire new army—the Army of the Meuse—which he thrust in the direction of Chalons, forcing the Army of the Alsace to deflect to the north, away from Metz, on August 29. The prudent move for Napoleon III would have been to turn back to the defense of Paris. This, at least, would have put him in position to negotiate something short of abject, unconditional surrender. Instead, the emperor led his 130,000 men to Sedan, a small fortress town on the Franco-German frontier.

Giving Napoleon III more credit as a commander than he deserved, Moltke had sent the Third Prussian Army, under Crown Prince Friedrich Wilhelm, marching toward Paris on the assumption that the Army of Alsace would take up a position to defend it. Discovering that the emperor had instead holed up at Sedan, Moltke telegraphed new orders to the Third Army, sending part of it to block the western exit from Sedan and the rest in an arc across the Moselle River to attack the Army of the Alsace from the north while the Army of the Meuse attacked from the south.

Thus, on September 1, 1870, the forces of Napoleon III were caught between the opposing teeth of a great steel trap. On September 2, the emperor tried to fight his way out, but the Prussian-Saxon encirclement held, and 3,000 of the Army of Alsace were killed, 14,000 wounded, and 20,000 taken as prisoners of war. Marshal MacMahon sustained a serious wound. With the situation hopeless, both he and his emperor surrendered their swords.

HUMILIATION

The French press condemned it as "the humiliation of Sedan." Two days after the battle, the Third French Republic was proclaimed, and its newly created Government of National Defense formally deposed Napoleon III, appointed Jules Favre as foreign minister, and sent him to negotiate with Bismarck. When the Prussian minister-president demanded Alsace and Lorraine, Favre broke off the negotiation, and on September 23 the Prussians laid siege to Paris.

But on October 27, Marshal Bazaine, his soldiers bottled up helplessly at Metz, surrendered the fortress along with the Army of Lorraine. Paris continued to languish under a patient Prussian siege until January 28, 1871, when the Third French Republic sued for peace. The Treaty of Frankfurt (May 10, 1871) bound France to yield Alsace and Lorraine and to pay a staggering billion-dollar indemnity.

A NEW EMPIRE

The victory brought to birth the German Empire, consisting of all the German states except Austria. Wilhelm I was crowned kaiser (emperor) in a ceremony conducted on January 18, 1871—not in Berlin, but in the Hall of Mirrors in the Palace of Versailles, where France had traditionally crowned its own kings.

As chancellor of the new empire, Bismarck was at the center of continental affairs for the next twenty years, exercising a brilliant if ruthless diplomacy to install a network of interlocking alliances aimed at isolating Russia and keeping a defeated France weak and demoralized. By the 1878 Congress of Berlin, the "Iron Chancellor" had essentially moved the capital of the Continent from Paris to Berlin. What the world came to call "Bismarck's system" brought a calm stability to Europe that prompted many to declare that the turbulent region had entered an age of almost utopian political and social progress.

It was true that nothing like Europe's diplomatic system existed in the rest of the world; however, Bismarck's epic diplomatic engineering, made possible by the German triumph against France, not only failed to bring permanent peace, but ensured that the next major European war would be fought on an unprecedented scale. The interlocking network of treaties, alliances, and secret agreements that bound the nations of Europe together also transformed them into armed camps.

Bismarck had once casually remarked: "If a general war begins, it will be because of some damn fool thing in the Balkans." Otto von Bismarck had been dead sixteen years when that "fool thing" came, at 11:15 on the morning of June 28, 1914, on a street in Sarajevo, Bosnia-Herzegovina, when a Serbian nationalist youth, Gavrilo Princip, shot the archduke of Austria and his wife the grand duchess. As a result, Austria attacked Serbia, and Russia, bound by treaty with Serbia, mobilized, setting into motion one alliance after another—all of which may be traced directly or indirectly to Bismarck—until, at the beginning of August 1914, all of Europe exploded into a "Great War," which eventually engulfed much of the rest of the world, including the United States. The U.S. president, Woodrow Wilson, wanted to ensure that the Great War would be the "war to end all wars," but terrible as it was it proved no more than a prelude to a conflagration even more cataclysmic, the second world war of the twentieth century.

EXPLOSION IN THE BALKANS: THE BALKAN WARS

1912–1913

As Austria-Hungary, Russia, and the Ottoman Empire rushed toward a common grave at the start of the twentieth century, the peoples of the Balkans took up arms against their dying masters and ignited the two world wars that defined the new century and nearly destroyed civilization in the process

C ombined, the two Balkan Wars that spanned 1912–1913 produced 130,000 dead soldiers, yet in the eye of history, they are mere brushfires nearly invisible in the cataclysmic glare of the two world wars to which they led.

Today obscured and obscure, they were nevertheless foretold, years before they erupted, by no less a figure than Otto von Bismarck. Instigator of the Franco-Prussian War of 1870 (Chapter 14), builder of the German Empire, architect of modern Europe, he was far more interested in looking forward than backward. After creating an empire, Bismarck used it to anchor an intricate web of treaties and military pacts, both public and secret, designed to impose on all Europe a "Pax Germanica," peace on German terms. Looking up from his military and diplomatic handiwork, the Iron Chancellor—Europe's "pilot," some called him—experienced the flash of a disquieting vision. A future war, all-consuming, was still a possibility, it occurred to him. If it came, he predicted, it would be the result of "some damn fool thing in the Balkans."

A TIME BOMB ARMED

At the start of the twentieth century, the house of Hapsburg, ruling the "Dual Monarchy" of Austria-Hungary, was perched precariously on the shifting sands of a polyglot "empire" composed of some five million Czechs and Slovaks, three million Serbs and Croats, an almost equal number of Romanians, two and a half million Poles, and perhaps a million Slovenes. A single aim united these otherwise disparate peoples: a longing to be free of the Dual Monarchy.

Austria-Hungary's emperor, Franz Joseph, aged and inept, his very throne creaky with corruption, struggled to accommodate the ardent ethnic nationalism of his fragmented realm without setting into motion its complete dissolution. His inclination was to expand, in the hope that making the Austro-Hungarian Empire bigger would somehow quell the discontent of its current constituents. The only way to expand, however, was at the expense of the Hapsburgs' ancient enemy, Ottoman Turkey.

◄

Aged and doddering, the Hapsburg emperor Franz Joseph symbolized the decline of the unwieldy Austro-Hungarian Empire during the era of the Balkan Wars.

If anything, the Ottoman Empire was more surely doomed than the Austro-Hungarian. True, at their height, the Ottomans had controlled most of Central and Eastern Europe, Western Asia, and North Africa, but that height had been reached some three centuries earlier. Ever since then, the Ottomans had been on the decline and were now all but bankrupted by continual warfare

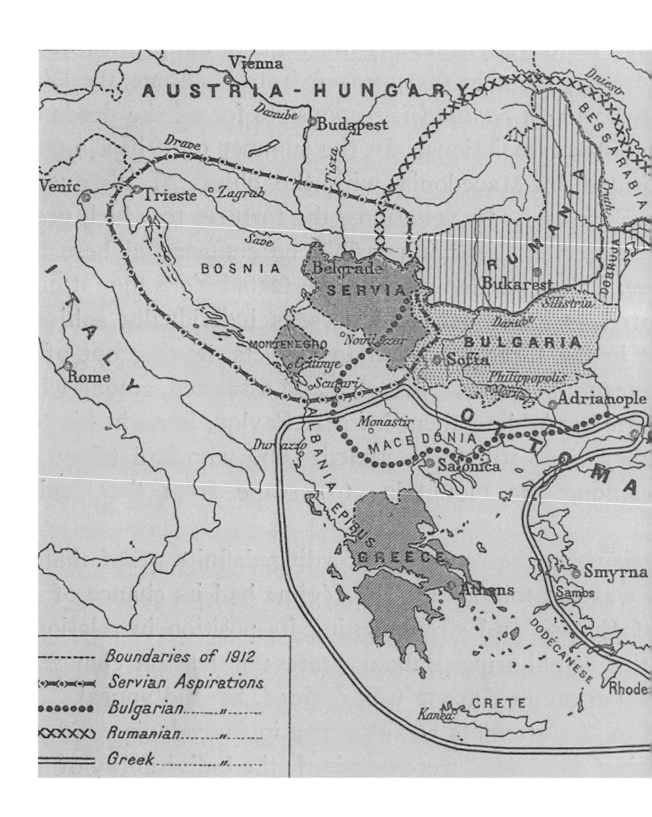

Boundaries of 1912
Servian Aspirations
Bulgarian .... "
Rumanian .... "
Greek .... "

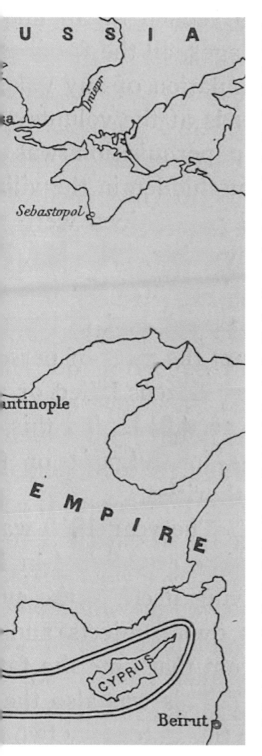

and an endless succession of degenerate rulers. By the beginning of the twentieth century, the Ottoman Empire consisted of the territory of present-day Turkey, in the Balkans, Albania, part of Serbia, and northern Greece; in the east, part of Armenia and Georgia were Ottoman possessions; and in the Middle East, Palestine (Israel), Syria, and Mesopotamia (Iraq) were under Ottoman control. The Turks were keenly aware that the three "Great Powers" of Central and Eastern Europe—Germany, Austria-Hungary, and Russia—lusted after pieces of this moribund empire, especially in the Balkans.

All that kept the Great Powers from immediately clawing the Balkans apart was their inability to agree on who should get what. As Bismarck had understood years earlier, the peace of Europe depended upon no single power staking a major claim to the Balkans, the crossroads at which Europe and Asia Minor met. For this reason, the nations of Europe did what they could to keep Ottoman Turkey going, even though it was so infirm that Western Europeans took to calling it by the name Czar Nicholas II had given it, the "sick man of Europe."

Recognizing that the patient could be kept alive only for so long, the Western powers also extended their support to the Austro-Hungarian Empire, which was only somewhat less critically ill. If the Dual Monarchy failed, the Russian bear, facing no resistance, would surely lumber in, seize as much of the old Ottoman Empire as its great claws could grasp, and then pose a more serious

◄

This period map illustrates the competing territorial "aspirations" of the principal combatants of the two Balkan wars. Note that Serbia is labeled "Servia"—a common Western spelling prior to World War II.

menace to Europe than the Ottoman Turks ever did. For this very reason, Bismarck himself had grudgingly called Austria-Hungary "a European necessity."

In all this, neither Bismarck nor anyone else bothered to consult the Balkan peoples themselves. As they in increasing numbers threw off the Ottoman yoke, so they wanted to be free of Austria-Hungary as well. By the early years of the twentieth century, German leaders still clung to the idea of the Dual Monarchy as a bulwark against czarist designs on Europe, but Britain, France, and Russia itself had come to believe that the Hapsburgs were rapidly becoming as feeble and dysfunctional as the Ottomans. By 1907, when treaties binding most of Western Europe to support Austria-Hungary lapsed, the Hapsburgs found themselves the troubled rulers of the most despised country in Europe, except of course for Turkey. Britain and France were no longer willing to carry either Austria-Hungary or the Ottoman Empire.

THE KEYSTONE CRUMBLES

As Czar Nicholas II saw it, Russia stood to gain from the decline and imminent collapse of both the Ottoman and Austro-Hungarian empires. What he completely failed to see was that his empire was also at the precipice. After suffering a humiliating defeat at the hands of the Japanese in the Russo-Japanese War of 1904–1905, then barely extinguishing an internal revolution the same year, the czar looked west to the Balkans as an opportunity for expansion, in which, much like Franz Joseph, he saw a means of increasing his hold over his own discontent people.

The Turks still controlled Macedonia, but it was enveloped by a nominally independent Greece, Montenegro, Serbia, and Bulgaria, all receptive to Russia's seductive promise of alliance. In 1912, these four nations, with the czar's blessing, would band together as the Balkan League; more immediately, however, Serbia posed the greatest threat to the continued rule of the Hapsburg dynasty because Serbia had powerful ethnic ties to the Serbs and Croats who still lived within the Austro-Hungarian Empire. In the past, Franz Joseph had simply bribed Serbia's ruling dynasty to keep its people in check, but a bloody 1903 Serb coup had elevated to power a vehemently anti-Hapsburg clan, and now Russia egged on Serbia and the rest of the Balkan League to rise against both Austria-Hungary and Turkey.

Britain and France, whose governments sympathized with the nationalist ambitions of Austria-Hungary's ethnic minorities, did not act to discourage the czar's Balkans meddling. Franz Joseph and his ministers surely recognized that the props were being knocked out from under them, but instead of seeking to come to terms with the nationalist forces within the Dual Monarchy, they chose to believe that they had only two choices: to die by inches, like the Ottoman Empire, or to die fighting.

Bismarck had identified Austria-Hungary as the fragile but vital keystone of European stability. Once the Hapsburgs lost the protection of the grand scheme of European alliances Bismarck had engineered in the previous century, the entire diplomatic structure of Europe was bound to come crashing down. All of the continent's nations were becoming increasingly resigned to the outbreak of a major war—the very war Bismarck had predicted as the outcome "of some damn fool thing in the Balkans"—and the major powers accordingly launched an arms race, which in self-fulfilling prophecy virtually ensured all-consuming war.

An Unhappy Compromise

Austria-Hungary claimed a huge space on the map of Europe, second in area only to the vast Russian Empire and third in population after Russia and the German Empire. Yet size can be a most deceptive measure of power. Austria and Hungary were ancient realms, but Austria-Hungary was the product of a recent compromise signed in 1867 by Emperor Franz Joseph of Austria and a delegation of Hungarian leaders chaired by Ferenc Deák. It was the emperor's desperate attempt to avoid losing Hungary, brimming with ardent nationalists, altogether. Under the compromise, the Austrian and Hungarian governments were legal equals, except that Franz Joseph exercised complete control over the armed forces, foreign policy, and a customs union. The impermanence of this Dual Monarchy was underscored by a provision in compromise that it be formally renegotiated every ten years—an arrangement that typically triggered destabilizing political crises at predictable intervals.

The Dual Monarchy bound together two ethnically and culturally different peoples, whose leaders deliberately sought to disrupt one another as often as they endeavored to cooperate. Thus, built into the government of the Dual Monarchy was the political engine of its own destruction.

CRIMES AND CONSEQUENCES

Before the nineteenth century closed, Sultan Abdul Hamid II sought to keep his ailing Ottoman realm alive by revoking the brittle empire's constitution and unleashing far and wide a secret police force to replace rational law with a brutality as mindless as it was unrelenting. As if this reign of terror were not sufficient to alienate his own subjects as well as leaders throughout Europe, the sultan, in a genocidal orgy, perpetrated the massacre of hundreds of thousands of Armenians in his empire during the 1890s. Ottoman Turkey was now an international pariah.

With the government on the verge of collapse, young officers from the Turkish Third Army Corps stationed in Salonika, Macedonia (now Thessalonika, Greece), organized the Ottoman Liberty Society and then staged a series of mutinies followed by a general uprising in Macedonia in 1908. Bulgaria exploited the resulting chaos to declare its independence from Ottoman rule in 1908, and that same year Austria-Hungary summarily annexed Bosnia-Herzegovina, plucking this province from Turkey's grip. Next, Turkish Crete proclaimed its union with Greece, though threats from the Ottoman government prompted Greece to delay its embrace of the breakaway island.

In 1911, Italy invaded and occupied Ottoman-held Tripoli (modern Libya) in the Italo-Turkish War. The powerlessness of Ottoman forces to resist the takeover inspired Serbia, Montenegro, Greece, and Bulgaria to act on Russia's suggestion of creating a Balkan League. On October 8, 1912, Montenegro, smallest of the League's members, declared war on Turkey and was quickly joined the other members.

FIRST BLOOD

Turkish forces available in the Balkans at the outbreak of the war included 140,000 troops in Macedonia, Epirus (a region straddling the Greek-Albanian border), and Albania, in addition to 100,000 in Thrace (a region spread over Bulgaria, Greece, and Turkey). The Balkan League mustered 180,000 Bulgarians, 80,000 Serbs, and 50,000 Greeks, all regular army forces. Montenegro contributed its diminutive force of 30,000—all of whom, however, were highly skilled in guerrilla warfare. If all of the combatants mobilized their reserves in addition to regular troops, manpower totals would approximately double. The Ottomans were capable of mobilizing a far larger force from within Turkey, but the Greeks controlled the Aegean, thereby blocking the transport of reinforcements into the Balkan theater.

The Turks had an even bigger problem than the Greek blockade. Wisely, Ottoman high command had employed German military advisers to modernize the empire's armies. Yet although this beneficial influence made itself manifest in organizing, equipping, and training the enlisted ranks, most of the senior officer corps vehemently refused instruction and clung to the old, outmoded ways of doing things. The result was an army as poorly commanded as the nation was governed. And that was poor indeed.

The armies of the Balkan League stormed into Turkey's eastern provinces during October 17–20, 1912. General Radko Dimitriev, whom a British military observer characterized as "a short and sturdily built man with quick brown eyes and a profile reminiscent of Napoleon," led three Bulgarian armies into Thrace, advancing against

Adrianople (modern Edirne, Turkey). At the same time Field Marshal Radomir Putnik, an ill-tempered introvert whose closest companions were the cigars he perpetually chain smoked, led his three Serbian armies into Turkish provinces from the north, even as Constantine, the Greek crown prince, led Greek army forces from the south.

Putnik and Constantine planned to crush Turkish force in a pincers movement converging on Macedonia's Vardar Valley. Constantine also detached a small force to invade Epirus in order to clean out Ottoman units there.

Constantine defeated the Turks at the Battle of Elasson, on October 23, 1912, forcing the Ottomans to fall back on Monastir in southwestern Macedonia. Ideally, the next step would have been pursuit. Constantine should have attacked the retreating force from the rear, but he saw that the Bulgarians had deviated from the agreed-on strategy. They were sending an entire division toward Salonika, obviously intending to snatch up this region. Turning from the Turks—and an opportunity to annihilate a large part of the Ottoman forces in the Balkans—Constantine advanced east to intercept the forces of his erstwhile ally. On his way to Salonika, however, Constantine encountered heavy Turkish resistance at Venije Vardar during November 2–3. A fierce battle ensued, which threatened to tear up the Greek forces. Constantine refused to give in to despair, regained the initiative, and turned the tables on the Turks, defeating them at Venije Vardar on November 5, 1912. While all Turkish forces remaining in the region withdrew—thoroughly demoralized—to Yannina (Ioannina), chief town of Epirus, Constantine resumed his march toward Salonika.

▲

An ill-tempered and solitary figure, Field Marshal Radomir Putnik led Serbia's army in the Balkan Wars, and with Constantine of Greece, he proved to be one of the ablest commanders in the conflict.

THE FOG OF WAR

As the Greeks advanced from the south, the Serbs descended from the north. At Kumanovo in northern Macedonia, Radomir Putnik glimpsed through the thick morning fog on October 23, 1912, what he believed was an Ottoman artillery battery in retreat. Although he was a military science professor, Putnik was abrasive, aggressive, and impulsive. His instinct was always to attack. And so he did now, only to discover that what he thought was a small unit in retreat was actually the right flank of the main Ottoman force. The Turks burst through the fog and pushed Putnik's men back.

But now it was the Turks' turn to be mistaken. This initial victory prompted Nizam Pasha, chief of staff of the Ottoman Army, to leap to the conclusion that the Serbs were vulnerable in this sector. Accordingly, he ordered a reluctant Zekki Pasha, commanding the Ottoman Vardar Army, to attack. Apparently taken aback by the order to strike against a numerically superior force, Zekki Pasha rushed his men into position, failing to prepare for the attack by emplacing critically important artillery. This allowed Putnik, unfazed by his initial defeat, to bring to bear attacks on both the Ottoman right and left.

Through the rest of October 23 and all day on October 24—a day of sunshine in contrast to the fog in which the battle had begun—Putnik pounded the Ottoman Vardar Army into panic and disorderly retreat. Drawing on his scholarly knowledge of battlefield tactics, Putnik deployed his forces in perfect textbook fashion, put-

Crown Prince Constantine of Greece led Greek forces against the Turks in the First Balkan War.

ting them in position for a double envelopment—the battlefield equivalent of a bear hug and a choke hold. With the Ottoman army already in full flight, however, Putnik was unable to envelop the enemy's main body, and he did not press the pursuit of the retreating men. Accordingly, Zekki Pasha fell back on Monastir (modern Bistola, in the far southwestern corner of Macedonia).

DECISION AT MONASTIR

Including the troops who had retreated to the town, Monastir was now defended by 40,000 Turks determined to stand fast. The battle began on November 5 with a bold Serbian thrust against the Turkish left flank. Putnik's objective was to wrest control of the high ground, but his attack bogged down, exposing the Serbs to a powerful counterattack. Turkish commanders rapidly transferred men from the center to reinforce the left for the strike. It was a timely action that enabled the Turkish forces to hold the high ground and to inflict heavy casualties on the Serbs. The price, however, was a center stretched fatally thin. Heedless of the losses on his right, Putnik sent his own center headlong into that of the Turks and readily broke through.

With the Serbs having broken through and the Greeks approaching from the south, the Turkish commanders lost their stomach to continue the fight. Will and resistance crumbled, and the Battle of Monastir turned into a catastrophe for the Turks. Half the Turkish troops at Monastir—20,000 men—were killed, wounded, or captured. The rest ran for their lives to the refuge afforded by the fortress at Yannina. They holed up there as the Greeks laid them under siege for nearly five months until on March 3, 1913, exhausted, hungry, and sick, the Turkish holdouts surrendered Yannina and its fortress.

Four days after the defeat at Monastir, on November 9, 1912, the 20,000-man Turkish garrison holding Salonika likewise surrendered to Greek forces. In this way, Constantine captured and occupied Salonika before the Bulgarians had arrived to claim it for themselves.

BULGARIAN FINALE

While the Greeks, Serbs, and fractional elements of the Bulgarian army fought in Macedonia, the principal Bulgarian forces, the First, Second, and Third Armies, marched into Thrace during October 22–December 3, 1912. They fought sharp battles in the western Turkish towns of Seliolu and Kirk Kilissa—the latter some thirty miles northeast

Saving Turkey

In 1889, cadets at the Ottoman military academy, correctly believing that the government of Sultan Abdul Hamid II was doomed, organized a political movement for progressive reform. The movement quickly spread far beyond the military academy, but its name reflects its student origin: the Young Turks.

The Young Turks were never a single organization; however, in 1906 they established the Committee of Union and Progress (CUP), essentially a political party, which agitated for a constitutional government in which a parliamentary system replaced the monarchy. On this all Young Turks were agreed; however, their ranks were sharply divided into those who supported a strong central government and those who believed the empire should be decentralized, with provinces and other constituents being granted a wide range of autonomy.

Although the Young Turks were a revolutionary political force, they also represented more broadly a progressive philosophy that supported modernization (synonymous with Westernization), religious reform, and an expansion of traditional Turkish intellectual and artistic boundaries. The Young Turks believed the empire needed a new government, but to save Turkey, they also believed that its society and culture had to be reformed from the ground up.

of Adrianople (modern Edirne, Turkey)—during October 22–25, defeating Turkish forces under Abdalla Pasha, who nevertheless was able to regroup and establish a 35-mile (56 km) entrenched front running north to south, from Lüle Burgas to Bunar Hisar, along the main road to Adrianople, near modern Turkey's western border with Greece and Bulgaria.

The Bulgarian Second Army laid siege to Adrianople as the First and Third Armies wheeled eastward to attack the Turks along the Lüle Burgas–Bunar Hisar line. That battle began on October 28 with a Bulgarian attack on the north end of the Turkish line, a blow so poorly coordinated, however, that the Turks easily repulsed it. The Bulgarian commanders recognized that the repulse was due to their botched attack, not the strength of the Turkish line, which was thin at this point. Turning from it as an objective of limited importance, the Bulgarians redeployed, concentrating their forces between the Black Sea and the Sea of Marmora to cut off all access to Constantinople, the Turkish capital. Laying siege to that city, the Bulgarians repeatedly attempted to breach the Chatalja Line defending the capital. In combat during November 17–18, the Bulgarians suffered sharp losses. Stalemated, the two armies ceased fire on December 3.

▶

Bulgarian troops "lay" (position and aim) a field gun during the siege of Adrianople, which was occupied by the Ottoman Turks. The photograph is from August 1913.

PEACE CONFERENCE AT LONDON

With Bulgarian troops just outside the walls of the Ottoman capital, Greek forces occupying Salonika, and Serbs in possession of the key Adriatic port city of Durazzo, the Ottoman government early in December 1912 begged for an armistice and peace talks.

Germany and Austria-Hungary were stunned by the victory of the Balkan League. Germany had been cultivating relations with the officers of the "Young Turk" movement, which was seeking to revitalize the Ottoman Empire, and the Hapsburgs had been looking

▲

The Second Balkan War was little more than a bloody coda to the First. Ottoman forces, which were now allied with former enemies Greece and Serbia against Bulgaria, are shown here repulsing a Bulgarian attack at Shatalaja, outside of Constantinople (Istanbul).

forward to the defeat of the Serbs, who posed the most immediate threat to the Austro-Hungarian Empire. The German government watched and waited, but the day Serbian troops marched into Durazzo, Austria-Hungary's Franz Joseph mobilized nearly a million troops and used them to back his demand that Serbia withdraw from the seaport. It was at this point that Russia flexed its muscle. Czar Nicholas II endorsed the Balkan League and defied Austria-Hungary by pledging to defend all that the League had conquered from Turkey. The message was unmistakable. If Austria-Hungary moved against Serbia, Russia would respond. If Russia responded, a great European war would surely follow.

Recognizing the imminent danger of a general war, England's foreign secretary Sir Edward Grey proposed an immediate conference of Europe's "Great Powers" in London. With Greece and Montenegro ignoring the prevailing armistice and continuing to fight the Turks, the London Peace Conference got under way on December 17, 1912, only to dissolve on January 13, 1913, without having concluded a permanent peace.

THE CURTAIN FALLS ON ACT I . . .

On January 23, 1913, Turkish nationalists of the Young Turk movement overthrew the Ottoman sultan at Constantinople and denounced the armistice he had made. On February 3, the war resumed. It did not go well for the Turks.

On March 3, 1913, the 30,000 defenders of the fortress at Yannina surrendered to Crown Prince Constantine. On March 24, Adrianople fell to a joint Bulgarian-Serb siege, the Bulgarian-Serb forces taking two full days to storm and defeat the city's defenses, absorbing 9,500 killed or wounded in the struggle. Shukri Pasha, commander of the fortress, surrendered 60,000 men to the Bulgarians and Serbs.

In April, Serb troops joined Montenegrin guerrillas in the siege of Scutari (modern Üsküdar), the part of Constantinople on the Anatolian shore of the Bosporus. With victory in their grasp, however, the Serbs and Montenegrins suddenly began fighting among themselves and finally withdrew on April 16. Even so, the Turks had had enough. They surrendered to Montenegro on April 22, returned to the peace table at the London conference, and joined the other combatants in appealing to the Western powers and Russia to impose a settlement.

The Treaty of London, signed on May 30, 1913, ended the First Balkan War. It was a brief document that satisfied no one, but was agreed to out of a common weariness. Its failure to fully spell out just how the territorial gains of the Balkan League would be distributed among the allies all but ensured the outbreak of a new war. Nevertheless, certain outcomes were clear enough: Turkey had lost all of its European possessions, except for the Chatalja and Gallipoli peninsulas. Montenegro, which had started the war and whose guerrillas had fought hard to win Scutari, was forced to yield this prize to Albania, which had been granted independence by the Treaty of London. Crete went to Greece, but Macedonia was to be partitioned among the Balkan states—though the treaty did not say how.

. . . AND RISES ON ACT II

In the Balkan League's dispute over the dissection of Macedonia, Serbia yelped loudest. That landlocked country bidding for access to the sea. As Russia thundered its opposition to Serbia's demands, the Bulgarians squared off against the Greeks and the Serbs. Bulgaria was greedy to gobble up the lion's share of the conquered territory.

On June 29, 1913, scarcely a month after signing the Treaty of London, Bulgaria attacked both Serbia and Greece, grabbed Salonika, and brushed aside the partially demobilized Serbian army. At this, Romania, which had remained neutral in the First Balkan War, leaped into the Second, attacking the Bulgarian army from its unprotected rear and then crossing the Danube and threatening Sofia, the Bulgarian capital.

Strangest of all, Turkey, catastrophically defeated just weeks earlier, joined Greece and Serbia against Bulgaria. Turkey recaptured Adrianople on July 10, 1913. After this city fell, Kaiser Wilhelm II announced Germany's support of Romania's King Carol I, and Nicholas II refused Russian aid to Bulgaria. This prompted the Bulgarian czar, Ferdinand I, to sue for an armistice. Yet again, the Western powers and Russia intervened, drawing up the Treaty of Bucharest. Signed on August 10, 1913, the new agreement obliged Bulgaria to cede Salonika to Greece, northern Dobruja (between the lower Danube and the Black Sea) to Romania, and a good deal of Macedonia to Serbia. Separately, by the Treaty of Constantinople concluded later in the year, Bulgaria also returned to Turkey most of Thrace, including Adrianople. It was a significant recovery, but overall the Ottoman Empire had lost more than 80 percent of its Balkan territory and more than 70 percent of its European population as a result of the two Balkan wars.

THE THIRD ACT

The "Great Powers" of Europe congratulated themselves on having prevented "some damn fool thing in the Balkans" from triggering a continental war. Yet the drama was far from ended.

The Balkan League allies, Bulgaria included, had all gained territory at the expense of the Ottoman Empire. But Bulgaria could not reconcile itself to the defeat it had suffered in the second war, and its restlessness proved contagious among the other Balkan states. Even more destabilizing was the situation of Austria-Hungary. Rid at last of its Ottoman rival, the empire found itself now facing the Balkan allies, whose example inspired the Croats and Slovenes, long under the Hapsburg heel, to dream of joining Serbia in an independent union of South Slavs: "Yugoslavia." Serbia became a hotbed of Balkan nationalism, in which a crop of secret societies flourished like weeds, each bent on creating Yugoslavia or a range of new nations. Serbia's major export quickly became cross-border political agitation, terrorism, and assassination.

The First and Second Balkan Wars, barely remembered now, destroyed the delicate balance of power among the nations of Europe and Asia Minor. Regionally, the wars exacerbated territorial, religious, nationalistic, and tribal instability. That was bad enough. But the more serious trouble was that Europe remained entangled in the network of alliances and enmities first woven by Otto von Bismarck, and the loose ends of that network were firmly tied to the Balkans.

On June 28, 1914, in Sarajevo, capital of the unhappy Austro-Hungarian province of Bosnia-Herzegovina, a Bosnian youth, Gavrilo Princip by name, shot and killed the visiting heir apparent to the Austrian throne, together with his wife. The murder weapon, a Browning revolver, had been put into his hand by the leader of a Serbian secret society. Accordingly, Austria-Hungary declared war on Serbia, and because of the complex alliances among Serbia, Russia, and the powers of Central and Western Europe, the assassination of Archduke Franz Ferdinand and the Grand Duchess Sophie drew Europe, its worldwide colonies, and eventually even the United States into the first world war of the twentieth century. That war, horrific as it was, left much unresolved and virtually ensured a second world war, far more destructive than the first. Long after that war had ended at mid-century with the detonation of two atomic bombs in faraway Japan, the Balkans remained a political and diplomatic "black hole," into which most of the powers of Europe and the United States were destructively drawn as the twentieth century ended.

TWENTIETH-CENTURY JIHAD:
THE WAR FOR AFGHAN INDEPENDENCE

1919

A monthlong "holy war" on the periphery of the British Empire signaled the end of colonial

empires and heralded a new mode of military-political-cultural combat called "asymmetric warfare"

The British developed the Handley Page V/1500 toward the close of World War I for a single purpose: to fly from East Anglia and drop bombs on Berlin by night. The Wright brothers had made their first flight, about three yards (2.7 m) in altitude, twelve seconds in duration, covering 120 feet (37 m) at 6.8 miles (11 km) per hour, just fourteen years earlier; so building a four-engine aircraft capable of flying 600 miles (966 km) with 7,500 pounds (3.4 metric tons) of bombs and then returning those same 600 (966 km) miles was a tall order.

By the time the airplane was ready to fly in 1918, World War I was almost over, and the V/1500 never bombed Berlin. But the Royal Air Force found a mission for its new bomber nevertheless. On May 24, 1919, Captain Robert "Jock" Halley lifted off from the hard-packed dirt of a rudimentary runway at Risalpur in the North West Frontier of British India (today Pakistan), flew for three hours at just under 70 miles (112 km) per hour to Kabul, capital of Afghanistan, and dropped four 112-pound (51 kg) bombs from wing-mounted racks and sixteen 20-pound (9 kg) bombs directly from the hands of Halley's "observer," Lieutenant E. Villiers. Four bombs hit the royal palace, sending the ladies of King Amanullah's harem screaming into the street, a scandal that created a greater sensation than the exploding bombs themselves. In any case, this was Britain's first use of "strategic bombing"—an air raid against a civilian target—and it prompted Amanullah to sue for peace, bringing an end to the war for Afghan independence in less than two weeks.

THE LONG HISTORY OF A VERY SHORT WAR

Although the fighting had spanned but a single month, for the Anglo-Indian troops in the field the end of what their government officially called the Third Afghan War couldn't have come soon enough.

In May, the weather prevailing in the Khyber Pass, which links Afghanistan to what is today Pakistan, is as hospitable as it ever gets, but the land took everything out of a person nevertheless. All was uphill, it seemed to the troops, in a landscape of rocks and rock walls forming narrow natural alleyways almost impossible to pull a supply train through and apparently designed—by Allah?—expressly for hiding a deadly ambush. To die here was one thing, but to fall wounded could be far worse. The Afghans, especially the fear-

A British bomber attacks the mountain fortress of the Afghani emir. Britain also used bombers to attack the Afghan capital city of Kabul—the first time that nation purposely conducted an air raid against a civilian target.

Rain of Terror

A number of historians have erroneously identified the British raid on Kabul in 1919 as the first instance of strategic bombing in the history of aerial warfare. While it is true that many World War I (1914–1918) military commanders and civilian politicians deemed the bombing of civilian targets immoral, the Germans used zeppelins (dirigibles) to drop bombs on cities for the purpose of demoralizing the enemy's civilian population by creating panic and demonstrating that a government was powerless to protect the citizens it governed.

The British and the other Allied powers did not purposely bomb civilian populations, but they did target war production plants, which were often in cities, and therefore civilian casualties were inevitable. On both sides, however, the vast majority of bombing missions in World War I were directed against enemy combatants, including personnel, vehicles, buildings, and encampments.

Throughout the war, all types of aircraft were used to drop bombs, but even before the war was under way, aircraft designers had been creating the first planes expressly built as bombers. On August 14, 1914—about two weeks after World War I began—a French Voisin, built on a sturdy steel frame (the prevailing standard was wood) and equipped with the most powerful aircraft engine available at the time, bombed the German zeppelin hangers at Metz-Frascaty. This was not only the first bombing mission of the war, it was the first bombing mission carried out by a purpose-built bomber.

The British soon developed their own bombers (including the Handley Page V/1500 that raided Kabul) as did the Italians. Most surprisingly, at least to the Western Allies, was the remarkable earlier heavy bombers developed by the Imperial Russian Air Service. Igor I. Sikorsky—who would much later become far more famous for his pioneering work in the United States on the helicopter—designed and built the *Ilya Mourometz*, the world's first four-engine airplane, which had its maiden flight before the outbreak of war, on May 13, 1913. The most advanced version of this early air giant was flown by a crew of four to eight, who were provided with sleeping quarters in the fuselage—though maximum endurance was five hours with its normal load and ten hours carrying extra fuel. The aircraft was more than 57 feet (17 m) long and had nearly a 100-foot (30 m) wingspan (top wing). Empty, the Ilya Mourometz weighed in at 6,930 pounds (3,143 kg); loaded with 1,100 pounds (499 kg) of bombs and fully crewed and fueled, it weighed more than 10,000 pounds (4,536 kg). Top speed was 85 miles (137 km) per hour and its service ceiling was 9,000 feet (2,743 m).

Although Germany continued to rely heavily on zeppelins for long-distance bombing missions, its Gotha G.V., developed in 1916, was the most infamous of World War I bombers. Driven by a pair of powerful Mercedes engines and with a wingspan of nearly 80 feet (24 m) (top wing), the Gotha could not only carry more than 1,000 pounds (454 kg) of bombs, it was also uniquely equipped with a "firing tunnel," essentially a hole through the bottom of the fuselage through which a gunner could shoot at the enemy below. It was Gotha fleets that carried out the deadliest civilian air raids of the war, beginning on May 23, 1917, when twenty-one of the aircraft bombed the English coastal town of Folkestone, killing 95.

▶

The storied Khyber Pass, as it appeared in 1919. Kipling called it a "sword cut through the mountains," and Lieutenant George Molesworth of the 2nd Somerset Light Infantry declared that its "Every stone . . . has been soaked in blood."

some *lashkars* (paramilitary Pashtun tribesmen), would slowly tear a wounded man apart on stony ground that bit into flesh like diamonds.

The month of war that spring cost His Britannic Majesty 236 killed, 615 wounded, and 500 or more dead from the cholera endemic to the region. Driven by a hunger for independence and a call to jihad (holy war), these Afghanis had a passion for the fight. But their weapons were antiquated, their commanders often inept, and they didn't have airplanes.

From the point of view of the British or Indian soldier, the reason for the fighting was clear and simple enough. On May 3, 1919, some 10,000 Afghan regular-army troops crossed the Afghan-Indian border via the Khyber Pass and occupied the Indian village of Bagh, water source for the key Khyber Pass trading town and military outpost of Landi Kotal. The Indian colonial government responded three days later with a declaration of war, and the 2nd Somerset Light Infantry, which had seen heavy fighting on the Western Front in World War I as well as in the Mesopotamian theater and Palestine, rattled through the Khyber Pass in a sixty-seven-truck convoy. It was a bone-shattering journey—the Somerset men jostling on hard wooden benches over wheels and axles mounted on primitive spring suspensions—through spectacular country, which no one got to see because the canvas canopies over the wagon box of each truck had been pulled down and buttoned up tight to keep the presence of the troops from tribal eyes.

But the roots of this war ran much deeper than a territorial violation at the Khyber Pass. The rugged country of southern Afghanistan is defined by a mountain range called the Hindu Kush. Officially translated as "Hindu Throne," but more commonly interpreted as "Killer of Hindus," especially by those who struggled to cross the range, the Hindu Kush region had been settled, albeit sparsely, since prehistoric times. It first entered history as Persian property in the age of Darius I (sixth century BCE) and repeatedly changed hands, passing through a succession of ruling dynasties before the Muslim conquest of Afghanistan beginning in the seventh century. Both Genghis Khan (about 1200) and Timur (some 150 years later) possessed the region for a time, and Timur's descendant Babur made it the epicenter of his mighty sixteenth-century Mughal Empire. Nadir Shah of Persia pushed his rule into the northern fringes of the Hindu Kush in the early eighteenth century, and after his death, one of his military commanders, Ahmad Shah Durrani, an Abdali Pashtun tribal leader, united Afghanistan as an independent empire in 1747.

Tribe of Honor

The largest population group in Afghanistan and the former North West Frontier of India (today Pakistan) are the Pashtuns (sometimes called Pathans), an ethnic grouping of at least forty-two million people, divided into perhaps sixty major Pashtun tribes, encompassing in turn some 400 clans.

Historically, the Pashtuns have been bound by language (although some dialects of Pashto are mutually unintelligible), by their Sunni Islam religion, and by a basic honor code that predates Islam and is called Pashtunwali. Key tenets of the code include hospitality and aid to those who come in search of help and Badal, a code of justice based on the principle of vengeance. The saying "Revenge is a dish best served cold," which entered U.S. popular culture via 1982's *Star Trek II: The Wrath of Khan*, is of Pashtun origin and a cornerstone of Badal.

Despite their historical, linguistic, ethnic, religious, and culture common heritage, the various Pashtun tribes proved resistant to political unity until Ahmad Shah Durrani founded the Durrani Dynasty in the mid eighteenth century.

These Mahsud warriors—the Mahsud are a subtribe of the Pashtun—are natives of Warziristan, in the North West Frontier. The photograph is from 1919.

The Durrani dynasty ended in 1818, leaving Afghanistan in political limbo until Dost Muhammed Khan became emir in 1826. And it was only then, practically for the first time, that Europe took notice of Afghanistan.

THE MOST DANGEROUS GAME

Arthur Conolly was a man of many guises. A noted writer-explorer, he was also a captain of the Anglo-Indian 6th Bengal Light Cavalry. But his true masters were the directors of the British East India Company, whom he served as an intrepid spy. For Conolly, international espionage was serious business, but that didn't mean one couldn't keep a sense of humor about it all. The swarthy Englishman roamed incognito throughout Afghanistan and India as Khan Ali, a Persian play on his distinctly Western surname.

In 1829, he wrote a letter to a friend, Sir Henry Rawlinson, another man of many vocations—soldier, diplomat, and student of ancient Persian texts—in which he coined

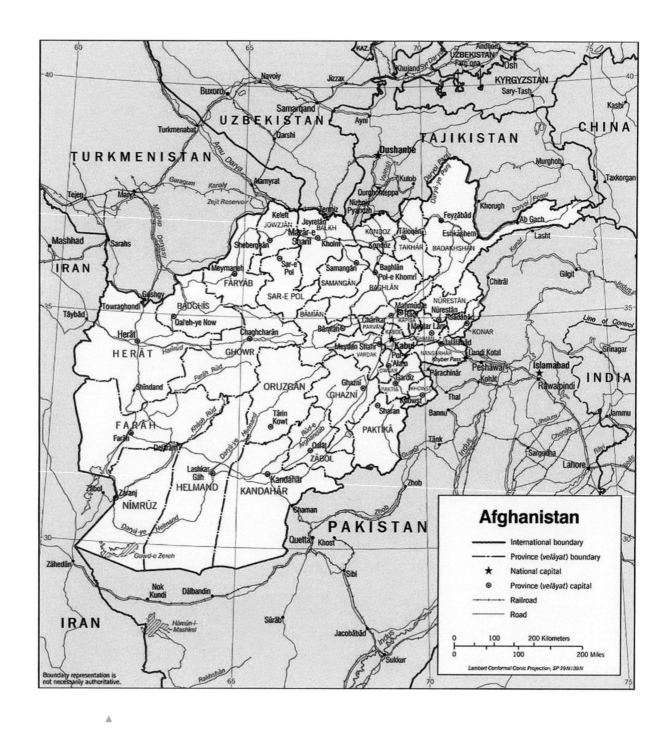

This is Afghanistan and the surrounding countries. In 1919, the country now known as Pakistan was the North West Frontier of British India. The Khyber Pass lies just to the southwest of the Indian (now Pakistani) town of Landi Kotal.

the phrase "Great Game" to describe the diplomatic contest that had developed between the British and Russian empires for political control over Central Asia.

The Great Game ended for Conolly in June of 1842, when the emir of Bukhara executed him as the British spy he undeniably was. The phrase lived on, however, as a historical label for the period roughly spanning 1813–1907, when Afghanistan became the prize in the Anglo-Russian struggle for dominance in Central Asia.

Treated as pawn in the Anglo-Russian Great Game, Dost Muhammed Khan, emir of Afghanistan, oscillated between loyalty to one empire and then another. In this uncertainty, the British had more to lose than the Russians. Afghanistan was the northwestern entrance to British India, and the imperial government was not about to allow its door to remain invitingly ajar. At first, the British played by the rules of the Great Game, maneuvering and manipulating instead of fighting. The crown's government tried to provoke the ouster of Dost Muhammed and his replacement by the former emir, who was reliably subordinate to Britain. But the game went too far, and the First Afghan War (1838–1842) broke out between Britain and Afghanistan. The immediate result was what the British wanted: the overthrow of Dost Muhammed in 1839. A popular revolt centered in the Afghani capital of Kabul, however, restored him to the throne in 1843. Sufficiently chastened, Dost Muhammed did agree to an alliance with the British in 1857.

Anglo-Afghan relations improved, but during the 1870s Russia began acquiring territory along the Amu Darya River on the border between Afghanistan and Uzbekistan and Tajikistan, both of which were under the czar's control. At this time, Dost Muhammed's third son and successor, Sher Ali Khan, abrogated his father's Anglo-Afghan alliance by declaring neutrality in the developing conflict between Britain and Russia. This touched off the Second Afghan War in 1878, and when British troops invaded Kabul, Sher Ali fled, intending to seek asylum with the Russians. He died before this was consummated, however, and his successor, Yakub Khan, immediately bowed to Britain, ceding the Khyber Pass (and other areas), thereby assuring the British control over India's northwestern portal.

Unfortunately for Yakub Khan, the assassination of a British diplomat prompted a military occupation of Kabul and despite his cooperation with the British, his ouster. Yakub Khan was replaced in 1880 by another compliant emir, Abd ar-Rahman Khan, whose reign, from 1880 to 1901, brought to the region a significant measure of stability. Afghanistan's borders were defined by international agreements between Britain

and Afghanistan as well as with Russia (1885 and 1895), British India (1893), and under Abd ar-Rahman Khan's son and successor, Habibullah Khan, with Persia as well (1905). In 1907, an Anglo–Russian agreement guaranteed Afghanistan's independence, albeit under British supervision in issues of foreign affairs.

ASSASSIN'S WORK

During World War I, Habibullah was pressured by both the British, to join the Allied cause, and by Turkey, which had sided with Germany, to join the Central Powers. Islamic law obligated one Muslim ruler to come to the aid of another, but Habibullah was unwilling to alienate the British. Claiming that the Turks did not practice "pure" Islam, he declared neutrality in the war. It was a highly unpopular stance, and after Turkey joined Germany in defeat in November 1918, anti-British sentiment swelled throughout Afghanistan.

Many Afghans condemned Habibullah for having failed to defend their religion. Moreover, in the revolutionary ferment that followed World War I, popular sentiment for a complete break from British influence mounted to fever pitch. There was a widespread belief that Habibullah had missed an opportunity to emulate the Russians' Bolshevik Revolution by fostering a union with all Central Asian Muslims in a bid for pan-Islamic

▲

The Amritsar Massacre, April 13, 1919, furnished a pretext for the Afghan invasion of British India via the Khyber Pass— the event that triggered the Anglo-Afghan War.

national freedom. On February 20, 1919, Habibullah was assassinated. In the prevailing political and emotional climate, it was perhaps inevitable.

By tradition, Habibullah's eldest son, Nasrulla, should have succeeded his father. But Nasrulla was a weakling, and his brother Amanullah, Habibullah's number three son, boldly proclaimed himself the new emir. To bolster his impertinent bid for power, Amanullah pledged revolutionary democratic reforms for a fully independent Afghanistan. For good measure, he ordered the immediate arrest of Nasrulla on a blatantly fabricated charge of having ordered their father's assassination. At Amanullah's behest, Nasrulla was summarily convicted and sentenced to life imprisonment.

A MASSACRE IN INDIA

Amanullah found himself in a precarious position. His promise of reform stood him in good stead with the country's progressive element, but Nasrulla had had the support of Afghani conservatives, and they were not pleased by his conviction and punishment. How, Amanullah asked himself, could he win over or at least mollify the conservatives?

On April 13, 1919, Amanullah believed he had been given his answer. On that day, in the Indian town of Amritsar, British General Reginald Dyer decided to teach the locals a lesson after an English schoolteacher had been assaulted by an anti-British mob. He led a detachment of troops and two armored cars, each with mounted machine guns, to the Jallianwala Bagh, where hundreds had gathered for an annual Punjabi cultural and religious festival.

The Jallianwala Bagh was a space of some six or seven acres (between 24,300 and 28,300 m²) surrounded by a wall through which there were just five entrances. Four of these were very narrow, accommodating a single-file line, and the fifth, though wider, was blocked by Dyer's troops and armored cars. From this position, Dyer ordered his soldiers to fire directly into the bustling festival grounds. In ten minutes, the machine gunners exhausted 1,650 rounds, following Dyer's directions to focus their fire wherever the crowd was densest and then turn to the four narrow exits, cutting down the throng trying to push its way through them. The official toll was reported as "at least" 379 civilians and approximately 1,200 wounded, but unofficial tallies, including some from stunned British civil servants, put the dead at about 1,000.

Seizing the "Amritsar Massacre" as his pretext for acting against colonial rule in Asia, Amanullah invaded British India via the Khyber Pass. He proclaimed a jihad and a war for absolute and final independence.

SQUARING OFF

On paper, Amanullah had a formidable regular army at his disposal, 50,000 troops to oppose the thinly spread Anglo-Indian North West Frontier Force. What is more, Amanullah's plan was to use his regular army as the nucleus around which a larger band of lashkars (Pashtun tribal fighters) would coalesce to create a total invasion force of about 120,000.

The reality in the field was far different from that on paper. The soldiers of the Afghan regular army were poorly trained and ill-equipped. Even worse, they were led by officers who had obtained their commissions not through military aptitude and experience, but largely through family and political connections. According to British assessments, the Afghan cavalry consisted of nothing more than ordinary infantry troops riding rather poor specimens of horseflesh. As for the infantry, it was mostly equipped with a hodge-podge of obsolescent hand-me-down rifles, few of which were equipped with bayonets. Artillery, horse-drawn rather than mechanized, was a mix of a handful of modern pieces plus cannons from the middle of the previous century. The army's machine guns were outmoded, barely a step above the Gatling guns introduced in the U.S. Civil War.

And there was worse. Ammunition was in critically short supply. There were no modern high explosives for the artillery, just old-fashioned (and quite feeble) black powder. Logistics was entirely improvised. Neither motorized transport vehicles nor any viable plans for transport and supply had been readied.

Yet it was folly to underestimate the Afghan fighting force. In contrast to the regular troops, many of the lashkars were not only equipped with relatively modern arms, but were superb fighters for whom combat was a cultural imperative.

On paper, the Anglo-Indian forces also looked impressive. After all, there were more than a quarter million troops in India. The reality of the field, however, was that only a fraction of this number, significantly fewer than the combined total of Afghan forces, was immediately available in the North West Frontier. British artillery overmatched that of the emir, to be sure, and British machine guns—.303 Maxims—while hardly state of the art in 1919, were far more modern and deadly than the badly outdated weapons in Afghan hands.

Because of the demands of the world war that had just ended, the best troops had been sent far away to the hottest war zones, leaving in India soldiers of a lesser quality. Many were "Territorials," a kind of home-guard reserve, typically overage and under-trained. Those Anglo-Indian troops who had fought in the Great War possessed the benefit of combat experience, but they also tended to be war weary, if not somewhat shell shocked or at least gun shy.

The Anglo-Indian forces did have a vast advantage in command and control, which was facilitated by motor transport and radios; they also possessed a number of armored cars and aircraft—weapons that put the British unmistakably in the twentieth century. Still, by and large, the troops immediately available were not well prepared for the rigors of combat in the North West Frontier.

A HARD FIGHT

The men of the 2nd Somerset Light Infantry attacked Afghan-held Bagh on May 9, but when they could not efficiently mass their forces to decisively overrun the town, the frustrated British commander called in three BE2c single-engine bombers to attack a nearby concentration of Pashtuns, hoping to shake the resolve of Bagh's defenders.

Developed early in World War I, the BE2c was slow—top speed, with an anemic ninety-horsepower engine, was seventy-two miles (116 km) per hour—and could carry only as many bombs as the observer, seated awkwardly in front of the pilot, could drop by hand—leaning precariously over the lip of his cockpit, to ensure that the bombs cleared the lower wing. Against tribal forces, however, it was effective enough, creating sufficient panic to make good combat organization impossible.

While the 2nd Somerset slugged it out at Bagh, the Afghans turned against nearby Landi Kotal. Afghan commanders threw everything available into the attack, including twenty-two outdated machine guns and eighteen artillery pieces, which fired from as a great a distance as their inadequate black powder charges would allow. After a half hour of continuous Afghan fire, the 2nd North Stafford Regiment and two battalions of the 11th Gurkhas charged the Afghan positions with their bayonets, driving them toward the Lower Khyber Pass. Here, however, Afghan mountain artillery opened up with intense fire. Had the nearby lashkar units organized a counterattack, the Anglo-Indian forces

▲

Amanullah Khan (1892–1960) invaded British India and went on to rule Afghanistan from 1919–1929.

would have been badly mauled, but the tribal warriors turned instead to looting the battlefield of the guns and equipment the retreating Anglo-Indian troops had shed. The result was that, by May 13, British and Indian soldiers captured western Khyber, which was not defended, and then gave chase, pursuing a mixed force of Afghan regulars and lashkars over the border to Dacca (Dhaka) in Bengal.

The purpose of the pursuit was to demonstrate to would-be tribal fighters in and around Dacca that the British superiority of arms was irresistible. The pursuing forces failed, however, to coordinate with Anglo-Indian troops already encamped in the area. The net result was that the pursuers drove the Afghans into a position from which they could pound the Anglo-Indian encampment with long-range artillery. After shelling the camp, the Afghans neatly converted their retreat into an infantry assault on the battered position. Only by dint of superior firepower were the British and Indians able to repulse the attack, sending the Afghans into retreat once again. The Anglo-Indian troops then counterattacked, forcing the Afghans to withdraw—and to abandon their precious long-range artillery—on May 17.

LAST GASPS

Their success against the Afghans at Landi Khotal and environs notwithstanding, the Khyber Rifles—one of eight paramilitary units that made up the Frontier Corps, whose troops were recruited by the British from tribesmen in the North West Frontier—began to desert, leaving the sole Anglo-Indian line of communication through the Khyber Pass poorly guarded and highly vulnerable.

Despite this, on May 16, British command sent a force of Sikhs to attack a fortified Afghan position the British had dubbed "Stonehenge Ridge." After a preliminary artillery bombardment, the Sikhs advanced for the attack, only to be forced to withdraw when their ammunition ran out. Resupply was slow through the now-inadequately-guarded Khyber Pass, and by the time fresh ammo arrived, the afternoon heat was nearly unbearable. Nevertheless, the Sikhs resumed their assault, following it up with a renewed artillery bombardment. After reaching the top of Stonehenge Ridge, they discovered that the Afghans had fled—leaving behind more equipment and artillery they could never replace.

Despite Stonehenge Ridge and other reversals, Afghan regulars and lashkars continued to make destructive hit-and-run raids in the eastern Khyber area, forcing the

British and Indians to abandon outposts throughout the Kurram Valley. Worse, British commanders found it nearly impossible to mount counterattacks because of the accelerating pace and volume of desertion, including the defection of two whole native units, the North Waziristan Militia and the South Waziristan Militia. This gave the Anglo-Indians no choice but to withdraw from their outposts in the Waziristan.

At a Waziri outpost called Wana, the local militia did more than simply decamp. The militiamen turned against their British commanders and those troops who remained loyal, surrounding them and holding them under sporadic fire. The trapped men made a desperate attempt to break out and were rescued by the timely arrival of the Zhob Militia, which had remained loyal.

Despite the discouragement spreading through the Anglo-Indian ranks, it was becoming clear the Afghan forces were starting to melt away. Even when they had the upper hand, the Afghanis were insufficiently supplied and too poorly commanded to sustain themselves for long in the field. When British high command called in the Handley-Page bombers against Kabul on May 24, the Afghan will to continue the fight was already waning. The bomb blasts pushed the emir past the tipping point.

On May 27, Afghan regulars mounted a half-hearted attack on a fort at Thal (today in Pakistan), but when the attacker's supporting artillery failed to arrive, they withdrew. On their way out, they noted that the local constabulary—native officials in British service charged with patrolling the region—had fled. Accordingly, the Afghans paused in their retreat to climb an abandoned constabulary observation tower just 500 yards (457 m) from the fort at Thal and use it as a sniper post, taking rifle shots at anyone who

"A Sword Cut through the Mountains"

Some anthropologists believe that the Khyber Pass, the rugged passage through the Hindu Kush linking Afghanistan with the North West Frontier (present-day Pakistan), was the prehistoric route by which the Indo-Aryan people came to populate India. Certainly, Persia's Darius I and Greece's Alexander the Great passed through it, and by the sixteenth century it was a major passage for trade and commerce. By 1879, Anglo-Indian work crews had cut a road through the Khyber.

The pass reaches an altitude of 3,510 feet (1,070 m) above sea level and at its narrowest is only 49 feet (15 m) wide, between steep canyon walls. Anglo-Indian armies passed through it during the three Afghan Wars—of 1839–1842, 1878–1880, and 1919—to invade Afghanistan from India. "Every stone in the Khyber has been soaked in blood," wrote Lieutenant George Molesworth of the 2nd Somerset Light Infantry. Earlier, Rudyard Kipling had called it "a sword cut through the mountains."

emerged from the fort's cover. In the meantime, others put to the torch the food dumps from which the fort was supplied, hoping to starve the garrison out.

Fortunately for the Thal garrison, none other than Brigadier-General Reginald Dyer—the officer who had commanded the Amritsar Massacre—was on his way with a relief force. After attacking Darsaman, nine miles (14 km) from Thal, at daybreak on June 1, he was approached by an Afghan officer bearing a white flag. Emir Amanullah, the officer explained, had ordered an end to the war.

Dyer did not trust "natives."

"My guns will give an immediate reply," he informed the envoy, "but your letter will be forwarded to the Divisional Commander." In other words, he intended to continue fighting until higher headquarters told him what to do.

Under the continued attack, the Afghans withdrew. Still unsatisfied, Dyer ordered his lancers (elite cavalry troops), who were backed up by armored cars, to harass the retreating troops. At the same time, bomber aircraft were called in to attack and disperse any lingering lashkars, lest they take up an attack on their own.

By the end of the day, the Third Afghan War was effectively over. Although Dyer had yet to receive his instructions from Divisional Command about whether to accept the ceasefire, there was no one left to fight. On June 3, British troops marched into a principal Afghan camp at Yusef Khel. It was deserted.

TACTICAL VICTORY, STRATEGIC DEFEAT

The two sides signed a formal armistice on June 3, followed by the Treaty of Rawalpindi on August 8. The British had achieved a tactical victory in forcing the Afghanis to withdraw from India, but this did not mean that Amanullah had been defeated. The treaty granted Afghanistan self-determination in foreign affairs—in effect, complete independence from Britain—in return for a pledge that Afghanistan would never again trouble the Khyber region. The British had come to believe that by granting the complete independence Amanullah had sought, Afghanistan would certainly not turn to Russia and allow itself to be occupied or otherwise controlled by that government.

As it turned out, this was more a fond hope than a reasonable belief. Vladimir Lenin, now at the head of a precarious Soviet government, courted Amanullah, and in May 1921, Afghanistan and the Soviet Union concluded a Treaty of Friendship. The British were chagrined, fearful that the Soviets would sooner or later attack India via Afghanistan and perhaps sow a communist revolution in "the Jewel in the Crown," as the British called India.

Although the Soviets supplied Afghanistan with money, technology, modern military equipment—including advanced aircraft—and technical and military advisers, Amanullah played them as deftly as he had the British, always suspicious of them, always keeping them at arm's length. Thus Afghanistan remained delicately perched between the capitalist British Indian Empire on the one hand and the communist Soviet Empire on the other.

Amanullah had exploited jihad as a means of consolidating his own power internally while wresting full sovereignty from Britain. For him, the political and diplomatic motives for war far outweighed the motive of jihad; therefore, having achieved his political and diplomatic ends, Amanullah was fully prepared to make peace. But, in a pattern that would come to characterize twentieth-century warfare at the fringes of Europe's colonies, the officially proclaimed peace proved nominal at best. Pashtun Lashkars continued to fight along the border until a formal reaffirmation of the Treaty of Rawalpindi, on November 22, 1921, accompanied by massive British subsidies, prompted Amanullah's government to end what was for the tribesmen a continuation of jihad.

The 1919 war was among several that heralded the dissolution of Europe's colonial empires and set up an enduring connection between political independence and religious war, as well as an equally enduring disconnect between warfare authorized by governments and warfare conducted by religiously motivated guerrilla movements. These latter "non-state" wars would increasingly dominate international relations in the post-colonial era. "Asymmetric warfare" —fighting between small non-state or stateless groups, often religious zealots, and such major powers as the United States—intensified in scope and volume as the twentieth century gave way to the twenty-first, becoming the dominant mode of modern warfare.

MIDDLE EAST MANDATE:
THE ARAB INSURRECTION IN IRAQ

1920—1922

The forced nationhood of Iraq, engineered by Britain in the wake of World War I,

created an environment that made possible the rise of ruthless dictator Saddam Hussein,

who in turn provided an irresistible target for a twenty-first-century incarnation of Western

ideological intervention under George W. Bush, forty-third president of the United States

War is such a serious, painful, and costly endeavor that we naturally think of it as the result of political, cultural, social, economic, and religious forces, collectively anonymous, which somehow make war inevitable. And this view is true, as far as it goes. But it does not go far enough. For whatever else goes into creating war, each particular war begins with decisions, which, of course, are made, not by anonymous historical forces, but by people—often by very few people, sometimes just a single person.

On March 16, 2003, President George W. Bush announced his decision to invade Iraq, issuing a televised ultimatum to Saddam Hussein, demanding that he and his inner circle (including his sons, Uday and Qusay) permanently leave the country within forty-eight hours.

The decision began a war that as of early 2009 (when these words are being written), has cost more than 100,000 Iraqi lives, nearly 4,300 U.S. lives, and the United States taxpayers some $600 billion—with economists projecting a total cost of $3–5 trillion, including military spending, broader economic costs, and the liability for many decades of benefits and medical care for combat veterans. Much harder to calculate is the war's cost in U.S. prestige, image, and influence, as well as the damage done to the always precarious stability of the Middle East. As of this writing, most Americans—indeed, most of the world—believed that President Bush's decision to make war was a bad one.

Seen in the context of the history that preceded it, the decision looks, if anything, even worse. For George W. Bush was not the first Westerner peering in from the outside who decided that he knew what was best for the Middle East. The decision of 2003 was not a new misjudgment, but a recapitulation of those of 1920–1922.

LAWRENCE OF ARABIA

Gorphwysfa, the country estate in Caernarfonshire (now Gwynedd), North Wales, where Thomas Edward Lawrence was born in 1888, was as far removed from the deserts of Mesopotamia as any place on earth could be. The young man was one of five illegitimate sons produced by a union between Sir Thomas Robert Tighe Chapman and Sarah Junner (who called herself "Miss Lawrence"), a governess chapman employed to look after his daughters. Thomas Edward grew up in Oxford, to which Chapman and "Miss Lawrence" had moved, living together under her preferred name. Young T. E. Lawrence was a solitary boy,

◄

T. E. Lawrence, Lawrence of Arabia, appears in this photograph as a dead ringer for matinee idol Rudolph Valentino in *The Sheik*.

among whose earliest passions was bicycling to country churches to make rubbings of the medieval brass monuments they contained.

Lawrence later claimed that he ran away from home in 1905 and joined the army, but no one has ever been able to corroborate this. What is indisputable is that he attended Jesus College, Oxford, from 1907 to 1910, and graduated with top honors, having written a thesis on the influence of the Crusades on European military architecture. It was based on a remarkable three-month, 1,000-mile (1609 km) solitary walking tour of Crusader castles in Syria. He briefly immersed himself in esoteric postgraduate work on medieval pottery before returning to the Middle East at the end of 1910 to become, he announced, a professional archaeologist.

To all appearances, T. E. Lawrence was just that. He learned Arabic, and he participated in archaeological digs near the Turkish border under the aegis of the British Museum. But in a world still dominated by the "Great Game"—the name British diplomats applied to the intrigue by which the great powers sought to manipulate one another to attain even greater power—nothing was exactly as it appeared. The young archaeologist took scholarly notes on the antiquities of Mesopotamia even as, acting on his own initiative, he took military notes on the Baghdad Railway, which ran near the digs. These he communicated to British authorities in Cairo, who passed them on to military intelligence,

By 1914—the eve of World War I—Lawrence had been formally recruited by the British military as a spy in the guise of an archaeologist. He thoroughly mapped the territory that soldiers of the Ottoman Empire—allied with Germany—would have to cross to attack British-held Egypt.

After the outbreak of the war, Lawrence served as an intelligence officer stationed in Cairo until the Arab Bureau of the British Foreign Office sent him on a covert mission to recruit and organize Arab "irregulars" (tribal warriors) in a guerrilla war against the German-allied Ottoman authorities who governed Mesopotamia—modern Iraq. Many of the Arabs, especially followers of Emir Faisal, son of Sherif Hussein of Mecca, were budding nationalists, eager to free themselves of the Ottoman yoke. The British objective was to exploit this hunger for independence by harassing the Ottomans—sabotaging the Baghdad Railway, raiding military outposts—to tie down large

▶

Far from the Western Front, the British army enters Baghdad during World War I.

numbers of Ottoman troops who would otherwise be employed against British forces or sent to invade Egypt.

Lawrence carried out his assignment brilliantly. He grasped precisely what generations of British colonial officials had refused to accept: that it was far more effective to approach indigenous peoples on their terms rather than to impose British terms on them. Accordingly, Lawrence shed his British army uniform and adopted Arab dress. He spoke, ate, and rode—both camels and ponies—in the manner of an Arab. His superiors back at headquarters believed it was all an elaborate act. But, in fact, T. E. Lawrence was in the process of becoming the man behind the name by which history would come to know him, Lawrence of Arabia. This Welsh-born, Oxford-educated bastard, a solitary

Lawrence of Arabia: Pop Culture Icon

By any measure, T. E. Lawrence was an extraordinary figure, an archaeologist-spy, guerrilla leader, and would-be nation founder. He was Indiana Jones long before filmmaker George Lucas, who created that archaeologist-adventurer, was born.

Although Lawrence was a solitary figure—never married, without close friends, apparently drawn to masochistic homosexuality—who protested his disdain for publicity, he collaborated with the popular U.S. writer, journalist, war correspondent, filmmaker, and broadcaster Lowell Thomas on the documentary film *With Allenby in Palestine and Lawrence in Arabia*, which Thomas took on tour in 1920, exhibiting it in the United States and England in movie houses that had been decorated with incense braziers and that featured performances by exotically (and minimally) attired dancing girls. Lawrence later called Thomas a "vulgar man," but as Thomas remarked, Lawrence of Arabia "had a genius for backing into the limelight."

In 1924, Thomas wrote *With Lawrence in Arabia*, a bestseller that, in its time, eclipsed Lawrence's own autobiography, the epic literary masterpiece titled *The Seven Pillars of Wisdom*, privately published in 1922.

Morally opposed to profiting financially from his adventures in the Middle East, Lawrence refused to take money from the subsequent 1926 public edition of *Seven Pillars* or from its abridgment, published the same year, *Revolt in the Desert*. At the height of his fame in 1922, Lawrence enlisted in the Royal Air Force (RAF) under the name John Hume Ross. Exposed in 1923, he transferred, as T. E. Shaw, to the Royal Tank Corps, then returned to the RAF in 1925, serving until 1935.

At the time of his death the following year as a result of a motorcycle accident, the forty-six-year-old Lawrence was far from being a wealthy man. As for Lowell Thomas, some 4 million people had seen his *With Allenby in Palestine and Lawrence in Arabia*, which earned him personally $1.5 million and launched a long and fabulously successful movie-making, writing, and broadcasting career. In 1962, the great British filmmaker David Lean completed *Lawrence of Arabia*, the sweeping epic based on Lawrence's life, which elevated its subject to an enduring status as a pop culture icon and catapulted its leading man, a virtual unknown named Peter O'Toole, into superstardom.

soul who struggled to find an identity for himself, had finally found fulfillment emulating Arab warrior leaders for the purpose of leading an Arab revolt. And when his mission for British intelligence had been accomplished and was at an end, he discovered that he could not simply quit and once again don the khaki of the regular British army.

Late in 1918, as World War I was drawing to a close, Lawrence participated in the capture of Damascus, Syria (at the time part of the Ottoman Empire), which he envisioned not as a British prize, but the capital of something unique in the world, an independent Arab state. He helped to engineer in Damascus the creation of a provisional Arab government under Faisal and then accompanied Faisal to the Paris Peace Conference in 1919, with the objective of ensuring that Arab independence would be part of the postwar world. Simultaneously, Lawrence befriended the celebrated U.S. travel writer and producer of travel films, Lowell Thomas, who featured him and his role in promoting Arab nationalism in a spectacularly popular documentary movie. It made "Lawrence of Arabia" famous, prompting no less a figure than Winston Churchill, at the time Britain's secretary of state for the colonies, to name him in 1921 an advisor to the Colonial Office.

DAYS OF MANDATE

By 1921, however, Iraq was already in armed revolt against the British. Neither Lawrence nor Faisal ever got much of a hearing at the Paris Peace Conference in 1919, and in the end the 1920 Treaty of Sèvres, one of several treaties drawn up to divide the world after the Great War, dissected the defeated Ottoman Empire, assigning to the care of Britain the provinces of Mosul, Baghdad, and Basra as a single political entity called the British Mandate of Mesopotamia. With this mandate, the Treaty of Sèvres, through the Western-dominated League of Nations (created by the Treaty of Versailles immediately after World War I), sought to conjure up a nation out of very diverse peoples. It would become Iraq.

Also in 1920, as a result of a conference held at San Remo, Italy, France was awarded the mandates of Lebanon and Syria, and Faisal ibn Husayn, who had been proclaimed king of Syria by a Syrian national congress a month earlier, was unceremoniously ejected in July by the French.

By the time the British organized a civil government for Iraq, under High Commissioner Sir Percy Cox, Iraq, Lebanon, and Syria were enflamed. Three major anti-colonial

secret societies, two created while World War I was winding down and one after it had ended, were already in place in Iraq when the mandate was proclaimed: The League of the Islamic Awakening, the Muslim National League, and the Guardians of Independence—the last, created in Baghdad in February 1919, was more strongly nationalistic than religious. It united members of two rival Islamic sects, Shia merchants and Sunni teachers and civil servants, with Iraqi military officers.

Almost immediately after the establishment of the mandate, a British officer was assassinated in Najaf, south of Baghdad, unleashing a string of British reprisals, which did nothing to endear the new administrators to the Iraqis. Not only did British administrators have to cope with violence directed against their rule, they also struggled to suppress violence among the diverse provinces that had been arbitrarily lumped into the mandate territory. And complicating the situation further, Assyrian refugees from Turkish oppression in the region began flooding through Kurdistan on Iraq's northern frontier in quest of asylum.

The grand *mujtahid* (religious ruler) of Karbala (a "holy city" in central Iraq), the Imam Shirazi, and his son, Mirza Muhammad Riza, recruited a well-organized

▲

With help from Lawrence of Arabia, Emir Faisal (1883–1933) became king of Syria (1920) and then the first king of Iraq (1921–1933).

insurgency against the British. Exerting the full weight of his religious authority, he issued a *fatwa* (religious ruling) calling for a *jihad* (holy war) against the British on the grounds that Islamic law forbade Muslims from allowing themselves to be governed by infidels. With this fatwa, the Arab revolt became a potent blend of nationalist revolution and religious war.

WEAPONS OF MASS DESTRUCTION?

As summer gave way to fall in 1920, the Iraqi revolt spread from Baghdad into the middle and lower Euphrates River valley. The southern tribes, all of which had long craved autonomy, rose up against the British. Only their unwillingness to unite under a single leader to coordinate their actions prevented the revolt from overwhelming the thinly spread British colonial forces. Perceiving the situation south of Baghdad as one of general anarchy, Churchill contemplated using RAF bombers to drop chemical

Spoils of War

The Treaty of Versailles, which officially ended World War I, created the League of Nations as a forum in which the states of the world could adjudicate their grievances without resorting to war. Article 22 of the "Covenant" that established the League provided for the orderly transfer of certain territories from the control of one country to another. These transfers were referred to as "mandates" and were intended to put former colonial possessions of the defeated Central Powers (mainly Germany, Austria-Hungary, and Ottoman Turkey) under the trusteeship of various victorious countries. There were three classes of mandates.

"Class A" mandates encompassed territories that had been controlled by the Ottoman Empire and that the European powers judged to "have reached a stage of development where their existence as independent nations can be provisionally recognized." Iraq, Palestine (today Israel), and Transjordan (today Jordan) were awarded to Britain as Class A mandates. Syria and Lebanon were awarded to France.

"Class B" mandates had all been German territories in the Sub-Saharan West and Central Africa. The European leaders determined that these territories required more control by the "Mandatory" (the nation awarded the mandate). Ruanda-Urundi (modern Rwanda and Burundi) were awarded to Belgium, and Tanganyika (modern Tanzania) went to Britain. Kamerun was divided into British Cameroons and French Cameroun, and Togoland was split into British Togoland and French Togoland.

"Class C" mandates were deemed to be "best administered under the laws of the Mandatory as integral portions of its territory." These were the spoils of war in the truest sense. They included territories in Southwest Africa and islands in the South Pacific. All had been German possessions.

German New Guinea went to Australia; German Samoa to New Zealand; various South Pacific islands to Japan; and Southwest Africa (today the Republic of Namibia) to South Africa, part of the British commonwealth.

Kaisarieh

Arablar · Kharput · Mürad su or R. · Geyra · Maku

vshehr · Gerun · Jaihun · MAMURES · Palu · Mush · Arjesh · Alchtot

Arjish Dagh · MALATIYEH · Sassoun · Bulis · L. Van · Van

ai · Hajin · Albistan · Adiyaman · A Z I T · Hazro · Hasuh · Sirt · Kotour · Dilman · Uru

ssar D. · Nigde · Kermes · D. Zeitun · Behesni · R. Tigris · Tulamerk · Urumiyah · Uru

ili · Sis · Shoon · Marash · Samsat · Zeitun · Mardin · Jelo · Dagh

har I. · Marash · Suverek · Nisibin · Zakhu · Soulsh

rsina · Adana · Aintab · Killiz · Urfah · EL JEZIREH OR · Nineveh

Iskenderun · Buyas · Kalat · Birejik · Harran · Senn · Erbil

G. of Iskenderun · Alexandretta · en Nejm · Mosnl · El Hadhr

HALEB · Rakka · Mesopotamia · Kerkou

Antakia · Kalat · Euphrates · El Hadhr · Suleir

(Antioch) · HALEB · Andrene · Khabour · Sab Asphal · Kerkou

Latakia · (Aleppo) · Deir · Kerkesiyeh

Banias · Hamah · Tayibeh · Werdi · Tekrit · Samara

Tartus · Homs · Syrian · Sakne · Anah · R. Tigris

(Tortosa) · Tadmor · Desert · Dasa · Sarifah · Samara

Tarabulus · Palmyra · Hit · BAGHD

(Tripoli) · Jebeil · Beyrout · Kubessa · Baq

el Kamr · Saida · DAMASCUS · Kalat Ramadi · BAGHL

Sur · M. Hermon · Kerbela · Babylo

Melakh · Hilleh · A

Kalaat Esrak · El Hamed · Meshed Ale · Diw

(Stoney Plain)

Dead Sea · Tafileh · Wady · Owsit Wells

Petra ruins · Sherarat · Magoua Wells · Leynah

Akaba · Maan · Palgrave 1862 · Wady Jowf

Howeitat · Jowf · Nefud or Sand Pass · Desert

Jeb. Tauran · Beni Ateeyah · J. Mukhtab · Tebouk · Jobbah · JEBEL · Shomer

Moilah

SEA

Karabagh
Ahor
Lenkoran
B. or Kizil Agatch
Astara
Hada Sta.
Darwau Tekk
Bam
Daman-i-Kul

Marand
Savalan D.
Yomut Turcomans
Tchikislar
R. Atrek

TABREEZ
Ardibil
Asterabad
ASTERABAD

BIJAN
Mt Sahud
Miana
GHILAN
Enzeli
Sefid Rud
B. BALFRUSH
Ashourada
Kizil Alan
Romiau
Jah

Maragak
Zinjan
Kizil Tzen
Resht
Lahijan
Sluee
Asterabad
Shahrud
Kuh-i

Mahamet Abad
Takhti Belkisse
Sultauid
Monuts of Elbuz
MAZANDERAN
Amol
Aseka
Taberistan
Cheshmeh Ali
Abbasa

kiz
IRAK
Kazbin
Mt Demavend
18,600
Damghan
Khanabad

Rivandere
Kizil Uzen
R. Kiveh
Demavend
Semnan
Salt Plain

ARDILAN
Ava
TEHERAN
AJEMI
Turut
(Kevir)

Senna
Mahran
Sava
Desert or Zarang
Habla
Great Salt Ste
KHO

Hamadan
Karasu
Kum
Sir Adja

Kermanshah
Mt Elwend
11,000
Awah
Nehavend
Sultanabad
Kashan

LURISTAN
Pushti Kuh
Sefid K.
Burujird
Khorremabad
Kuh
K-i Darbish
11,700
Ardisan
Sadaru
Chur
Tel

PAN
Gargish
Khonsar
Anarak
Rasabad
KUH

R. Tigris
Jubeiler
Kerkhah
Dizful
Kuren R.
Nedjerabad
Senda Rud
ISPAHAN
Julfa
Nain
Agda
Risab
Illaha

Susa
Shuster
Kumishch
Ardakan
Kuh-i Marva
11000
Yesd
Bafk

BASRA
Havezza
Ahwaz
KHUZISTAN
K. Alidjuk
14000
Esfandian
Yezdekhast
Anar

Kornah
Jerrahi
Ram Hormuz
Abadeh
Kashkizerd
Kub-i-Bul
Murghab
Bahramab

Dorak
Decair K.
12000
Babahan
Pebor R.
Dabek

BASRA
Mohammerah
Zobeir
Hindyan
Istakhur
Persepolis
Shehri Babek

El-Kurweit
Bubiyan I.
FARISTAN
Shiraz
L. Niris or
Bakhtegan
Ki

in 8
Wafrah
Koweit or Korein
Feleje I.
Karak I.
Kasrun
L. Neniek
Niris
Kotro

jman
Khubba I.
Sabukah
Garrow I.
Bushire
Dekrud
Fasa
Darab
Sashken Mts
Baft

Firusabad
Jarun

weapons, including the poison gas that had been the scourge of the Western Front in World War I.

A year earlier, in May 1919, he had written a memorandum to the War Office. "I do not understand this squeamishness about the use of gas," he declared. "We have definitely adopted the position at the Peace Conference of arguing in favour of the retention of gas as a permanent method of warfare. It is sheer affectation to lacerate a man with the poisonous fragment of a bursting shell and to boggle at making his eyes water by means of lachrymatory [tear] gas. I am strongly in favour of using poisoned gas against uncivilised tribes." This was a reference to the doctrine, popular among colonial powers, that the weapons and tactics "civilized nations" might find unacceptable to use against one another were perfectly acceptable when directed against "uncivilized" peoples. In fairness to Churchill, he wrote that it was "not necessary to use only the most deadly gasses: gasses can be used which cause great inconvenience and would spread a lively terror and yet would leave no serious permanent effects on most of those affected." This form of attenuated terrorism, he believed, would produce the desired "moral effect" yet reduce "loss of life . . . to a minimum."

In the end, the British almost certainly did not use the gas (although some historians have advanced dubious claims that they did), but in Kurdistan, which extended into northern Iraq, where the revolt proved the most violent and persistent, British aircraft did resort to dropping white phosphorus bombs against Kurdish villagers. In World War I, this substance had been used in artillery shells and aerial bombs mainly to create smokescreens to mask troop movements; however, when employed in antipersonnel weapons, white phosphorus burns intensely, setting fire to anything even remotely combustible, including dwellings, the cloth of clothing, and human flesh.

RE-ENTER LAWRENCE

By the time Churchill turned to Lawrence of Arabia for advice in 1921, the revolt in the Mesopotamian "mandate" was amorphous and general, directed against the British and

◀

This is Mesopotamia at the end of the nineteenth century, before the map of the Middle East was high-handedly redrawn by the post-World War I League of Nation "mandates."

against one tribal or religious group by another. The British statesmen themselves were by no means agreed on what Britain's Iraq policies should be. There was no consensus within the official British circles on what kind of government should be set up. Most officers in the Colonial Office proposed exercising permanent, direct control of Iraqi affairs for the purpose of protecting British interests in the Persian Gulf and in India. Other leaders, mostly outside of the Colonial Office, thought it best to accommodate and conciliate Arab nationalists by means of a system of indirect control in which an indigenous government operated with ostensible autonomy but under some degree of British supervision.

The British public, weary of war in any form and for any purpose, increasingly demanded the wholesale withdrawal from Mesopotamia. Encouraged by Lawrence, the British government in 1921 offered the Iraqi throne to Faisal, who as Iraq's first Hashemite monarch established a quasi-autonomous Arab government under a limited British mandate. Faisal did not jump at the proposition, however, but instead responded that he would accept the throne only if it were offered by the Iraqi people themselves. It was a brilliant reply because it gave Faisal a nonaggressive means of coaxing the British to replace the mandate entirely with a firm treaty of alliance between two sovereign nations. This would still bind Iraq to Britain, but without the charade of a mandate, which made a mockery of Iraqi sovereignty.

Assisted by Lawrence, Churchill presided over a conference in Cairo, which on July 11, 1921, proclaimed Faisal king of Iraq—with the proviso that his government be "constitutional, representative, and democratic." In compliance with Faisal's condition that the offer of the crown be made by the people, Churchill directed High Commissioner Sir Percy Cox to conduct a plebiscite. The people accordingly voiced their approval of Faisal, who was duly crowned on August 23, 1921. On October 2, 1922, the new king gave preliminary approval to a treaty of alliance with Great Britain, which was then submitted to the new Iraqi assembly for ratification.

DIPLOMATIC SLEIGHT OF HAND

For their part, British negotiators were as canny as Faisal had been. In the treaty of 1922, the British pledged to prepare Iraq for membership in the League of Nations—the final mark of sovereignty—"as soon as possible." It was a vague phrase that gave the British an indeterminate amount of time to continue to conduct themselves in Iraq pretty much as they had under the mandate. In fact, all that was different was that the word mandate was no longer used.

Faisal was willing to accept the fiction of sovereignty, but many in the Iraqi Constituent Assembly were not. Here the treaty met with strong opposition, which was overcome only through unremitting British pressure. On June 11, 1924, the Anglo–Iraqi Treaty of Alliance was finally ratified. It still would not go into effect until King Faisal I definitively signed it, and his delay in doing so once again threw the British off-balance as Iraqi nationalists, extremely dissatisfied with the treaty, continued to demand immediate independence with no strings attached. Faisal delayed long enough to fan the flames of popular discontent. He did not want to rule a kingdom whose subjects were permanently willing to serve two masters. At length and at last, he put pen to paper on March 21, 1925.

This done, the independence movement continued to agitate, the prospect of renewed anti-British revolt always simmering. On June 30, 1930, Britain and Iraq signed a new treaty, which stepped back from the full alliance of the 1922 document and instituted instead a vaguely defined "close alliance" based on a promise of conducting "frank talks" on any matters of foreign policy affecting the "common interests" of the two nations. Most important, the new treaty stipulated Iraq's admission to the League of Nations as a fully sovereign state on October 3, 1932.

WESTERN VISIONS, IRAQI REALITIES

This should have been a rare happy ending to what was a long colonial story. But an underlying and very basic problem remained. "Iraq" was an ancient name for an ancient region, but as a nation Iraq was a modern improvisation—and an awkward one at that. Lawrence of Arabia, brilliant, adventurous, and romantic, had found among the Arabs an identity he had never had as a child, as a man, or as an Englishman. Operating among leaders who wanted nothing more than to rid themselves of the Ottomans and the Europeans, Lawrence goaded them into accepting what was, finally, a Western definition of nationhood. He presented this as if it were the only alternative to continued colonial domination. Perhaps it was. But what the Arabs desired was the tribal independence they had long enjoyed. Independence on Western terms was no real independence at all.

Lawrence's vision for the Arabs, well-meaning though it was, was further co-opted by the League of Nations' mandate system, which not only decreed for the Arabs

◄

These are British soldiers with Arab scouts during the Mesopotamian campaign of World War I, about 1916.

nationhood on a European model, but imposed on them a heterogeneous "national" population that, left alone, would never have chosen to coalesce into a nation. Thus Iraq came into the world as a kind of Frankenstein's monster, an awkward, unwieldy, arbitrary, unhappy facsimile of a nation-state rather than an authentically organic nation. As such, its disparate people, treaties and proclamations notwithstanding, were never really independent.

Where no natural attraction exists to hold a country together, force is the only alternative to dismemberment. King Faisal died in 1933 and was succeeded by King Ghazi, whose rule was chronically undermined by one attempted military coup after another. Rashid Ali al-Gaylani, prime minister under Ghazi, took over the government after the king's death in 1939. With World War II underway, the British, now fearful that al-Gaylani would ally Iraq with the Germans and cut off oil supplies to the Western allies, invaded Iraq in 1941, restored the Hashemite monarchy, and occupied the country until 1947, well after the war had ended.

The regime of the Hashemites ended in a 1958 military coup d'etat known as the 14 July Revolution. Brigadier General Abdul Karim Qassim assumed the reins of government and promptly aligned Iraq with the Soviet Union. In 1963, another military officer, Colonel Abdul Salam Arif, overthrew the Qassim government and served as president of the Iraqi Republic until his death in 1966, at which point his brother, Abdul Rahman Arif, became president. Two years later, the Arab Socialist Baath Party overthrew Rahman Arif, and Ahmed Hasan Al-Bakir became the first Baath president of Iraq. Shortly after this, Saddam Hussein al-Tikriti ascended to power through the ranks of the Baath Party, and in 1979, by means of assassination and the threat of assassination, Hussein became the new president.

The same tools Hussein had used to attain power he used to maintain power. Secret police forces, paramilitary units personally loyal to himself, imprisonment, torture, assassination, execution, and the institution of a chronic state of warfare against dissident populations within Iraq (especially the Kurds) and outside with neighboring Iran, were the means by which Saddam Hussein sustained Iraq and his power over it. Independence became a hollow word and a meaningless concept. Hussein played the Western powers, especially the United States, off both the Soviets and the extreme Islamic anti-Americanism of Iran. At times, the United States propped up Saddam Hussein, supplying him with military hardware to fight Iran and to keep oil-rich Iraq out of the Soviet sphere. At other times, the United States fought against Saddam Hussein. In either case, the "enemy" was as much a Western creation as it was the product of indigenous forces. The war against Saddam Hussein that unmistakably began with a U.S. president's decision in 2003 was nevertheless born in the heart and mind of T. E. Lawrence in 1919 and nurtured from that time through the late 1940s by the increasingly desperate policies of a Britannic empire in the throes of dissolution.

CHAPTER 18

OUT OF AFRICA:
THE MAU MAU UPRISING

1952–1956

Although the British military defeated the luridly bloody Mau Mau Uprising in Kenya, the war

inspired many other independence movements throughout Africa, most of which came to fruition

in the 1960s, bringing about an end to European colonial hegemony on the African continent but

also establishing a tradition of extreme violence associated with political change in the region

Under British eyes, Senior Chief Waruhiu wa Kungu of the Kikuyu tribe was a pillar of Kenyan colonial society. A virile figure, father to the many children his five wives had borne him, he was every inch the tribal chief, except that instead of an animal-skin toga draped over his right shoulder, Waruhiu wore the European suit of the landowner, Christian mission teacher, and community leader that he was. His clothes, relative prosperity, profession, religious conversion, full collaboration with white colonial officials, and reputation among many of the Kikuyu themselves as a source of wise council and a solver of problems endeared him to the British. If only all Kikuyu would emulate Waruhiu, they remarked to each other over tea or gin and tonics.

On October 7, 1952, Senior Chief Waruhiu wa Kungu was being chauffeured along a broad, British-built road just outside of Nairobi. By the early 1950s, Kenya's capital was gobbling up more and more of the Central Highlands (called the "White Highlands" because Europeans owned the vast majority of its fecund land), the city's population swollen by desperately poor Kikuyu who had come from the country in search of whatever work the white man might toss their way. Today, though, was a bright fall day, crisp and clear enough to glimpse Mount Kenya, snowy summit and all, looming picturesquely over the ramshackle shanties and European commercial buildings of Nairobi. A Kikuyu man in khaki shorts, which had been liberated from a British military supply depot, lifted a rifle to his shoulder, drew a bead on the automobile carrying Waruhiu wa Kungu, and squeezed off a succession of shots. Two found their mark, one tearing through the chief's neck, the other drilling into his chest.

Just days before, Waruhiu had spoken out against the rising violence of independence agitators who called themselves, variously, the Muigwithania ("The Understanding"), the Uiguana ("The Unity Oath"), or the Muingi ("The Movement'), but who were universally known as the Mau Mau.

The assassination stunned the 30,000 British and other European settlers in Kenya. Sir Evelyn Baring, who had just arrived as the new governor the day before, telegraphed the Colonial Office in London asking for troops. They began arriving within two weeks, concurrent with Sir Evelyn's published proclamation on October 21 that stated "A public emergency has arisen which makes it necessary to confer special powers on the Government and its officers for the purpose of maintaining law and order."

◄

The face of war: Mau Mau forces recruited young men and as many African revolutionary armies still do, even child warriors.

ROOTS OF REBELLION

The Portuguese explorer Vasco da Gama was the first European to explore Kenya, at the end of the fifteenth century. He discovered a fertile realm whose ample highlands made for a climate far gentler than much of the rest of eastern Africa. During the sixteenth century, Portugal established a strong presence in Kenya, which, however, was soon challenged by the British, the Dutch, and the Omani Arabs, all of whom founded competing colonies. In 1885, Germany belatedly bid to start a colonial empire by establishing a "protectorate" over what had been the domain of Sultan Barghash of Zanzibar on the East African coast, but in 1890, the Germans ceded their holdings to the British, who penetrated the region's interior with their Kenya–Uganda Railway. After World War I, all of Kenya became a British colony, and by the 1930s British and other European settlers had hewed out vast coffee and tea plantations in the Central Highlands, which offered the choicest soil and climate in all of Kenya. They drove out Kikuyu farmers by the hundreds of thousands, forcing them to scratch out their subsistence on far less favorable lowland tracts or to seek menial employment in Nairobi and Mombasa.

In 1948, colonial authorities created a reservation system in which 1.25 million Kikuyu were confined by law to 2,000 square miles (5,180 km²) of what had been their country, whereas some 30,000 British and other European colonists were free to settle and farm 12,000 square miles (31,080 km²) of Kenya's best land. The colonizers permitted approximately 120,000 Kikuyu to become tenant farmers in the White Highlands, working small plots on European farms in exchange for their labor. As tenants, they had no legal rights to the land whatsoever and were perpetually at the mercy of landowners' demands for more days of labor in exchange for the privilege of continuing to occupy their patches of land. Throughout the 1940s, most Kikuyu farmers, tenants, as well as many on the reserve, suffered relentless annual reduction in income.

But not all of them. A small but significant Kikuyu minority owned good lands and seeing their economic future with the colonists rather than with the Kikuyu masses, they supported the colonial administration. Thus conditions were established not only for an anti-colonial uprising but for an accompanying civil war.

Toward the end of the 1940s, an underground organization called the Kikuyu Central Association (KCA) planned a campaign of civil disobedience in the manner of the noncooperation movement Mohandas Gandhi had used to lead India to independence from British colonial rule. The KCA began by strictly adhering to nonviolence, but it also required its members to take special oaths, which reportedly included sacrificing animals and drinking their blood. White Kenyans also heard rumors that oath rituals sometimes involved cannibalism, bestiality, and necrophilia. These stories—which were probably based on at least a grain of truth—were sufficient to terrorize Kenya's European community, despite the KCA's otherwise nonviolent orientation.

During 1949–1950, Kenya's African urban workers staged numerous strikes and demonstrations, first in Nairobi and then in other cities, some of which turned violent—though the violence was primarily between African radicals and African loyalists, not between blacks and whites. By the early months of the 1950s, Africans in Kenya were joining the KCA, unions, and the "Forty Group," which was made up of former African soldiers who had been conscripted by the British for service early in World War II.

Syllables of Terror

Some believe the name "Mau Mau" (rhymes with "cow cow") was intended to evoke the cry hyenas make when they forage for food. That was an activity so familiar and so frantic in appearance that the Kikuyu still use the phrase "mau-mau" to describe eating in great haste. It seemed to the guerrillas of the uprising an apt description for their own stealthy rapacity in combat.

Others have pointed out that the syllable mau is in many geographical names throughout Kenya, attached to hills, rivers, and villages. Some have seen it as an acronym for a Swahili slogan, *Mzungu Aende Ulaya; Mwafrika Apate Uhuru*, "Let the white man return to Europe; let the African be free." Still others believe "Mau Mau" to be a linguistic shuffling of the Swahili phrase *Uma uma*: "Get out! Get out." A few sources think that "mau mau" was an elixir proffered to Mau Mau soldiers with a promise that it would make them impervious to English bullets. Some historians report that it is nothing more than a pair of nonsense syllables, which the white colonists invented to mock the Kenyan independence movement.

Unlike the KCA, the Forty Group made no show of nonviolence. It set about collecting money to buy guns and ammunition and began plotting a revolution.

Late in 1947, Jomo Kenyatta, a mission-educated Kikuyu who had worked for Nairobi's municipal water department and was a KCA leader who briefly flirted with Communism, won election as president of the Kenya African Union (KAU). British authorities welcomed this because Kenyatta was comparatively moderate; however, he soon found it impossible to resist the call of KAU radicals for independence. In May 1951, Kenyatta presented James Griffiths, who was touring Kenya in his capacity as colonial secretary of the British government, with a set of demands for fair representation in the colony's government. Griffiths neither accepted nor rejected the KAU demands, but pointedly ignored them and instead proposed creating a Legislative Council consisting of fourteen representatives for the 30,000 white settlers, six for Kenya's 100,000 Asians, and one for its 24,000 Arabs. The African majority, some five million people, were allotted just five representatives—who would be elected from among candidates nominated by the government.

Griffiths's outrageous proposal radicalized the entire KAU, which now spawned a secret "Central Committee" that organized "oath campaigns" throughout the country. Once again, there were stories of oaths solemnized with blood rituals, cannibalism, bestiality, and necrophilia. Accounts surfaced of a "seven-stage oath," in which participants consumed blood, ate pieces of human flesh, performed sexual acts on animals, and ate morsels of brain recovered from disinterred human corpses. Although contemporary commentators and current historians have discounted many of the details of these reports as lurid exaggerations, others believe that the accounts were accurate and that organizers of the uprising used the extreme nature of the blood oaths to bond adherents irrevocably to the movement. Far from being "typical" of "savage" African culture, all of the practices associated with the oaths were taboos in Kikuyu and Maasai tribal culture. That was the point. Those who took the oaths were ashamed ever to return to their villages. Their only loyalty now could be to the movement.

From Prisoner to President

Jomo Kenyatta was born in 1889 or 1894 (sources vary) on the far outskirts of Nairobi in a village of the Kiambu District. As a boy and youth he was educated at the Scottish Mission Center at Thogoto and was baptized a Christian, taking the name John Peter, which he later changed to Johnstone. Nevertheless, Kenyatta took a great interest in his native culture and customs and even served as an assistant to his grandfather, a traditional tribal medicine man.

During World War I, Kenyatta lived with Maasai relatives in the Rift Valley district of Narok in western Kenya. He made his living as a clerk to an Asian trader, and then after the war became the manager of a European-owned store. It was during the post–World War I years that Kenyatta began to reconnect with his African roots. He left Narok for Nairobi, where he worked in the Nairobi City Council water department from 1921–1926. He lived cheaply on the outskirts of the city, in a hut in Kilimani, but also worked his own shamba (small farm) in Dagoretti, west of Nairobi.

Kenyatta became active in the African rights movement, and in 1925 emerged as a leader of the KCA, often serving as the liaison with and representative to the white government. In 1928, he founded Muigwithania, a newspaper that eschewed direct involvement in politics, but covered in depth Kikuyu culture and promoted new, efficient farming methods accessible to the small Kikuyu farmers. In these practical ways, he sought to cultivate independence among the Kikuyu.

Sponsored by the KCA, Kenyatta traveled to Britain in 1929 in an effort to win government and popular support for enhanced tribal land rights. On a second trip to Britain in 1931, he formally petitioned Parliament for African representation in Kenya's government, met Mohandas Gandhi in London in 1932, and then went to Moscow, where studying Marxist economics, he briefly flirted with Communism. When he returned to Britain in 1933 and spoke out against the government usurpation of gold-rich land in the Kakamega reserve, British politicians labeled him a Communist.

Kenyatta remained in London, teaching Gikuyu (the Kikuyu language) at University College, and wrote a book on the subject, which was published in 1937. He also took up the study of anthropology at the London School of Economics, and in 1938 published Facing Mount Kenya, a book devoted to Kikuyu customs and culture. It was at this time that he adopted Jomo as his Kikuyu name.

With the outbreak of World War II, Kenyatta worked on a farm in England in preference to conscription into the army and after the war became active in the Pan-African independence movement. He returned to Kenya in 1946 and in 1947 was elevated to the leadership of the Kenya African Union. Although he was a moderate force in the organization, he soon embraced the call for immediate independence raised by the more radical faction. This was sufficient, in 1952, to bring his arrest, trial, and conviction as a Mau Mau supporter. He was sentenced to seven years of hard labor, to be followed by "restriction" in a native district.

Kenyatta was released from prison in 1959 and remained "in restriction" until August 1961, when he was permitted to return to his home in Gatundu. Although his imprisonment was a hard act of injustice, it did keep Kenyatta out of the Mau Mau violence, and he emerged associated with neither the Mau Mau nor those who favored accommodation with the colonial government. Elected president of the Kenya African National Union (KANU) in October 1961, he took a leading role in talks with the British government that led to complete independence in 1963 and served as the nation's first prime minister. When Kenya became a republic within the British Commonwealth on December 12, 1964, Kenyatta was elevated to the presidency. He died in 1978 at age eighty-nine.

◄
Jomo Kenyatta was president of the Kenya African Union and was later the first president of an independent Kenya.

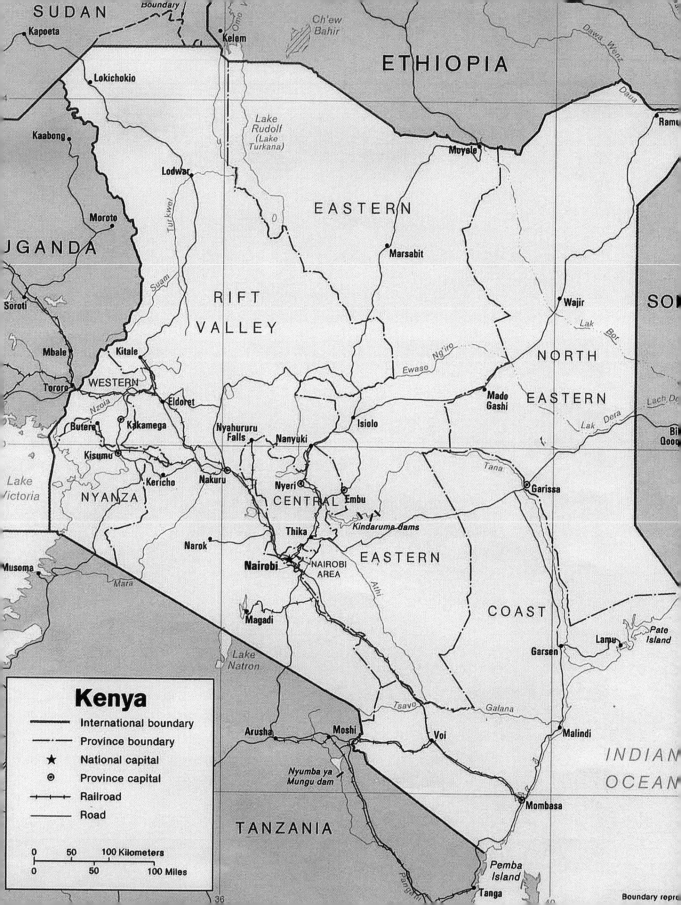

STATE OF EMERGENCY

The KAU's Central Committee became the nucleus of the Mau Mau Uprising. It organized and equipped armed terror squads, which forced others to join and intimidated or killed those who resisted. Government informers and collaborators with the colonial police or British army were butchered; however, through October 1952, when the state of emergency was declared, not a single European had been attacked.

On October 21, the very day of the emergency declaration, government authorities launched Operation Jock Scott, in which British soldiers and colonial police rounded up almost 100 Africans identified as leaders of the still-incipient uprising, including Jomo Kenyatta. Over the next month, they would arrest some 8,000 Africans.

Kenyatta and five others were charged with "managing and being a member" of what was now widely called the Mau Mau Society. The truth was that, if anything, Kenyatta was one of the few African leaders who might have been able to rein in the Mau Mau violence. His speeches against Mau Mau excesses in 1952 drew mortal threats from Central Committee radicals even as colonial authorities, seeking a scapegoat, convicted and sentenced him on April 8, 1953, to seven years' hard labor.

British authorities had not only made the error of silencing a moderate voice among the African activists, but had also created a martyr to the very cause they were trying to suppress. Following Kenyatta's arrest, Mau Mau terrorism spread beyond Nairobi and throughout the White Highlands as well as Kikuyu reserves. Two weeks after the emergency was declared, the first European fell victim to the Mau Mau Uprising.

MAU MAU ASCENDANT

Having arrested so many, British authorities had good reason to believe they had decapitated the leadership of the Central Committee and the Mau Mau movement. But they had underestimated the scope of the rebellion. True, many leaders were now locked up, but many others had fled into the bush. Moreover, although authorities had reasonably accurate intelligence concerning Mau Mau activities in Nairobi, they knew almost nothing about the local rebel committees that had been formed throughout the countryside. It was these local organizations that now rose up.

◄

This is Kenya. The fiercest Mau Mau activity was in the Nairobi area.

Mau Mau gangs—they cannot properly be called military units—were armed with a few European-made rifles and homemade firearms (many of which exploded on first use), but most numerous were the traditional African weapons, including short swords called *simis*, whips fashioned of rhinoceros hide (*kibokos*), as well as native spears. The weapon of choice, however, was the *panga*, a broad-bladed machete, which was used to hack apart and mutilate victims. It became the bloody trademark of the uprising.

Frank Kitson, who had served in the British army as a major during the uprising, related in a postwar memoir what he had heard from an eyewitness to a typical Mau Mau raid. He described how the raiders "slashed around" with simis and pangas. When the raiders descended on the village, everyone ran for their lives, but when the Mau Mau caught up with an old man who was "slower than the rest," they hamstrung him, drawing their simis across the hollow of his knees, severing the tendons, so that he collapsed helplessly at the feet of the pursuers. Unable to run away, he could do nothing but cover his face with his arms in an effort to ward off the blows of simi and panga.

"A mouse in a mechanical mincing machine would have had a better chance of survival," Kitson observed. One of the helpless man's tormentors "hacked off a foot, and another sliced off the testicles to use later in [a cannibalistic] Oathing ceremony. A third gouged out his eyes with a staple"—a U-shaped metal loop with pointed ends used to fasten pipe or wiring to a wall or ceiling. He then "put them in his pocket for the same purpose." The rest of the "gang came by to cut and stab the twitching corpse." They licked the blood from their weapons and set fire to "all the huts they could see."

Aside from the mayhem, the most telling feature of this account is that it describes Africans attacking Africans. Before the Mau Mau Uprising ended in 1956, 11,503 Kenyans—Mau Mau and victims alike—had been killed. This is the official toll, which does not include Africans executed by authority of the courts, a number exceeding 1,000 by 1959, when the state of emergency was finally lifted. But even a total of 12,500 is far fewer than what most historians believe. Scholarly estimates of casualties range from 20,000 to 70,000; a few authorities believe the death toll actually exceeded 100,000. There is no dispute about losses among the British and colonial military, which numbered 590 killed and 1,500 wounded, and deaths among European civilians numbered no more than 32.

While contemporary British reports went into lurid detail concerning the nature of the Mau Mau attacks even as they downplayed the numbers of Kenyan casualties, early accounts made no mention at all of the brutality of British troops and Kikuyu Home

Guardsmen in British service. Soldiers made little effort to distinguish the Mau Mau from noncombatant Kenyans. If a person was African, he—or she, for that matter—was a target. Like the Mau Mau, British and colonial soldiers, turned loose, created a killing field. Soldiers avidly gathered the severed hands of Mau Mau, bringing them back to their encampments, where each hand earned a five-shilling bounty. The bounty was unofficial, but the practice of severing the enemy's hands had been formally authorized by British military headquarters for the purpose of identifying the dead by means of fingerprints.

BATTLE LINES DRAWN

Some 55,000 British military personnel, including soldiers, Royal Marines, and members of the Royal Air Force, were sent into combat against the Mau Mau—though British regular forces fielded never exceeded 10,000 at any one time. British regulars were augmented by the Kenya Police, the Kenya Tribal Police, and the Kikuyu Home Guard.

No one knows how many Mau Mau were involved in the uprising, which rose to its height during 1953 after the Nairobi Central Committee, renaming itself the Council of Freedom, resolved in January of that year to prosecute a full-scale "war of liberation." The Council of Freedom struggled to bring strategic, tactical, and logistical order to what was up to this point the uncoordinated violence of gangs. The secret committees operating throughout the Kenyan countryside were designated the Passive Wing of the liberation movement. Their assignment was to find weapons, ammunition, food, and finance, to gather intelligence, and above all to acquire recruits. This was more often accomplished by force than by patriotic persuasion. The recruits were incorporated into the movement's Active Wing, which consisted chiefly of the Land and Freedom Armies— a name that succinctly expressed the two objectives of the war.

On the face of it, the impulse to rationalize the military struggle seemed a laudable one; however, Council of Freedom leaders failed to recognize that it was the very irrational—wild, random, and unpredictable—nature of the uprising that most terrorized the colonists and colonial authorities and that most perplexed the thinly spread British military. Worse, the Council of Freedom was unable to furnish a big-picture strategy. It was one thing to proclaim the creation of Land and Freedom Armies, but the warrior gangs in the field had not been trained in guerrilla warfare and except for members of the Forty Group, they had no military experience at all. Nor did the Council of Freedom devote time and attention to acquiring modern weapons and other supplies required by a genuine army. Finally, the uprising was almost exclusively concentrated in the White Highlands and the surrounding native reserves. This meant that the uprising was never truly national in scope. Had the Council of Freedom organized significant resistance across the entire breadth of Kenya, the British would have been hard-pressed to counter and contain the uprising.

Still, through the early summer of 1953, the Land and Freedom Armies raided with near impunity, striking throughout the forests of the White Highlands and environs, terrorizing and killing Kenyans loyal to the British, and hitting police outposts and Home Guard facilities, scavenging weapons from both. The raiders focused on Christian converts and Kikuyu landowners, but also targeted remote white-owned farms. Even the outskirts of bustling Nairobi were not safe from attack.

As the casualty figures suggest, deaths among European civilians were relatively rare. The Mau Mau strategy was to kill a sufficient number of Europeans to terrorize the community, but to concentrate on depriving the colonial government of the cooperation and loyalty of the Africans by slaughtering any who sided with the whites. To go up against the mighty British nation was foolhardy, the Mau Mau believed; but if the British had no one left to govern in Kenya, they would have no choice but to leave. The effect of these few white killings on Kenya's European community was nevertheless profound. After Mau Mau raided a white farm on January 24, 1953, using pangas to hack to death the farming couple and their six-year-old son, Europeans throughout the country summarily fired their Kikuyu servants and other household workers, fearful that they would turn against them. Men, women, and even children took to carrying arms at all times, including guns, knives, hatchets, clubs—whatever their homes and ingenuity could furnish. Those living in outlying districts fortified their houses as best they could in an effort to transform them into miniature self-sufficient fortresses.

But it was always the Africans who bore the brunt of the attacks. Most raids were small, carried out by no more than a hundred Mau Mau—a hundred men being the standard size of a Mau Mau combat unit; however, during the night of March 25/26, 1953, approximately 1,000 raiders swept through the village of Lari, a loyalist stronghold. The Mau Mau rounded up nearly 200 villagers, mostly women and children who were the families of Home Guardsmen, and struck at them with their pangas. Many of those

▶

Lieutenant General Sir George W. E. J. Erskine led the successful British campaign against the Mau Mau.

Crimes of War

We tend to think of the concentration camp as the horrific invention of Adolf Hitler and his henchmen before and during World War II. In fact, concentration camps—called "reconcentration camps"—had been employed by the Spanish administrators of Cuba to contain Cubans who agitated for independence in the years leading up to the Spanish-American War in 1898. The British themselves had built concentration camps in South Africa, in which they confined Boer civilians during the Second ("Great") Boer War of 1899–1902.

The camps the British constructed in Kenya were miserable, both overcrowded and underfunded. Rations were barely sufficient for subsistence, especially for men subject to hard labor, and the whip was the primary instrument by which order was enforced. As in the Nazi concentration camps of World War II, the British camps were disease-ridden, with cholera taking a heavy toll among inmates. British medical officers assigned to the camps wrote scathing reports on conditions and appealed for food and medicines. The Colonial Office turned a blind eye and a deaf ear.

who escaped the panga were burned alive in their huts. About 120 villagers were killed or severely wounded, some suffering lifelong disfigurement.

The Lari raid triggered massive retaliation by the Home Guard, which shot and killed suspected Mau Mau or Mau Mau sympathizers on sight. Additionally, any African who carried a firearm was subject to capital punishment, sometimes after due process of law, but more often on sight.

THE TIDE TURNS

General Sir George Watkin Eben James Erskine had served in France and Belgium during World War I; in India during the turbulent 1930s; in Europe during World War II, participating in the D-Day Normandy invasion of June 6, 1941; and in Egypt and the Mediterranean after the war. In 1953, he assumed the post of General-Officer-Commanding-in-Chief, East Africa Command, and in June of that year, he installed himself in Nairobi, where he appointed himself director of operations in the war against the Mau Mau.

Erskine was given his pick of the latest crop of young British men drafted as part of the United Kingdom's post–World War II national service program. He used the fresh troops to patrol the Kikuyu reserves, which he designated as "Special Areas," meaning that anyone who did not instantly obey the commands of British soldier or a local

▶

Rounded up in a sweeping British crackdown in 1954, suspected Mau Mau warriors, supporters, and sympathizers were herded into concentration camps by the thousands.

police officer or Home Guardsman would be shot. After many Africans, pursuant to this regulation, were indeed shot, Erskine deemed that his point had been made and suspended the harsh provision. Anyone who ventured without official permission into the "Prohibited Areas," the region on and around the Aberdares Range and Mount Kenya, places of most intense Mau Mau activity, could also be shot on sight. This order Erskine did not rescind.

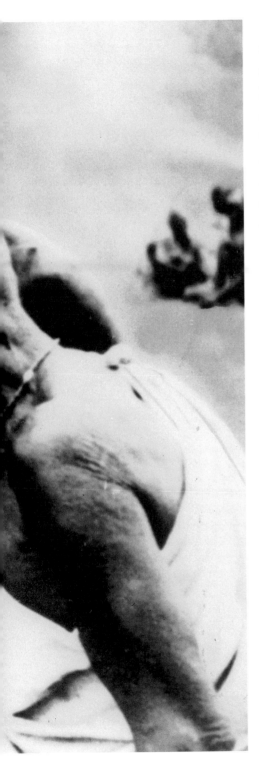

In addition to regular British troops, Erskine recruited former Mau Mau, who were duly "de-oathed" and organized into units designed to resemble the Mau Mau gangs, each unit commanded by a white British officer disguised with makeup to look like a Kikuyu. These counterfeit gangs infiltrated Mau Mau ranks and destroyed them from the inside. The Mau Mau leadership had assumed that their elaborately gruesome oaths were an infallible means of guaranteeing loyalty. They were mistaken, and once this system had proved vulnerable, the structure of the Mau Mau Uprising was fatally compromised.

Yet despite the success of the infiltration methods, Erskine's efforts at achieving a decisive victory were repeatedly frustrated. Only after British intelligence finally revealed the fact that Mau Mau organization was rooted in the cities—even though the raids themselves were mostly against villages and farms—did Erskine make a breakthrough. On April 24, 1954, he launched Operation Anvil in Nairobi, putting the entire city under martial law. While it was firmly locked down, security forces made mass arrests of more than 17,000 individuals, most of whom were later proven innocent. At the same time, some 15,000 Kikuyu from Nairobi and elsewhere were rounded up and internally "deported" to designated Kikuyu reserves west of Mount Kenya.

◄

Mau Mau adherents swore elaborately gruesome blood oaths to the insurgency. Those who later renounced their Mau Mau affiliations were "rehabilitated" in cleansing ceremonies. Two Kikuyu women, former Mau Mau, lick a "twigsm-part" proffered by a shaman called a mundo mugo. Dipped in goat's blood, the talisman spiritually reverses and undoes the Mau Mau blood oath.

Erskine turned next to the trade unions, rounding up labor leaders along with the rank and file, badly crippling the Council for Freedom's Passive Wing, thereby disrupting Mau Mau recruitment and supply. They herded those plucked from the unions into detention centers, which were neither more nor less than concentration camps. By the end of 1954, these camps held 77,000 Kikuyu inmates. That same year, more than 100,000 of the 120,000 Kikuyu farmers who had worked white farmlands as tenants had been internally deported to the reserves.

Erskine and other colonial authorities turned their attention to those reserves in the summer of 1954, instituting a policy of "villagization," by which Kikuyu residents were forced together into villages where they could be effectively contained—and observed. By the fall of 1955, more than a million Kikuyu had been "concentrated" into what amounted to 854 rural ghettoes.

WHOSE VICTORY?

By the end of 1953, the Mau Mau were fighting what was clearly a losing war. Infiltrated, their supply system—such as it was—almost completely destroyed (the Passive Wing was virtually nonexistent), and their supporters executed, languishing in prison and concentration camps, or eking out subsistence in one of the "villagized" rural ghettoes, the Land and Freedom Armies ceased to be an effective revolutionary force. Nevertheless, an estimated 15,000 Mau Mau fighters still roamed the countryside by the beginning of 1954. Accordingly, in December of that year, Erskine assigned the King's African Rifles—whose enlisted personnel were East African askaris (native soldiers)—to carry out Operation Hammer, a massive sweep through the forests in the heart of Mau Mau country.

By the fall of 1956, no more than an estimated 500 Mau Mau diehards were still known to be holed up deep in the bush. The colonial government called off Operation Hammer and decided to cope with the diehards by offering amnesty to any who surrendered. This gesture brought about peace talks, but on May 20, 1955, negotiations broke down, and Erskine once again dispatched his counterfeit Mau Mau gangs to locate and infiltrate the holdouts. They discovered that the surviving Mau Mau were close to starvation and had almost completely exhausted their stock of ammunition.

When Kikuyu Tribal Police captured Dedan Kimathi, the last known Mau Mau leader, on October 21, 1956, the Mau Mau Uprising was declared to have ended—though the state of emergency remained in effect, lest a new outbreak develop.

There could be no doubt that the British had militarily defeated the Mau Mau Uprising. Yet despite the military victory, colonial authorities nevertheless granted to the KAU the demands for equitable political representation it had made (and colonial secretary James Griffiths had ignored) back in 1951. In addition, the government repealed laws banning Africans from growing coffee, the crop white farmers found so profitable, and the villagization program was turned into a means of allowing more Kikuyu to consolidate larger land holdings. In this way, the decline in Kikuyu income was reversed and began to rise. Equally important, more Africans were given reason to believe that they had a stake in the colonial government.

The liberalization of colonial government in Kenya was a victory for the Kikuyu and for all African Kenyans. But the effects of the Mau Mau Uprising did not end with it. The episode had demonstrated two things about Africa in particular and empire in general: first, political repression had consequences—as much for the oppressor as for the oppressed; second, the colonies of the African continent—and elsewhere—having watched the Mau Mau Uprising closely, did not deny that it was a native military defeat, but what they paid closer attention to was just how much that "defeat" had won for the Africans. No sooner did the decade of the 1950s give way to the 1960s than one by one all of Europe's African colonies sought and secured their independence, thirty-seven countries by 1968, among them Sudan, Morocco, and Tunisia in the north, Nigeria in the west, Congo in the continent's heart, and Kenya itself, on the east coast. The strange, brutal, singularly ugly Mau Mau Uprising heralded the end of Europe's ownership of Africa and of so much of the rest of the world.

BIBLIOGRAPHY

CHAPTER 1
A Woman Against Rome: Boudicca's Revolt, *60 CE*

Andrews, Ian. *Boudicca's Revolt.* Cambridge: Cambridge University Press, 1973.

Hunt, Richard. *Queen Boudicca's Battle of Britain.* Staplehurst, U.K.: Spellmount, 2002.

CHAPTER 2
The First Holocaust: A Messiah Rebels Against Rome, *132–135 CE*

Josephus, Flavius. *The Works of Josephus.* Peabody, MA: Hendrickson, 1980.

Morgan, Julian. *Hadrian: Consolidating the Empire.* New York: Rosen Central, 2002.

Neusner, Jacob, ed. *History of the Jews in the Second Century of the Common Era.* New York: Garland, 1990.

Tacitus. *Histories.* London: Heinemann, 1923.

CHAPTER 3
Triumph of the Caliphate: Islam Conquers Spain, *711–718 CE*

Armstrong, Karen. *A Short History of Islam.* New York: Random House, 2002.

Holt, P. M., Ann K. S. Lambton, and Bernard Lewis. *The Cambridge History of Islam,* 2 vols. New York: Cambridge University Press, 1970.

Torrey, Charles C., ed. *History of the Conquest of Egypt, North Africa, and Spain.* New Haven: Yale University Press, 1922.

CHAPTER 4
Shoguns Rising: The Genpei War, *1180–1185 CE*

Hall, John W. *Japan: From Prehistory to Modern Times.* Tokyo: C. E. Tuttle, 1971.

McCullough, Helen Craig, trans. *The Tale of the Heike.* Palo Alto, CA: Stanford University Press, 1990.

Murdoch, James. *A History of Japan,* 3 vols. New York: Routledge, 1996.

Samson, George B. *A History of Japan,* 3 vols. Palo Alto, CA: Stanford University Press, 1958–1963.

CHAPTER 5
Revolt and Reaction: The Peasants' War in Germany, *1524–1526 CE*

Engels, Frederick [Friedrich]. *The Peasant War in Germany,* reprint ed., New York: International Publishers, 2000.

Miller, Douglas. *German Peasants' War.* London: Osprey, 2003.

Stayer, James M. *The German Peasants' War and Anabaptist Community Goods.* Montreal: McGill–Queens University Press, 1994.

CHAPTER 6
"The Third Rome": Ivan the Terrible and the Boyars' Revolt, *1547–1572 CE*

Hosking, Geoffrey A. *Russia and the Russians: A History.* Cambridge, MA: Harvard University Press, 2001.

Pavlov, Andrei. *Ivan the Terrible.* London: Pearson/Longman, 2003.

Troyat, Henri. *Ivan the Terrible.* New York: Sterling, 2001.

CHAPTER 7
The Beaver Wars "No Ink Black Enough to Describe the Fury of the Iroquois," *1638-1684 CE*

Axelrod, Alan. *Chronicle of the Indian Wars: From Colonial Times to Wounded Knee.* New York: Prentice Hall, 1993.

Jennings, Francis. *The Ambiguous Iroquois Empire.* New York: Norton, 1984.

Richter, Daniel K., and James H. Merrell, eds. *Beyond the Covenant Chain: The Iroquois and Their Neighbors in Indian North America, 1600–1800.* Syracuse, NY: Syracuse University Press, 1987.

CHAPTER 8
King Philip's War: America's Costliest Conflict, *1675–1676 CE*

Axelrod, Alan. *Chronicle of the Indian Wars: From Colonial Times to Wounded Knee.* New York: Prentice Hall General Reference, 1993.

Drake, James David. *King Philip's War: Civil War in New England, 1675–1678.* Amherst, MA: University of Massachusetts Press, 2000.

Jennings, Francis. *The Invasion of America*. New York: Norton, 1975.

Lepore, Jill. *The Name of War: King Philip's War and the Origins of American Identity*. New York: Random House, 1999.

CHAPTER 9
Ottoman Eclipse: The Austro–Turkish War, *1683–1699 CE*

Murphey, Rhoads. *Ottoman Warfare: 1500–1700*. New Brunswick, NJ: Rutgers University Press, 1999.

Parry, V. J., and M. J. Kitch. *Hapsburg and Ottoman Empires*. London: Sussex Publications, 1982.

Setton, Kenneth Meyer. *Venice, Austria, and the Turks in the Seventeenth Century*. Darby, PA: DIANE Publishing, 1991

Young, William. *International Politics and Warfare in the Age of Louis XIV and Peter the Great: A Guide to the Historical Literature*. Bloomington, ID: iUniverse, 2004.

CHAPTER 10
Cold Ambition: The Great Northern War, *1700–1721 CE*

Frost, Robert I. *The Northern Wars: State and Society in Northeastern Europe, 1558–1721*. New York: Longman, 2000.

Hattan, R. M. *Charles XII of Sweden: Union, Disunion, and Scandinavian Integration*. New York: Weybright and Talley, 1969.

Oakley, Stewart. *War and Peace in the Baltic, 1560–1790*. New York: Routledge, 1992.

Roberts, Michael, ed. *Sweden's Age of Greatness, 1632–1718*. London: Macmillan, 1973.

CHAPTER 11
The First Wars on Terror: The United States vs. the Barbary Pirates, *1801–1815 CE*

Chidsey, Donald Barr. *The Wars in Barbary; Arab Piracy and the United States Navy*. New York: Crown, 1971.

De Kay, James Tertius. *A Rage for Glory: The Life of Commodore Stephen Decatur, USN*. New York: Free Press, 2004.

Howarth, Stephen. *To Shining Sea: A History of the U.S. Navy, 1775–1998*. Norman, OK: University of Oklahoma Press, 1999.

Wheelan, Joseph. *Jefferson's War: America's First War on Terror, 1801–1805.* New York: Carroll and Graf, 2003.

CHAPTER 12
Eastern Sunset: The First and Second Opium Wars, *1839–1842 and 1856–1860 CE*

Beeching, Jack. *The Chinese Opium Wars.* New York: Harcourt, 1977.

Hsin-pao Chang. *Commissioner Lin and the Opium War.* Cambridge, MA: Harvard University Press, 1964.

Fay, Peter Ward. *The Opium War, 1840–1842.* Chapel Hill, NC: University of North Carolina Press, 1975.

Hanes, W. Travis, and Frank Sanello. *The Opium Wars: The Addiction of One Empire and the Corruption of Another.* Napterville, IL: Sourcebooks, Inc., 2002.

Hurd, Douglas. *The Arrow War: An Anglo-Chinese Confusion, 1856–1860.* New York: Macmillan, 1967.

CHAPTER 13
Rising Sun: The Meiji Restoration, *1860–1868 CE*

Beasley, William G. *Meiji Restoration.* Palo Alto, CA: Stanford University Press, 1972.

Hall, John W. *Japan: From Prehistory to Modern Times.* Tokyo: C. E. Tuttle, 1971.

Murdoch, James. *A History of Japan,* 3 vols. New York: Routledge, 1996.

Samson, George B. *A History of Japan,* 3 vols. Palo Alto, CA: Stanford University Press, 1958–1963.

CHAPTER 14
Germany in the Saddle: The Franco-Prussian War, *1870–1871 CE*

Bucholz, Arden. *Moltke and the German Wars, 1864–1871.* New York: Palgrave Macmillan, 2001.

Howard, Michael Eliot. *Franco-Prussian War: The German Invasion of France, 1870–1871.* London: Routledge, 2001.

Lerman, Katharine Anne. *Bismarck.* New York: Pearson Longman, 2004.

Wawro, Geoffrey. *Franco-Prussian War: The German Conquest of France, 1870–1871.* New York: Cambridge University Press, 2003.

CHAPTER 15
Explosion in the Balkans: The Balkan Wars, *1912–1913 CE*

Erickson, Edward J. *Defeat in Detail: Ottoman Army Operations in the Balkan Wars, 1912–1913.* Westport, CT: Greenwood, 2003.

Gerolymatos, André. *The Balkan Wars: Conquest, Revolution, and Retribution from the Ottoman Era to the Twentieth Century and Beyond.* New York: Basic Books, 2003.

Mazower, Mark. *Balkans: A Short History.* New York: Random House, 2002.

Turfan, Naim. *Rise of the Young Turks: Politics, the Military and Ottoman Collapse.* London: I. B. Tauris, 1999.

CHAPTER 16
Twentieth-Century Jihad: The War for Afghan Independence, *1919 CE*

Clements, Frank. *Conflict in Afghanistan: A Historical Encyclopedia.* Santa Barbara, CA: ABC-CLIO, 2003

O'Ballance, Edgar. *Afghan Wars, 1839–1992.* New York: Brassey's, 1993.

CHAPTER 17
Middle East Mandate: Arab Insurrection in Iraq, *1920–1922 CE*

Lawrence, T. E. *Seven Pillars of Wisdom,* reprint ed. Ware, U.K.: Wordsworth Editions, 1997.

Marr, Phoebe. *The Modern History of Iraq.* Boulder, CO: Westview, 1985.

Tauber, Eliezer. *The Formation of Modern Syria and Iraq.* Ilford, U.K.: Frank Cass, 1995.

CHAPTER 18
Out of Africa: The Mau Mau Uprising, *1952–1956 CE*

Anderson, David. *Histories of the Hanged: The Dirty War in Kenya and the End of Empire.* New York: Norton, 2005.

Elkins, Caroline. *Imperial Reckoning: The Untold Story of Britain's Gulag in Kenya.* New York:Macmillan, 2005

Maloba, Wumyabi O. *Mau Mau and Kenya: An Analysis of a Peasant Revolt.* Bloomington, IN: Indiana University Press, 1999.

Odhiambo, E. S. Atieno, and John Lonsdale, Eds. *Mau Mau and Nationhood: Arms, Authority, and Narration*. Columbus, OH: Ohio University Press, 2003.

GENERAL WORKS

Asprey, Robert B. *War in the Shadows: The Guerrilla in History*. Garden City, NY: Doubleday, 1975.

Atterridge, A. Hilliard. *Famous Land Fights*. London: Methuen, 1914.

Beckett, Ian F. W. *Encyclopedia of Guerrilla Warfare*. New York: Checkmark Books, 2001.

Black, Jeremy. *European Warfare 145--1815*. New York: St Martin's Press, 1999.

Black, Jeremy. *War in the Early Modern World*. Boulder, CO: Westview Press, 1999.

Chambers, John Whiteclay, II, Ed. *The Oxford Companion to American Military History*. New York: Oxford University Press, 1999.

Clodfelter, Michael. *Warfare and Armed Conflicts: A Statistical Reference to Casualty and Other Figures, 1500–2000*. Jefferson, NC: McFarland, 2002.

Daffy, Christopher. *Siege Warfare: The Fortress in the Early Modern World, 1494–1660*. London: Routledge and Kegan Paul, 1979.

Delbruek, Hans. *History of the Art of War*, Westport, CT: Greenwood Press, 1985.

Dupuy, Ernest, and Trevor N. Dupuy. *The Encyclopedia of Military History*. 4th ed. New York: HarperCollins, 1993.

Eggenberger, David. *An Encyclopedia of Battles*. New York: Dover Publications, 1985.

Fuller, J. F. C. *Military History of the Western World*. New York: Da Capo Press, 1955.

Gallay, Allan, Ed. *Colonial Wars of North America, 1512–1763: An Encyclopedia*. New York: Garland Press, 1996.

Harbottle, Thomas, and George Bruce. *Dictionary of Battles*. Briarcliff Manor, NY: Stein and Day, 1971.

Heller, Charles E., and William A. Scoffer. *America's First Battles, 1776–1965*. Lawrence, KS: University Press of Kansas, 1986.

Jones, Archer. *The Art of War in the Western World*. Urban-Champaign, IL: University of Illinois Press, 1987.

Keegan, John. *The Mask of Command*. New York: Viking, 1987.

Keegan, John. *The Price of Admiralty: The Evolution of Naval Warfare*. New York: Viking Penguin 1989.

Keegan, John, and Joseph Darracou. *The Nature of War.* New York: Holt, Rinehart and Winston, 1987.

Koch, H. W. *The Rise of Modern Warfare: From the Mercenaries Through Napoleon.* London: Bison Books, 1981.

Kohn, George C. *Dictionary of Wars*, rev. ed. New York: Checkmark Books, 1999.

Laffin, John. *Brassey's Dictionary of Battles.* New York: Barnes and Noble, 1995.

Margiotta, Franklin D., Ed. *Brassey's Encyclopedia of Military History and Biography.* Washington, DC, and London: Brassey's, 2000.

Montgomery, Bernard. *A History of Warfare.* Cleveland, OH: World Publishing, 1968.

Peers, Douglas M. *Warfare and Empires.* Aldershot, U.K.: Ashgate Publications, 1997.

IMAGE CREDITS

ABOUT THE AUTHOR

Alan Axelrod is the author of many books on military history, including *Bradley: A Biography* (2008), *Miracle at Belleau Wood: The Birth of the Modern U.S. Marine Corps* (2007), *Horrid Pit: The Battle of the Crater, the Civil War's Cruelest Mission* (2007), *Blooding at Great Meadows: Young George Washington and the Battle that Shaped the Man* (2006), *Patton: A Biography* (2006), and *Encyclopedia of Wars* (2005). He has been a creative consultant and on-camera personality for several television documentary series and has appeared on the Discovery Channel, MSNBC, CNN, and National Public Radio.

ACKNOWLEDGMENTS

I am grateful to the driving forces behind this book, Will Kiester and Cara Connors of Fair Winds Press, and to my agent, Ed Claflin.

INDEX

Note: Page numbers in italics indicate figures.